"Grace M. Cho's memoir richly braids Korean meals, memories of a mother fighting racism and the onset of schizophrenia, and references ranging from Christine Blasey Ford's testimony to the essays of Ralph Ellison."
—*VANITY FAIR*

"A wrenching, powerful account of the long-term effects of the immigrant experience."
—*KIRKUS REVIEWS*

"As a member of the complicated postwar Korean diaspora in the US, I have been waiting for this book all my life. *Tastes Like War* is, among other things, a series of revelations of intergenerational trauma in its many guises and forms, often inextricable from love and obligation. Food is a complicated but life-affirming thread throughout the memoir, a deep part of Grace and her mother's parallel journeys to live with autonomy, dignity, nourishment, memory, and love."
—**SUN YUNG SHIN**, author of *Unbearable Splendor*

"What are the ingredients for madness? Grace M. Cho's sui generis memoir of her mother's schizophrenia plumbs the effects of colonialism, war, and violence on a Korean American family. Her moving and frank exploration examines how the social gets under our skin across vast stretches of space and time, illuminating mental illness as a social problem as much as a biological disease."
—**DAVID L. ENG**, coauthor of *Racial Melancholia, Racial Dissociation: On the Social and Psychic Lives of Asian Americans*

"Raw, reaching, and propulsive, Grace M. Cho's *Tastes Like War* creates and explores an epic conversation about heritage and history, intergenerational trauma, and the connective potential of food to explore a mother's fractured past. This is both a memoir and a reclamation."
—**ALLIE ROWBOTTOM**, author of *Jell-O Girls: A Family History*

"*Tastes Like War* is a requiem and a love song for a brilliant, elusive mother whose traumatic past shadows her daughter's present. This searingly honest, heartbreaking memoir evokes the ways in which food in the immigrant household may just as easily be a path to assimilation, alienation, and forgetting as it can be to remembering, connection, joy, and possibility."
—**GAYATRI GOPINATH**, author of *Unruly Visions: The Aesthetic Practices of Queer Diaspora*

"Exquisitely crafted, *Tastes Like War* will break readers' hearts as it engages them in a daughter's search for her mother in the traumatic effects of war, immigration, and mental illness. Cho brilliantly shows the possibilities of the genre to bring together thought and affect in the pursuit of understanding the ghosts of our historical present."
—**PATRICIA TICINETO CLOUGH**, author of *The User Unconscious: On Affect, Media, and Measure*

"Grace M. Cho's debut memoir follows and forages alongside her mother in the shadowed gendered histories of the unending Korean War in the United States. This is a book of care and homage to the persistent creativity of a Korean mother, her daughter's love, and their resilience despite the ghosts of US militarism. *Tastes Like War* signals a powerfully evocative new voice."
—**JENNIFER KWON DOBBS**, author of *Interrogation Room*

"In excavating the origins of her mother's schizophrenia, Grace M. Cho untangles not only her own family history but that of a generation of survivors and their descendants marked by war. Her exploration leads readers on a poignant journey across time and space, revealing the scars on the human psyche wrought by the legacy of violence underpinning US-Korea relations. A moving tribute to all those 'never meant to survive,' *Tastes Like War* suggests that healing can't always be achieved through solitary effort but requires a collective reckoning with the past."
—**DEANN BORSHAY LIEM**, director of *First Person Plural*

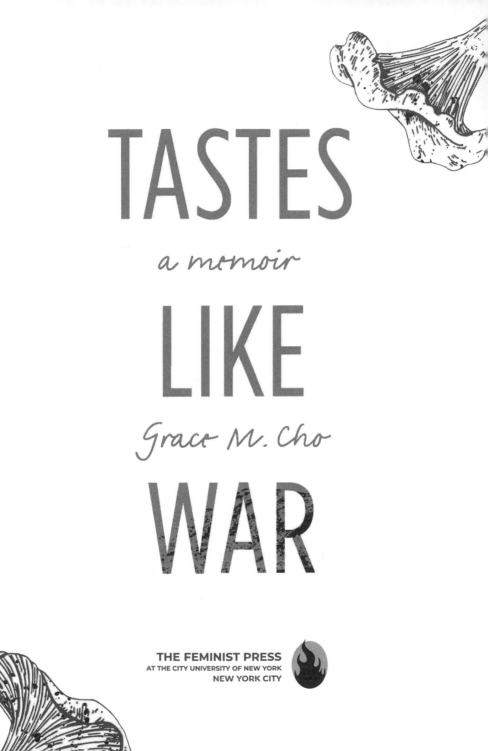

TASTES

a memoir

LIKE

Grace M. Cho

WAR

THE FEMINIST PRESS
AT THE CITY UNIVERSITY OF NEW YORK
NEW YORK CITY

Published in 2021 by the Feminist Press
at the City University of New York
The Graduate Center
365 Fifth Avenue, Suite 5406
New York, NY 10016

feministpress.org

First Feminist Press edition 2021

Some names and identifying details have been changed to protect the privacy of individuals.

  This book is supported in part by an award from the
National Endowment for the Arts.

 This book was made possible thanks to a grant from New York State Council on the Arts with the support of the Governor and the New York State
Legislature.

This book was published with financial support from the
Jerome Foundation.

Third printing March 2022

Cover design by Suki Boynton
Text design by Frances Ross

Library of Congress Cataloging-in-Publication Data
Names: Cho, Grace M., author.
Title: Tastes like war : a memoir / Grace M. Cho.
Description: First Feminist Press edition. | New York, NY : The Feminist
  Press at the City University of New York, 2021. | Includes
  bibliographical references.
Identifiers: LCCN 2020051100 (print) | LCCN 2020051101 (ebook) | ISBN
  9781952177941 (paperback) | ISBN 9781952177958 (ebook)
Subjects: LCSH: Cho, Grace M. | Cho, Grace M.--Family. | Korean American
  women--Biography. | Children of the mentally ill--United
  States--Biography. | Food habits--Korea (South) | Cooking, Korean. |
  Korea (South)--Social life and customs.
Classification: LCC E184.K6 C4733 2021 (print) | LCC E184.K6 (ebook) |
  DDC 305.48/89519073--dc23
LC record available at https://lccn.loc.gov/2020051100
LC ebook record available at https://lccn.loc.gov/2020051101

PRINTED IN THE UNITED STATES OF AMERICA

*For all of my mothers, each of whom fed me in her own way,
and for everyone whose voices have gone unheard.*

PROLOGUE

Chehalis, Washington, 1976

I AM FIVE YEARS OLD, walking down Main Street with my family. The usually sleepy downtown is a riot of balloons and streamers; a marching band thunders past. "It's America's two hundredth birthday," says an old lady with short curls as she hands me a red-white-and-blue popsicle. Funny to have a birthday party for a country, I think, yet I am far too young to consider what it means to be patriotic, or American, or Asian in America. I'm ignorant of the raging wars in Southeast Asia, the stalemated war in Korea, or the ways in which Asian migrations are intimately intertwined with American imperialism and the grossly misnamed "Cold War" that slaughtered seven million innocents in the name of anti/communism.

I think only about the icy-sweet chemical flavor on my tongue, the sticky syrup dripping down my fingers. With my clean hand, I hold on to my father as we push our way through the revelers—my father, a fifty-seven-year-old white Anglo-Saxon farmer turned merchant marine, born and raised in Chehalis, who married my mother, the foreign girl, the China Doll, the war bride, the lovely lotus he saved from third world Korea.

Her waist-length black hair betrays her effort to style herself like a Western woman in a halter top, shorts, and platform sandals. Her sun-kissed skin is noticeably brown against the

1

backdrop of an all-white crowd. My mother stands out because she's the Oriental.

Then, for a moment, she pulls away from the celebration and grimaces slightly from the noise or the glare of the sun. Though I do not yet understand what it means to be an alien, even at the age of five, I can see that she's on the outside, that maybe she doesn't feel like she belongs at this party.

In my lifetime I've had at least three mothers.

The first was the mother of my childhood. I adored and admired her, my beautiful mama. A charismatic and savvy micropolitician, she fought tirelessly to gain acceptance in my father's rural hometown, and in so doing made life more livable for her children. Food was her first line of defense against a deep and abiding fear of the Other that permeated the collective unconscious of the white working-class community in which we landed. She possessed the gift of being a social chameleon, at turns a glamorous and alluring party hostess who introduced our rural American neighbors to the exotic flavors of Korea, an enthusiastic cook who fed everyone that set foot in her kitchen, and a rugged and fearless forager who supplied the whole town with wild edibles.

Feeding others was a way of making a living and learning to live among people who saw her as always and only a foreigner. It was at once a gesture of nurturance and an act of resistance. And in the repetition of these acts, she created her own worth.

By the early 1980s my mother had begun to metamorphosize, like a pupa growing its wings. She wore her once long and lustrous hair cropped close. *So much easier this way*, she would say each time she snipped it away, black snow falling on our white kitchen table. The no-fuss hair matched her homemade power suits, her style an expression of her aspirations to be a career woman, no matter how low the pay or status of her actual job.

With what she had made of herself, she sponsored relatives to come to the United States and supported others in Korea. All the while, my father sailed the Pacific for six months out of the year, leaving her to be a half-time single mother. Out of necessity, she had become the pillar of our family.

And then came the break.

What started as an interest in local and national politics quickly careened into "delusions of grandeur" and "paranoia." Her mind had become so absorbed by the machinations of Ronald Reagan that there was no room left for thinking about food. Her shrinking pantry was perhaps the first sign, the prelude to a mental agitation that would turn our garden fallow and our cupboards empty for years to come.

In 1986, when I was fifteen, she developed what psychiatrists call "florid psychosis." *Florid.* Such a beautiful image to describe the terror. A field of flowers from which my second mother bloomed.

This was the mother of my adolescence and early adulthood, the one that loomed so large in my consciousness that she overshadowed the other mother of my childhood and made me cower in the corner, not because she was violent, but because I had somehow, despite never having known a mad person, internalized the stereotype that equated madness with danger.[1] Because *schizophrenics are seen as some of the most dysfunctional members of society . . . homeless . . . inscrutable . . . murderers . . .*[2]

I was afraid of my own mother, but even more terrifying was the prospect of losing her, as she became prisoner to the voices that told her to stop doing the things she used to do: *Stop talking to strangers. Stop answering the phone. Stop going outside. Stop cooking. Stop eating. Stop moving. Stop living.*

And I did in fact lose her to a kind of death—one where she withdrew from the social, a death in which society rendered her worthless and disposable. It was a stereotype that erased her personhood, and especially her motherhood. Because psychotics are not viewed as capable of loving or being loved.

My socially dead mother sat on the couch for years on end with the curtains closed, completely cut off from the outside world. This was the mother whose voices told her to make herself invisible and small, to sit in the dark, eat as little as possible, and let no one from the outside see her. This was the mother of my coming-of-age, the one around which my adult psyche formed, the one I could not let disappear, but could not yet fully embrace.

It seemed as if she heeded the call of the xenophobes to "go back to where you came from," for her origins were not so easy to locate, and therefore the place she came from was a kind of no place. She was a Korean born in imperial Japan under conditions of forced labor, who returned to a divided, occupied, and war-torn Korea and was later exiled for her transgression of sleeping with my American father. Her retreat inward seemed to take her back to these places of conflict, making her want to stamp out her own existence and vanish into nothingness.

The town to which we migrated was not a refuge but another place of imperial violence, where the rescued must continuously pay a psychic price for their purported salvation. The town in which she became American was the same place in which she became schizophrenic.

At the age of fifteen, when I sought explanations for my mother's schizophrenia, everything I found said that she had a broken brain, nothing more than the result of a bad gene. Even then, I knew that her madness had been mixed from more than one ingredient, though I couldn't begin to understand what the others were. Seven years later I would begin to search for the exact recipe, and the search would lead me to research, in the form of a doctoral dissertation.

I began the project of writing my mother back into existence at a time when I only had two mothers, the before-schizophrenia and the after-schizophrenia mothers. Although I knew that I would never get the first one back, I hoped to at least understand the forces that had killed her.

The ten-year-long journey of my research and writing, from the start of my PhD program through the completion of my first book, coincided exactly with the time period in which I cooked for her. I had initially chosen academia as the method of investigating the personal because it felt like a safe and familiar place in which to take risks; cooking, on the other hand, had always been forbidden terrain to me, a distraction from what my mother envisioned as my true calling of becoming a scholar. Ultimately, cooking became an equally important part of my education about the past.

Whenever her hunger was satisfied, she showed me flashes of the first mother that had raised me. And in turn, that fed my hope. I continued to look for her traces in every book I read and every meal I cooked. In trying to understand how I got from mother one to mother two, a third mother was born.

This third mother was the mother of my thirties, who gradually accepted me as her cook and taught me to prepare the dishes my grandmother once cooked for her. And slowly, through eating these foods, she found a way home. Through cooking the foods of her childhood and getting a glimpse into her early life, I found one too.

No longer held hostage by visions of her as a madwoman, I was able to zoom the lens out and see her from a wider angle. This was the mother who gave me permission to investigate the very past that she had been hiding from me, and thereby let me imagine her before she was my mother—an adolescent in postwar South Korea under the regimes of Park Chung-hee and rising US military hegemony, who worked at a US naval base, selling drinks, and probably sex, to American military personnel. Although the second mother was the impetus to start the research, it was the third mother who gave me sustenance to finish it.

Through my academic work, I encountered many voices— of scholars and activists, of Korean War survivors, both civilian and combatant, and of sexual laborers in varying positions on the continuum between forced and free. Cooking and sharing meals with my mother amplified these voices as I began to tune in to hers.

Feeding her brought me closer to her schizophrenia and allowed me to break bread with her voices. I came to understand that the voices were not alien to her, but part of her, perhaps voices from a suppressed and violent family history that were searching for a witness. They were probably there all along in the first mother. Lying dormant in her mind and poised to leave traces of a fractured history on the future. Through the act of communion with her voices, I learned to stop being afraid of them and listen to what they had to say.

After the completion of my first book, I hadn't planned on writing another one about my mother, but her untimely death churned up new memories that needed to make their way onto paper. As Maggie Nelson said about *Jane: A Murder*, a collection of poetry about her aunt's murder, "It took the writing of not only that book, but also an unintended sequel [*The Red Parts*], for me to undo this knot, and hand its strands to the wind."[3] This book, too, is an unintended sequel.

Paradoxically it was my mother's very absence that gave her a new presence in my life. My grief was so powerful that it unearthed long-forgotten memories that had been buried beneath the weight of her illness and the traumatic history that I spent a decade researching. These were memories of the engaging, competent, and incredibly productive first mother that was perhaps the polar opposite of the stereotypical schizophrenic.

Food was always in the foreground of these memories, whether as a source of pleasure, a source of income, or something more basic—a means of survival. By returning to the scene of eating, I discovered not only things that broke her but also things that kept her alive.

I want to take the fragments of my mother and weave them into a story about her survival. I want to write her back into existence, to let her legacy live on the page, and in so doing, trace my own.

PART I

For those of us
who were imprinted with fear
like a faint line in the center of our foreheads
learning to be afraid with our mother's milk
for by this weapon
this illusion of some safety to be found
the heavy-footed hoped to silence us
For all of us
this instant and this triumph
We were never meant to survive.

And when the sun rises we are afraid
it might not remain
when the sun sets we are afraid
it might not rise in the morning
when our stomachs are full we are afraid
of indigestion
when our stomachs are empty we are afraid
we may never eat again
when we are loved we are afraid
love will vanish
when we are alone we are afraid
love will never return
and when we speak we are afraid
our words will not be heard
nor welcomed
but when we are silent
we are still afraid

So it is better to speak
remembering
we were never meant to survive.

—AUDRE LORDE, "A Litany for Survival"*

1. TASTES LIKE WAR

Princeton, New Jersey, 2008

I WALKED UP THE STAIRS for the last time into the one-room studio my mother never left except when it was "absolutely necessary."

I had never before entered her apartment without her there, and rarely had I seen it with the curtains drawn. Sunlight streamed in through the glass doors of the balcony, illuminating everything in the room. She was really gone.

The cream-colored couch was gray and worn in the center of the seat cushions, where her skin had touched the fabric.

The stains on the couch, a visible imprint of her sudden absence. The balcony, a bitter reminder of her inability to step outside and take a breath of fresh air.

The apartment had been a labor of love and filial duty. In 2001 my older brother and his wife had turned the office above their garage into a granny flat so that my mother could have a permanent home.

Her life had consisted of a series of displacements, the beginning disrupted by colonization and war, the end by schizophrenia and near homelessness. Though she never went a day without housing, her situation was precarious, moving from one temporary place to another, living with my brother or me when she didn't have a place of her own.

They had planned out the renovation with painstaking detail. The building codes did not allow for a full bathroom, so they put in a shower with a small wooden bench so that she could still sit down. Nor did the codes allow for a kitchen, but they installed a stainless-steel sink, marble counters, a bar fridge, and counter-top appliances that transformed the nonkitchen into a functional cooking space.

They furnished and decorated the apartment in a dozen shades of off-white—the couch, the walls, the rug, the bedding, and the heavy floor-to-ceiling curtains that opened onto the picturesque balcony, overlooking an acre of lawn surrounded by woods. Her favorite colors had always been neutral earth tones like beige, ivory, taupe—colors that reminded me of the creamy mushroom casseroles I had seen on the dinner tables of the distant American cousins on my father's side. To my mother, these colors were "high class," a status she'd always aspired to but could never achieve.

She was in her eighth year as a shut-in when she moved there. If it was a place she was literally never going to leave, at least she should love it.

I don't know if she actually loved it, though she did once say it was "okay." Regardless, it must have been a step up from my New York City apartment's guest room, where she lived for seven months during the renovation. At my place, there was no idyllic scenery or classy color palette. Instead it was all bright, mismatched colors with hand-me-down furniture and a view of traffic congestion on the Brooklyn–Queens Expressway.

My sister-in-law had really talked up the balcony, telling me on several occasions that what the apartment lacked in space it would make up for in charm.

"We're going to put a bird feeder out there and a nice little table and chairs," she said, tucking a strand of dirty blond hair behind her ear. Her Arkansan drawl was still prominent after ten years in the Northeast.

"She won't go outside," I said.

"You don't know that. At least she can watch the kids play in the backyard."

Her certainty made me doubt my pessimism. Maybe. Maybe, I thought, she'll look out the window if someone else opens the curtains.

My mother opened the sliding glass door only once, though she didn't actually set foot outside. Shortly after moving into the apartment, she put a potted flower that my then eight-year-old niece had picked out for her as a housewarming gift onto the balcony. And she left it there the whole winter, to die.

"That was a present from her granddaughter! Why would she do something like that?" My sister-in-law was annoyed. She took it as an act of disrespect or carelessness, or at the very least, another sign of her ever-deteriorating mental health.

"It's hard to know what she's thinking," I said. But I was curious about my mother's motivations, so the next time I saw her, I asked about the flowers.

"Ma, how come you kept those flowers outside? Didn't you like them?"

She looked irritated and waved her hand at me, as if to shoo away my questions. But after a long pause, she answered.

"Because of the name. I hate the name."

"Why? What's the name?"

"Cyclamen. It sounds like cycle." She contorted her face as if she were disgusted, but when she resumed talking it sounded like she was about to cry. "I am tired of the same thing over and over. I wish things would change."

Vicious cycle. Cycle of violence. My mind free-associated into my research and my imagined family history.

My memory flashed to an incident that had happened a few months earlier when we'd been watching TV together after dinner. A soap commercial came on, showing a woman lathering up in the shower, the camera's gaze fixed on her hands and bare shoulders. My mother turned her face away from the TV and shaded her eyes with her hand. There was a vacant, disconnected look in her eyes and her affect had gone flat. Even the suggestion of a naked body was too disturbing for her to watch.

I later told my friend, a doctoral student in psychology, about what had happened. "A soap commercial?" she said. "Now *that* is some trauma."

I looked out at the balcony and remembered the cyclamen, the cycle.

Maybe the cycle referred to the relentless repetition of her lonely days, economized into the fewest possible movements:

Get out of bed at 6:00 a.m. and eat a breakfast of plain toast, apple juice, and instant coffee while standing at the sink. Take medication. Go to the bathroom, flush toilet, wash hands and face, brush teeth. Sit down on the couch and watch the daylight begin to filter through the cracks in the curtains. Open the blinds in the kitchen only to send a signal to my sister-in-law that she needed something. Otherwise, keep them closed. Watch the hands on the clock slowly revolve until twelve noon. Get up and eat lunch: ramen or a peanut butter sandwich if there's nothing left of whatever meals my sister-in-law or I have put in the fridge. Resume sitting on the couch and watch more time go by. Get up at 5:00 p.m. and eat the same thing for dinner. Wash dishes. Sit some more until the sun goes down. Do the bathroom routine again. Lie down in bed and stay still until falling asleep sometime around midnight.

Repeat.

Once a week she'd take a shower. The only other things that disrupted this monotony were visits from one of her children or grandchildren. On days without visitors, her voices were her only company.

Despite how devastated I felt by her death, I told myself that at least she would never have to live another day like that.

When my mother moved into the apartment in December 2001, she'd hardly been eating. Her diminishing appetite had ebbed and flowed for years, hitting a low earlier that fall, when she was living with me in Queens.

She spent most of her time at my place sitting on the futon in her room, keeping the TV on for a few hours each morning, sometimes just as background noise.

On the morning of September 11, I popped my head in to say goodbye to her before I left for LaGuardia Community College, where it was my second day working as a writing fellow. She was hanging her head down, staring at the floor as she listened to the local news. The volume was low, and I didn't notice what was flashing across the screen. The first plane had already struck, yet my mother said nothing about it as I walked out the door.

Later that day, I would return home in hysterics, having run miles along Roosevelt Avenue after the subways shut down and the phone circuits jammed, demanding to know why she didn't warn me, why she didn't try to call my brother, who worked across the street from the World Trade Center.

She said simply that she had failed. That she let me go to work because she thought she could stop it. And not to worry about my brother because she wouldn't allow anything to happen to him.

"Mom, this has nothing to do with you! This is not in your control."

She then put me in my place.

"Why so much crying? You think you are so special? You are not the only one in the world who go through something like this."

Me and my first world privilege, never having known such destruction.

I wondered about the family members she had lost in the war and whether she had somehow felt responsible for their demise. I wondered what it was doing to her already-traumatized mind to watch the images of New York as a war zone, replaying over and over, in the aftermath of the event.

A few weeks later she started complaining about her stomach. For two days she vomited bile into a metal bowl, and then I made an executive decision.

"Mom, we have to get you to the hospital."

"I am not going anywhere," she said.

"But you're sick! Or you'll get sick if you don't start eating. Look, it might be something simple to treat, like an ulcer."

"An ulcer? If you are so worried about my getting ulcer, why would you feed me spicy food? Huh?" She looked me dead in the eye, spitting venom. It was the first time since my teenage years that I felt afraid of her.

There was no way to force her to go anywhere if she didn't want to, and the only way I could get her to eat was to tell her I was about to throw something away and then leave it outside her door. It must have appealed to the scavenger in her, the one that emerged during those months that she lived with me.

At the end of the day, the food would always be gone.

My brother and his wife seemed to think that things would improve once my mother had a place of her own. I suppose it was a reasonable assumption.

During the first few months, she still didn't want to eat.

They tried some of the same tricks I'd resorted to when she was at my place in Queens, like leaving food for her in the hopes she'd eat it, knowing how much she hated for things to go to waste.

They also stocked her pint-size kitchen with large quantities of packaged foods that required no more preparation than adding water or opening a can. According to my sister-in-law, my mother was eating the ramen and fruit cocktail, but had barely touched the powdered milk. Although I felt some relief knowing that she wasn't starving, I also felt ashamed that her diet was so bereft of nutrition.

"Mom, are you getting enough to eat?" I asked.

She nodded.

"What about protein?"

She nodded again, then snorted. "They got me powdered milk."

"Oh yeah?" I said, feigning surprise.

She became quiet as if she had already lost her train of thought and was deep in some hallucinatory reverie.

"I can't stand the taste of it," she said. "Tastes like war."

It was only the second time she ever brought up the war without my prompting. Her words jolted me into a reverie of my own, as fragments of my research tumbled around in my head. Images of babies sitting on dirt roads next to the bodies of their dead mothers and napalmed women bandaged like mummies. The words of a woman who survived the Nogeun-ri massacre, who lost her child when American planes dropped bombs from above: *That day I saw the two faces of America.*[1] The words of a war bride who remembered American food aid: *I had heard of the "Yankees" and how they were here to save us. . . . We were all hoping for rice or barley, and we drooled at the thought of so much food . . . but it was an endless supply of powdered milk that caused all who drank it to suffer for days with diarrhea.*[2]

In February 2002 my mother finally went to the hospital after my brother and sister-in-law called an ambulance and had her admitted on the grounds that she was trying to starve herself to death.

After the hospitalization, she started meds again, started to eat again, but still not much. Not everything. Her resistance still took the form of rejecting food, but the foods she couldn't or wouldn't eat were very specific, like the powdered milk.

After Arnold Schwarzenegger was elected as California's governor, she asked me to stop buying her Arnold bread.

"Mom, you know it has nothing to do with him, right? The name is just a coincidence," I said.

She smiled and let out a little laugh, as if she knew how crazy it sounded.

She always seemed to put a great deal of thought into her choices to eat or not eat something. In time, I recognized these choices as an expression of agency, tiny acts of rebellion against enormous structures of power.

It is not simply the "what" of what one eats that matters. . . . Most important, it is the many "whys" of eating—the differing imperatives of hunger, necessity, pleasure, nostalgia, and protest—that most determine its meaning.[3]

My mother never wanted me to cook for her, but over the years, she reluctantly taught me to make Korean food. Maybe she got tired of eating instant ramen and canned fruit cocktail. She wanted, instead, to eat a steaming bowl of fluffy white rice with saengtae jjigae: an old-fashioned stew of pollack and radishes laden with garlic and red pepper flakes, spicy and bubbling hot. The first spoonful of it made her sigh and say, "I haven't tasted this in forty years."

By her second year living in the apartment, it had become the norm for her to give me a grocery list of Korean products and tell me what meal I should cook on the next visit.

The last time I saw her, she asked me to get fish pancakes from the Korean market and some Pepcid because her stomach had been bothering her. She'd also recently had diarrhea. The grocery list was one of several things that nagged at me for months after my brother found her lifeless on the floor.

The official cause of death was "myocardial infarction."

I tried to imagine the way my sister-in-law described my mother's body. "She was curled up on the rug with her head resting on her hands, like she was asleep. She looked like she was at peace." I had seen my father have a heart attack, and I knew it didn't look like a peaceful slumber.

A few weeks before my mother's death, during one of my visits, she got up off the couch and walked over to the small black mother-of-pearl vase on top of her TV cabinet.

"This is where I keep my pearl earrings. In case something happen to me."

She gently lifted a wad of paper towels out of the vase, unwrapped them, and placed a pair of pearl studs into her cupped hands. She gestured them toward me.

"For you. Don't forget."

Part of me wondered if she was planning another suicide attempt, but just as quickly as the thought arose, I dismissed it. She was so different now. Fourteen years had passed, and she was an entirely different person from the suicidal mother of my early twenties. Plus, she seemed upbeat when she said it, so I filed the comment away as part of the generalized catastrophic thinking and emergency readiness that had long been a part of her mindset.

After she died, I remembered the earrings and the Pepcid, and debated whether it was more likely that she had overdosed or had been hiding a serious illness. And then there was my brother's speculation: "Who knows what all those drugs were doing to her?"

The pearl earrings were still there, inside the layers of Bounty, inside the vase. I put the little bundle in my backpack and a gut-wrenching feeling gripped me: she had known she was going to die.

I took one last look around the room and let it sink in. This was the place of my mother's mysterious death, the final scene of her lonely, tedious life, but it was also the place of her redemption. This was where she had spent the best years of her life after the schizophrenia had set in, where she learned to enjoy food again and ask for what she wanted. Where we shared the meals that she hadn't eaten since her youth.

As she talked about the things she ate or wished to eat or had been deprived of eating when she was young, she also shared minute details about her past, a trail of crumbs that would lead me to my family history.

2. AMERICAN DREAMS

Korea, 1961

BY THE TIME MY MOTHER reached the age of twenty, half of her family had already died. My grandmother gave birth to at least four children between the years 1922 and 1941: one boy and three girls. My mother was the youngest. If my grandmother had given birth to more than four children, no one ever spoke of them.

They were all born when Korea was a colony of Japan, and Gyeongsang Province, where my mother's family lived, endured the greatest violence by virtue of its proximity to Japan. Under Japanese colonial rule, Koreans were dispossessed of their land and homes and forced into various forms of labor. Young women and girls were taken to Japan to work as sex slaves for the imperial army. Most were teenagers, and some were as young as ten.

Korean subjects were ordered to speak only Japanese or risk having their tongues cut out, so my grandparents raised their children to speak their oppressors' language.

My mother and her siblings lived through their colonized childhoods, but two of them, along with my grandfather, would be lost in the Korean War and its aftermath. My mother and her eldest sister were the survivors.

The end of Japanese colonial rule in 1945 did not mean the end of occupied Korea, but rather, a change in occupier.

In August 1945 the United States became the only country in history to use nuclear weapons, bombing Hiroshima and
Nagasaki, an event later commemorated by an American holiday
called "VJ Day." Victory over Japan.

The atomic bombs killed not only the two hundred thousand
Japanese that the United States saw as an enemy people but also
some twenty thousand Koreans, a people that the United States
claimed to have liberated and saved. My mother's family was in
Osaka during World War II, and so they were spared annihilation.
But the United States would continue to kill Koreans in order to
save them from themselves.

At the end of World War II, when my mother was four years
old, the US drew a line at the 38th parallel, dividing the country
in two and ceding the North to the Soviets. As soon as Japanese
occupation of Korea ended, American and Soviet occupation
began, and Korea became the United States' first "laboratory of
communist containment," the first "theater of the Cold War," in
which an experiment in mass destruction would play out. The
dead, the wounded, the motherless or fatherless, the homeless, the families permanently torn apart when the border was
closed—each of these categories numbering in the millions.

Buried beneath the ashes of the cities and towns that burned
to the ground during the Korean War, beneath the sobering sta-
tistic of three million identifiable bodies, were the others that
could not be easily calculated among the casualties. Bodies that
could never be found and counted as dead. Bodies too decomposed to be identified. Entire families wiped out in a single blow
with no one left to claim them. People who died of seemingly
natural causes in a country too devastated to sustain the life of the
remaining population. Dire circumstances that led to the exodus
of its survivors.

My mother's words about the past, scattered across two
decades:

My brother disappeared during the war, when I was nine.

My father died during the war, when I was ten.

My sister Chunja—oh, she was my favorite! She was closest to me in age, you see. My sister died when I was twenty, in 1961.

It would take me twenty-five years to locate my family beneath the rubble.

Chehalis, Washington, 1980

THE FIRST TIME I get an inkling of my family history is when my third-grade teacher assigns our class a family-tree project.

With my father in some faraway port—Manila or Guam or Singapore—I plan to interview only my mother. She hates to talk about the past, but for the benefit of my education, she's willing to do just about anything.

I know my grandmother and aunt, my halmeoni and imo, and the two cousins I met during our summer trips to Busan, so I think I know what my mother's side of the tree will look like.

I sit down at the high counter in the living room that looks out onto the kitchen. The white wooden shutters that divide the two rooms are open, allowing me to face my mother as she works. This is my favorite spot in the house because I feel tall in the swiveling yellow vinyl barstool, and it's within arm's reach of the ceramic cookie jar in the shape of Goofy's head. I plan to eat a cookie once I finish my family tree, but for now, I open my Garfield notebook and focus on the task at hand.

"What's Halmae-ya's name?" I ask, picturing my grandmother's hands swish rice under running water. My mother has just fed our two cats and has begun to chop scallions at the pull-out cutting board next to the sink.

"Cho Sung-woon. C-H-O. First name you spell S-U-N-G-W-O-O-N."

"What's your father's name?" I don't call him Halbae because I've never even seen a picture of him, and therefore haven't made the emotional connection that he's my grandfather.

"Ha Jum-eul." Again she spells out the name.

"What were your grandparents' names?"

"Huh. I don't know," she says, shaking her head. "Koreans don't call old people by their first names."

"Okay, then . . . what are the names of the children?" I draw two lines for my mother and her sister, my imo.

My mother spells out Imo's name, as well as her own. Then she wipes some bits of scallion off the cutting board and leans against it. She focuses her eyes on the wall two feet in front of her and says, "I had a brother and another sister too."

I nearly drop my pencil as I look up, mouth agape.

"My brother disappeared during the war. I don't know what happened. I just never saw him again."

"How old were you?"

"Oh, about your age," she says, still staring at the wall.

I try to imagine what it would be like to suddenly never see my brother again, and even though I don't see him much anymore because he's a big kid, already planning for college, the word "never" still crushes me. An urge comes over me to tear my homework assignment into little pieces, but then I worry that I'll disappoint my parents and teacher, the people who believe in me and have invested in my education.

My mother seems lost in a dream.

"What about your sister?" I ask.

"My sister Chunja . . . she was by far the best looking out of all three of us girls. She was my favorite . . ."

"What happened to her?"

"She died before you were born." Her gaze finally connects with mine, and the two of us stare in silence, amplified by the humming of the long fluorescent bulb mounted on the wall. She closes her eyes and sighs the words, "Aigu! Dap-dap-eu-rah."

"Dap-dap-eu-rah"—*I'm suffocating*—an expression of stifling sadness.

My mother's brother, my grandmother's first child and only son, disappeared at the start of the war in 1950. His body was never found, and the family could not officially claim him as dead, nor did they want to believe that he was gone forever. Historical records would later file his disappearance under the ambiguous category of "missing or wounded" along with some two million others.

When the armistice agreement was signed in 1953, it spelled out a contract between the United States and North Korea that the war would be resolved with a peace treaty and the divided country would be put back together within six months. Over a third of the surviving population had been separated from their loved ones because they ended up on opposite sides of the border, and the armistice gave them a promise that they would soon be reunited.

This meant that my missing uncle might resurface once the border reopened. But none of these promises was fulfilled, the signatories of the armistice have remained locked in a stalemate ever since, and my mother's family never found out whether he died, defected, or simply had the misfortune of being in the wrong place on July 27, 1953.

Other families—the ones who were lucky enough, and lived long enough—would wait forty, fifty, sixty years to spend a few hours with their lost brothers and sisters during state-supervised visits. The family reunifications would begin during the fourth decade of the armistice and take place every few years, as gestures of goodwill between the two Koreas, each time granting visits to a handful of applicants.

For example, in August 2018, only eighty-nine out of 57,000 applicants would meet their missing family members after more than sixty-five years apart. One woman, ninety-two-year-old Lee Keum-seom, would see her son again for the first time since 1950, when they lost each other in the chaos of the war. *I didn't know what to do but cry for a whole year, calling out his name. . . . He was only four years old.*[1]

But when my mother lived in Korea in the 1950s and 1960s, South Korean families had to act as if their missing kin were dead. If the government suspected that they had any ties to the North, even if such ties were accidental, they could have been persecuted as enemies of the state. So my family was to never again speak my uncle's name, and my grandmother took in his five-year-old boy, Jinho, one of millions of children who lost parents to the war, and raised him as her fifth child.

Natural cause: an illness or internal malfunction of the body not directly caused by external forces.

For years, the only thing my mother could say about my grandfather was that "he died during the Korean War." I would eventually learn that he wasn't killed by bombs or bullets, but by stomach cancer.

What complicated my grandfather's illness was that all the hospitals had burned to the ground during the first six months of the war, as part of an American policy that destroyed civilian institutions, calling them "military targets" in the official record. By the time he knew of his cancer, there was no place left for the sick to go.

The lack of infrastructure, the food insecurity, the postwar suffering of survivors would continue throughout the 1950s and into the 1960s.

My mother's sister Chunja would also die of stomach cancer, in 1961, at the age of twenty-six.

I would come to question not only the state of health care when Chunja was sick but also what could have caused such a young woman to develop stomach cancer. I would remember the stories from my research of Koreans who survived by scavenging half-eaten hot dogs and hamburgers from the dumpsters at American military bases and wonder how much of her illness had been linked to her impoverished diet. I'd remember what my mother told me about the kinds of things her family ate during the (post)war era: *We used to catch spiders and grasshoppers, sometimes little birds, and roast 'em over a fire. The spiders tasted pretty darn good, but those little birds hardly have any meat on 'em. Hardly worth all the trouble of plucking and cleaning, 'cause we practically eat it in one bite, bone and all!*

There are no pictures of my dead aunt or anyone else from my Korean family prior to the 1963 glamour shot of my twenty-two-year-old mother in a beehive hairdo, an off-the-shoulder faux-fur stole, and black kohl eyeliner, flashing her wide smile and dimples for the camera. I had internalized this image as the epitome of feminine beauty, so it was hard for me to imagine a sister who was more stunning than my mother. My surviving aunt would later confirm that my dead aunt was a vision of such otherworldly proportions that she could make any woman look ordinary by contrast.

She would corroborate other parts of the story, too, answering my broken Korean with a single word: "Geu-reh." *Correct.*

"Chunja Imo died of stomach cancer?"

"Geu-reh."

"Your oppa was lost in the war?"

"Geu-reh." And then she would add questions of her own:

"Do you suppose he's still alive? He would be almost ninety now. Could he be still alive in North Korea?"

Princeton, New Jersey, 2006

MY MOTHER AND I are sitting in her apartment eating a meal of ssam, grilled meat and rice wrapped in lettuce leaves. In between bites of food, she lets loose a secret about her beautiful dead sister.

"My sister had two children, you know. Boys."

"No, I didn't know! Where are they now?"

"No one knows. They just disappeared." She puts the ssam in her mouth and begins chewing.

"What do you mean 'they just disappeared'?" I wait as she chews and swallows, pushes more of the ssam into her mouth, chews and swallows again, until she has eaten the entire wrap in one continuous bite.

"You see, in Korea, children belong to their father," she says, as she assembles the next piece of ssam. "No one knows what he did with them after she died."

The thought enters my mind that they were given up for adoption and are living somewhere in America, with names like Andrew and Christopher, or maybe in France. André and Christophe.

I think about some of the adopted kids I knew growing up who were renamed Cathy, Cody, and Robert. Their Korean names forgotten, replaced. Their birthdays rewritten as the date of their adoption. Their Korean families rendered dead through official documents, the children told to never again speak their names.

At the time that I learned of my missing cousins, I had also recently researched the ways in which my own family history was implicated in the history of transnational adoption. Although it began as a rescue mission in 1954 to find American homes for Korean war orphans, it quickly turned into a substitute for social welfare and a government policy to rid the country of an unwanted population.

South Korea's first president, Syngman Rhee, whose motto was "one race, one nation," publicly denounced the presence of "Yankee wives and mixed race children" as a "social crisis." He signed a presidential order for the placement of these children in transnational adoption as a solution to the "GI baby problem." American propaganda depicted the poor, socially rejected biracial child as the most vulnerable of all creatures to the clutches of communism, and therefore, Americans would be exercising their patriotic duty by rescuing them.

At the same time, Korean social workers launched aggressive campaigns to convince mothers working in the camptowns that Korea could offer nothing of value to their children and the only rightful place for them was in their father's country. And indeed, the law was structured to make it so. Children born to Korean mothers and foreign fathers would not be allowed to attend public schools or register as South Korean citizens. Long before I was born, Rhee's policies had already determined the conditions of our exile.

South Korea's adoption program and American campaigns to save Korean children from communism and the "Asian disregard for human life" had become so successful that, by the 1960s, Korean social workers had to expand their recruitment efforts to other marginalized populations.[2] Single mothers and poor families of "pure" Korean descent became the new targets. Instead of finding homes for needy children, adoption agencies began looking for children to place in homes, thus continuing the steady supply of Korean adoptees westward. One former Korean social worker spoke openly about this practice: *I misunderstood my job and thought I was supposed to make the birth mothers relinquish their children.*[3]

In the minds of many Koreans, America became a mythical place where there was no poverty or racism, and anyone could make it big. In the words of one woman who gave her two Amerasian children up for adoption: *One time my older one came home with his trousers soaked and frozen with his own pee. Children bullied him by saying, "You must have a big penis. Let me see." . . . I talked to them for about a month and said, "We have been waiting a long time for your father who has never come. If you stay here, you will face constant discrimination. However, in the US there is no such thing."*[4]

Chehalis, Washington, 1977

IT IS A MILD fall day in first grade, and I have just gotten off at the bus stop near my house. The neighborhood blond bully calls after me.

"Wait! Wait! I want to show you something."

I turn around and watch her crouch down and peer into the shady grass beneath a small grove of oak trees. Tentatively, I stop and move in her direction. When I'm close enough to almost see over her shoulder, she springs to her feet with a rusty hammer in her hand and waves it at me. I begin to run and think I've lost her before I realize that she has stopped to dip the hammer into a mound of fresh dog poo. She begins chasing me again, aiming her shit-smeared weapon at my head. Another child from the bus stop joins in and tackles me. He pins me down as the blond bully holds the hammer above my face, but somehow I wriggle away and run.

Panic pulses through my body as I feel myself slipping on mud and falling into a ditch. I land on my back and look up through the tops of the gold and green sun-dappled trees at a rare blue sky. A trickle of cold water runs down my neck and soaks through the back of the red corduroy jacket that my mother had just washed that morning. I picture how upset she'll be that it's already dirty, and the tears start. I squeeze my eyes shut so that the blond bully cannot see me crying, but I hear her cackling at the top of the ditch.

"Dog eater!" she calls out as she drops the hammer into the water next to me, splashing mud and feces onto my jacket.

Sometime between the ages of fifteen and twenty-one, my mother journeyed from her family's ancestral town of Chang-nyeong to the port city of Busan in search of work. This I know by putting together two pieces of evidence: according to my cousin in Korea, she went to high school for one or two years in Changnyeong; she was pregnant with my brother in Busan by age twenty-one. Only the second one can be proven.

Not once did my mother ever narrate a clear story about her coming of age, but she did drop a few crumbs of information during our dinner conversations over the last ten years of her life. Once in a while, she would flesh out a character or scene from postwar Korea that had stayed in her memory, and in so doing, she gave me the outline of a story.

Though my mother had lost half her family, it seemed as if her heart remained open. She spoke with compassion about the other survivors among whom she lived. Around her were people of all ages trying to make a living in a country still reeling from the devastation of the war: the grandmothers who carried heavy bundles of cabbages into the city to take to market, the girls who quit school to toil long days in the factory, the men who stole and butchered dogs to sell for meat. She couldn't admit that she

pitied the dog traders, because they were regarded as the dregs
of society, and no respectable person could excuse the filthiness
and dishonesty of their work. One of her own dogs even fell
victim to them and was turned into meat. As much as she hated
them for snatching her pet, and as much as she internalized public opinion that they were unworthy of her concern, she could
not help but wonder what circumstances led them to that fate. In
some small way, she felt for them too.

There was a young boy in her neighborhood whom she
watched with particular tenderness. He was a peddler of red-
bean ice, about eight or nine years old. At the height of summer,
his covered basket was no match for the sun, and his ices turned
to slush at a rate much faster than he could sell them. On those
sweltering days, the boy crumpled up on the side of the road
and cried in frustration as drops of red-bean syrup formed little
rivers in the dust. Whenever my mother had enough change to
spare, she would buy an ice or two to save him from the humiliation of failure.

These were some of the fragments of experience that my
mother shared with me, but she never spoke about her work. I've
always wondered if she moved to Busan already knowing what
she would do there, or if she went with another purpose, only to
be lured into a different kind of occupation. Maybe she had seen
the US naval base where local girls walked hand in hand with
American soldiers, who showered them with gifts of sweets and
perfume, and marveled at their comfort. It must have seemed as
if they wanted for nothing. Did she know from the beginning that
she was going to be one of them?

My surviving imo, sixteen years my mother's senior, was like
another mother to her. Indeed, my imo's children were only
a few years younger than my mother. So when my aunt's husband died and her sons were grown, she could spend more time

looking after my mother. But as much as she fretted over her baby sister, she could not protect her from everything.

My mother dreamed of getting an education, but she was a girl. Girls helped pay for the educations of their brothers instead of going to school themselves. Jinho was preparing to go to university while my mother was working in Busan.

In the 1960s, South Korea was in the throes of massive transformation: postwar reconstruction, urbanization, and rapid industrialization. Rural people moved to the cities in search of work in the burgeoning factories. In 1963, when Park Chung-hee seized power, he implemented a series of economic plans that would put industry first and social welfare last. He would tell the people that their job was to rebuild the nation by working more and earning less. Misery would become the measure of good citizenship.

Bars and nightclubs were established around American military bases so that the soldiers could feel comforted by a feminine touch. Aspiring performers sang and danced. Pretty girls sold drinks on commission and chatted with men at the bars. Koreans went to the bases in droves, if only to beg for scraps or search for leftovers in the garbage. For some women, it was a small leap from eating out of the trash to exchanging services for food. Exchanging sex for dinner. Selling food on the black market for money with which to buy more food. Selling sex in nightclubs to pay for things more expensive than food, debt mounting with each passing day. These were the kinds of things people did to survive.

Because the Korean War was never resolved, American bases and the service industry catering to them flourished, and public sentiment toward the American presence in Korea remained ambivalent. The emerging South Korean nation depended on the United States for both national and economic security, and the bases provided much of the currency that the average person needed to get by. Koreans were grateful for the opportunities to work, but resentments still ran high because Americans enjoyed privileges that most Koreans had never imagined—spacious accommodations, an endless supply of food, and the guaranteed company of women.

There were two places of employment designated for young women who weren't from elite families: the factory or the army base. I imagine that my mother, being a person of great ambition, chose the latter. She may have been attracted to the American base for its wealth of exotic foods, for its day-to-day life filled with small luxuries and opportunities to sometimes sing on stage. Most of the jobs in the camptowns offered shorter hours and greater earning potential than did those in the factory. More importantly, it promised the glamour of America and the possibility of one day moving there by building a life with an American soldier. The chances of that actually happening were slim, but my mother, and a million other women like her, made a wager.

I wonder if Imo tried to convince my mother that such a place would lead to her certain ruin. Or maybe my mother knew this already, and it was the prospect of ruin itself that drew her in. Maybe there was nothing about her life before the camptown that she wanted to keep pristine, and in a reckless moment, she plunged headfirst into the uncharted waters of America town. After all, what did she have to lose?

The women who flocked to the American bases could not have foreseen the consequences. The barmaids, the club hostesses, the singers, the dancers, the prostitutes, the waitresses, the shopkeepers who supplied convenience items to the soldiers, the beauticians who coiffed the entertainers, the black-market peddlers who traded in PX goods, the casual passersby who paid attention to catcalls—all of these women were branded "Western princesses" and "Yankee whores." It was bad enough that they casually mingled with men who were unacceptable to their families, and that they did so in seedy settings, but what made it worse was that these men were Americans—the very Americans to whom the Koreans were indebted and subordinated. It was an affront to the nation. Although South Korea profited greatly from US military presence, to the point that the government aggressively promoted the sex industry around the bases as a form of "foreign diplomacy," the women workers were gradually stripped of their rights. Korean society reviled these women so much that life in "normal" society became impossible. Fathers legally disowned the very same daughters whose labor paid off their families' debts. Some women even died at the hands of their abusers—men who were never brought to justice.

The allure of America obscured the hazards of the work— that drunken soldiers with extraterritorial protections could be lethally violent. That club owners sent "slicky boys" after girls who didn't play by the rules. That their children would become stateless subjects. That they would soon be sinking in quicksand and there would be only two ways out—death, or marriage to an American.

Chehalis, Washington, 1987

IT'S THE SPRING of my sophomore year of high school, and I am in history class. A boy named John is sitting behind me, whispering my name. I try to ignore him because his comments are often vaguely sexual, drawing attention to my developing body, but at the same time he is one of the smart kids in my school and sometimes my ally against the tide of ignorance that I face daily. This time he says something that catches me off guard.

"Hey, Grace? Was your mom a war bride?" He says this in a
slightly mocking tone. I don't respond. He asks again, "Was your
mom a war bride?"

I don't understand the question and mull over in my head how
my mother could be a war bride when the Korean War was in the
1950s but my parents married in 1971.

"I heard that she was," he says.

I want to put the question to rest, so I say, "My mom's from
Korea, not Vietnam."

I do not yet realize that Korea is still at war.

Neither of my parents ever talked about how or when they
met, but from the keepsakes my father left behind after he died,
I know that he was stationed in Vietnam in 1968. By 1970 my
mother was pregnant with me, and my parents were planning to
get married.

According to my aunt, an insatiable hunger consumed my
mother throughout her pregnancy. There were a lot of things she
was hungry for, but some of her hungers were so big and beyond
her reach that it was hard to translate them into words, so she
asked for the nameable things she knew she could get. She would
say to my aunt, "Unni-ya, cook for me please." Of all the things
my mother could have eaten, she singled out one dish in particular. "Unni-ya, please make me some nokdu-juk." She ordered the
mung-bean porridge almost every day, and if my aunt suggested
she eat something else, my mother insisted, "But nokdu-juk is
what baby wants to eat." Even when my mother wasn't pregnant,
she had a habit of seeking out her craving and overindulging in
that one thing.

She was a single mother at the time, raising my then six-year-
old brother against the odds. In those days, and still today, sex
outside of marriage was such a serious transgression of Korean
cultural norms for women that the men in their families would

sometimes forge adoption papers to send away children born to single mothers. Women who carried the physical evidence of their sexual deviance—in the form of children and pregnancies—were pushed to the margins of society. My mother was no exception. The only women Koreans despised more than single mothers were the women who "mixed flesh with foreigners," because they were whores, and traitors too.

Despite the constant reminders that she was condemning her child to a future of despair, my mother would not let go of my brother. Instead, she became determined to make a home with him in America, and my father was about to make that dream come true. Although her impending marriage to my father may have been a relief to my aunt and grandmother, it did not earn my mother any modicum of respect from other Koreans.

At fifty-one years old, he was a father figure whose promises of a life far away, where she could start over, offered my mother some solace. His very presence was a reminder of brighter days to come, but for most of their early relationship, he lived in the States while she waited in Korea. My father had important matters to attend to back home—namely, divorcing his first wife so that he could marry my mother.

My mother became lonely while she waited for him. I wonder if she hadn't also started to fear that he was like so many other American soldiers who disappeared and left a trail of children in their wake. Without a marriage certificate, there was nothing obligating my father's return. Alongside her beautiful dream of a new American life was the shadow of a nightmare—the possibility of another mixed race child that she would either have to give away or bring into a hopeless, stateless future.

To keep her spirits up, she sometimes went to the beauty salon, but her preference for Western hairstyles and clothing marked her as a Yankee's girlfriend. One day after having her hair set in a flip, she was walking home, her bouncing hair and click-ing heels adding a special jauntiness to her stride. A man called after her, "Hey! Hey! Miss Korea! Where are you going?" He per-sisted with his call and followed her down the street: "Hey, Miss Korea! Where do you think you're going?"

The story, as my mother told it to me, ended there, but in my mind this episode led to another. Maybe he spat in her hair, or grabbed her arm and pushed her to the ground. Maybe he raped her as a symbolic reclamation of Korean territory from the Americans. Maybe this rape caused the pregnancy right before me, the one that my mother aborted, for which my father beat her until her eardrums broke. My imaginings were fueled by the violent incidents I had visualized through my research on Korean women who were sexual companions of US military personnel. Equally, they were fueled by childhood memories of the conflict between my parents. *Go ahead, break my eardrum again, you no-good so-and-so!*

During her pregnancy with me, she called on my aunt to visit frequently. Whenever Imo came, she massaged my mother's feet, brushed her hair, and rubbed ointment on her belly. Over a game of cards one day, my mother told Imo a secret that would have shocked anyone who might have been eavesdropping: "I hope this baby is a girl."

She had already given birth to a boy, and that fact gave her permission to wish that the second child be a girl. Besides, this baby was going to grow up American, and my mother had gotten the notion that women could do great things in America.

As I grew inside her, so did her loneliness. Whenever it was time for my aunt to leave, my mother became desperate. She would hide Imo's shoes and plead, "Please stay a little longer, Unni. You don't have to leave right now." Their separations became more and more fraught, and the following year, when my parents were married and my mother was about to board a plane to America with my brother and me, it was my aunt who begged my mother not to go.

The scene would repeat each summer, climaxing with our final departure in 1976, my last and most enduring childhood memory of Korea.

A boarding gate at Gimhae International Airport, the air thick with cigarette smoke and steamy August haze. Imo on her knees, clinging to my mother's arm and wailing the word for "little sister." "Dong-saeng-aaah! Dong-saeng-aaah! Dong-saeng-aaah-aaah . . . Dong-saeng-aaah-aaah . . ." Imo in her hanbok, getting dragged across the floor. My mother, mortified and breaking free. Imo grabbing handfuls of her short permed hair. Imo with her voice trembling, "Gaji mara, Dong-saeng-ah. Gaji mara." *Don't go.*

3. THE FRIENDLY CITY

Chehalis, Washington, 1977
Population: 5,727
Korean population: 3

"*CHINESE, JAPANESE.*" A child tugs his eyelids upward, then downward, to slant. "*Dirty knees, look at these.*" He grabs at his nipples with his thumb and forefinger, pulling out the fabric on his chest to simulate a woman's breasts.

At first I am stunned to silence, then find a retort. "I'm not Chinese or Japanese."

The scene repeats every few days at recess, as I play alone on the always-damp log toys of my elementary school playground. It's usually a boy or group of boys that taunts me. Each time, my reply is a little quicker. "I'm not Chinese or Japanese." Sometimes I add, "I'm Korean."

Over time my response evolves. "I'm half Korean." I want to distance myself from the words that make slanted eyes and women's breasts seem shameful, but it's too late. The shame is already inside of me.

Chinese, Japanese . . .

"I'm half American," I say. "My father is American." With enough time I learn to make my mother disappear.

Drive along the I-5 corridor from Seattle to Portland, and where dense evergreens start to give way to sprawling pastures, you will see a double-sided billboard off the highway with a picture of Uncle Sam. Passersby in both directions can read his words: *Bangladesh has clean air, but would you want to live there?* and *AIDS: the wonder disease that turns fruits into vegetables.*[1] The billboard belongs to the children of Alfred Hamilton, a farmer who erected it in the early 1960s in defiance of Ladybird Johnson's Highway Beautification Act, which outlawed advertising on interstate highways. The purpose of the sign was to spread his "archconservative views in big block letters."[2] *No Mexican Olympics team? All the runners and swimmers are here!*

Just as you begin to digest Uncle Sam's serving of right-wing patriotism, you will see Exit 76: 13th St, Chehalis, Washington—my father's hometown, the place where I grew up. In the summer of 1972, when I was one-and-a-half and my brother was eight, we immigrated with our mother from Busan to Chehalis to join my father.

We were the first Asians to settle there, the first immigrants in decades.

Neither of my parents ever talked about why we moved to the United States, yet growing up in the 1970s and 1980s, I internalized a story about it nonetheless: it was better than Korea. Despite not knowing the circumstances of our immigration, somehow I knew we were supposed to be Grateful.

My father's roots in Chehalis ran deep, going back to the 1800s. His grandparents had been homesteaders who traveled westward from Tennessee and Nova Scotia to live off the bounty of the Pacific Northwest, on land stolen from the Indigenous people that Chehalis was named after. While people like my paternal great-grandparents were glorified in American history as brave pioneers who helped found the Pacific Northwest, the Chehalis were not even acknowledged as a people—they were disembodied, reduced to a foreign language. *An Indian word meaning "shifting and shining sands,"* according to the town's official website.

The stories of people like my mother were written out of that history too. Her bravery went unacknowledged, and unlike my father's grandparents, she traveled alone. In the 1970s Korean women who traveled without the company of a Korean man wore the stamp of impropriety, and Korean women who traveled to America with or for an American man became so sullied that they were no longer considered Korean. Like all Korean women who ran off with their American husbands, my mother was treated as a casualty. Once they crossed over to America, these women could never really return.

She may have had her doubts about my father and the new world she was about to inhabit, but she also must have known that there was nothing left for her in Korea, no possible way of carving out a livable future. So she got on that airplane bound for America to start fresh in a place where she had heard that mixed race relationships and children were accepted. But in 1972, the United States had not yet undergone what the news called the "browning of America." It had only been a few years since the 1965 Immigration Act, which lifted restrictions against nonwhite immigrants, and we arrived ahead of the big waves of Koreans that would come a few years later to cities like Los Angeles, New York, Chicago, and Seattle. Not to my father's economically depressed town of five thousand.

Most people in Chehalis had never come face-to-face with a real live immigrant until my mother moved to town. If they had looked beyond the surface, they might have seen that she was not one of *those* immigrants who clung to their foreign ways, spread them like a pestilence, and took everything from the rightful Americans. *Those* immigrants didn't actually exist in our town; they were a mere abstraction, a composite of right-wing media images: The Yellow Peril. The Alien Invasion. The fabric of American society come unraveled at the hands of foreigners.

No, my mother *wanted* to be American. She *tried* to be

American, conforming to every new custom she learned. She took nothing except the jobs that other people didn't want, working subminimum wage or in the middle of the night. Even after the immigrant haters came face-to-face with her, they still couldn't see her, and so she became their flesh-and-bones straw woman.

When we first arrived to Chehalis, however, the sign off Exit 76 was promising: *Welcome to the Friendly City.*

Chehalis was a neighborly kind of place where you could show up on someone's doorstep unannounced, and if they knew you, they'd invite you inside for a cup of coffee or a soft drink and some cookies.

My father was the only one in my family who most people in town actually knew. Everywhere we went they seemed to like and respect him. Sometimes they'd pull me aside and say, "Your dad's a great guy, ya know."

My mother's acquaintances were fleeting, as she tended to associate with other outsiders and immigrants who arrived after her, but most of them didn't last long in Chehalis. There was a Black man named Ollie and a Filipina whose name I don't remember. She did develop one close friendship with a longtime local woman, a white woman, who was old enough to be her grandmother. Her name was Ethel and she lived in the St. Helen's Apartments, upstairs from the Book and Brush, the town's bookstore and art-supply store. She visited Ethel regularly until she died in the mid-1980s, which was around the same time that my mother began to show signs of schizophrenia.

I'm not sure what it was like for my brother. Because of our age difference, we lived in different worlds. When I was in my early twenties, he told me that he didn't think Chehalis was as bad as I made it out to be. "That's because you were a boy," I said. "The racism was worse in Korea," he shot back. Both statements are probably true. Regardless, he seemed to have had something of a social life when he was in high school.

As for me, I had one true and lasting friend.

1978

IT'S RECESS AND I'm playing by myself on the log toys, holding on to a slide pole with one hand and walking around it in circles. A blond girl from my class grabs the pole next to me and begins to copy me. I glance at her, nervous about what she'll say. The tension builds as we continue to quietly rotate around the poles. Finally, she breaks the silence.

"Are you Korean?"

I'm amazed by her question. "How did you know?" Instantly I like her, the first child to not call me Chinese or Japanese.

"My parents hosted a family from Korea, and they also went to Seoul," she says.

Decades later I will marvel at the rarity of a small-town white American couple vacationing in 1970s South Korea.

We exchange names—hers is Jenny—and then go back to walking in parallel circles. We play together the next day at recess, and again the next, and soon we begin seeing each other every day after school too. At her house we eat homemade Finnish cardamom pastries and Wasa bread with cubes of cream cheese. At mine, my mother wakes up early from her daytime nap to set the big dining table with orange linen napkins that she sewed by hand, crystal plates, and tiny silver forks for our afternoon snack, which is usually fresh fruit: strawberries and chunks of honeydew melon dipped in powdered sugar. Jenny becomes my dearest friend, my psychic armor for the onslaught ahead.

The people in my family's immediate midst—schoolteachers, next-door neighbors, and my father's friends and relatives— were generally kind and well-meaning toward us. At the outer limits of Chehalis's six square miles were the hicks, the rednecks, the shitkickers, as the kids in my high school called them, and as they sometimes called themselves too. They had a reputation for holding the same views as Uncle Sam on the Hamilton Farms billboard. But the divide between town and country was an open border, and so we lived among both people who tolerated immigrants and those who wanted us to "go home."

To survive my father's hometown, we sometimes had to make ourselves invisible. My mother tried to wring the foreignness out of her tongue by speaking only English, except for the names of Korean foods and things for which there was no translation, even at home with us, her Korean children. And so I became an outsider, not only to the place where I grew up but also to the language of my birth country. I would always be excluded from the *we* of "woori mal"—*our language*, as Koreans call Korean. Decades later, after summers of studying Korean in windowless classrooms in Seoul and conforming the sound of my speech to the standard dialect, I still could not utter the words "woori mal" to Koreans without an interrogation. *Where are you from? Why don't you speak Korean well? Are both your mother and father Korean? No*, they would conclude, *you are not Korean.*

1980

FOURTH GRADE. I've just arrived at Jenny's house for one of our marathon playdates. Instead of her usual chatter and excitement at my arrival, she's quiet and avoids eye contact.

"What's the matter?" I ask, and then her words spill out.

"My neighbors asked my mom who your real dad is!" Her face turns red, and she begins to cry. "They don't believe that your dad is really your dad. My mom got so mad and told them it's not true, but they wouldn't believe her!"

I'm awash in emotion, feeling vulnerable but protected by Jenny's family—her mother's anger a reflection of her sense of justice, possibly of her own identity as a Finnish immigrant's daughter. More than anything, I feel shocked. It's the first time I realize that my family is a scandal, the first time I'm able to see myself through the adult locals' eyes.

How can they not see how much I look like my father? We have the same angular jawline, the same full cheeks, the same cupid's-bow dimple; my mother marvels at the similarities almost every time she looks at me. Yet the white people can't see it. All they see is the Korean in me. The Korean they call "Chink" and "Jap."

Who am I without my father to claim as my own? Now that my relationship to him has been called into question, I'm even more of a foreigner in this town. Illegitimate to the core.

The racism in Chehalis was not of the colorblind variety. All colors but white were highly visible. You could count the nonwhite people on two hands, a few fingers each of Black, Brown, and Yellow. While the numbers slowly increased over the years that I lived there, it wasn't a linear progression. Sometimes there'd be a sharp decline in the people of color census because of some tragedy. A Black boy named Chris in my brother's high school class who died by suicide, I can't remember if by hanging or gunshot. A Korean adoptee who survived slitting her wrists, her scars the object of other people's ridicule or pity. She was in my high school for a year or so before she disappeared. A Mexican girl named Kari in my junior high class who went away after she became pregnant, at the age of twelve.

Then there was Sheena, a Cambodian girl who arrived in 1987. We were in the same gym class, and she always talked to me in the locker room: "You are the only one here who is nice to me."

Jenny came to me one day, upset about something that had been going on with Sheena in her typing class. Sheena sat next to her each day, her keys clicking out *Everyone hates me. They call me ugly and stupid. They call me bitch.* Line after line of vitriol.

"Isn't Miss McPherson going to do something?" asked Jenny. "Or is she just going to keep giving her papers back with her words per minute written at the top?"

By 1987 some of the immigrant haters had gotten used to my family, but they still saw the Asians that were settling along the Pacific Coast as a threat. At some moments, their fear of the Other rose up in waves, against newer immigrants like Sheena, and at others, it manifested as tiny ripples, the microaggressions that weren't yet part of a public conversation.

I hate the Chinks and Japs. They're taking over everything. Oh, but I'm not talking about you! You're okay. You're different.

These were words I heard from people I considered to be my friends.

Part of me also saw myself as different, an Americanized half American, but the rest of me felt the full sting of the insult. My Amerasian double consciousness.

The self-effacing part of me couldn't process the unrelenting hostility. And as hostile as the environment was for me, it was more so for my mother, who for years had to navigate unfriendly waters by herself while my father was at sea. She had such high hopes for becoming American.

When I was eight or nine, I woke up one school day to find that, instead of changing into her nightgown after returning from her 11:00 p.m. to 7:00 a.m. graveyard shift, my mother had put on a blue polyester pantsuit and was blotting her lipstick in the mirror.

"Mama, where are you going?"

"Seattle," she said as she smoothed the creases in her pants. I was surprised that no one had mentioned this earlier. Seattle was the place we went for cultural events and "important matters."

"Really? What for?"

"I'm taking citizenship test."

"What's that?"

"It's for Mama's becoming American citizen today. I put cereal on the table for you. Go eat."

She got into her car to drive ninety miles to Seattle, spent the day at the Immigration and Naturalization Service center, drove ninety miles back in the afternoon, began cooking dinner when she got home, and left herself almost no time to sleep before her next shift.

"What happened with the test?" I asked when I saw her that night.

"Nothing happened."

"What do you mean 'nothing happened'?"

"What do you mean 'what do I mean'? Nothing happened. I just took test and now I'm becoming American citizen."

Such a simple statement of fact, but what new privileges would that status grant her? In what tangible way would it make her life better? Maybe in another place I could have seen the difference.

1983

I AM TWELVE years old. My mother comes to pick me up from school, and as we start the drive home, she becomes suspicious that a car is following us. She turns suddenly to test the driver. "I lost that sonofabitch," she mutters to herself, but a moment later, he reappears in the rearview mirror. Fear begins to grip me as I start to wonder if we're his prey. Images from *Friday the 13th* and *Halloween* fill my head, of a masked killer knifing us to death after a long harrowing chase. Then I come back to reality. If he's going to kill us, it'll probably be with a shotgun. My mother speeds up and so does he. Each move she makes, he makes in turn. The cat-and-mouse continues all the way to our home, where she pulls over to the side of the road and parks in front of the ivy-covered oak tree at the edge of our front yard instead of pulling into the driveway. The other car parks right behind us. I think that she must have parked on the street so that the stalkers wouldn't know that this is our house, especially since we are living there alone, with my brother gone away to college and my father somewhere in the Pacific.

She gets out, rushes over to the stranger, and bangs her fist against the windshield. "Get out of the car," she says sternly.

I'm too scared to move from my seat, but I turn around to see who's been following us. There are four young white men, and their windows are rolled down. The driver doesn't move.

My mother pounds the windshield again. "Get out!" She yells this time.

He opens the door and emerges from behind the wheel. It's a lanky boy of sixteen or seventeen with a mop of brown curls. He's a head taller than her, but she stares him down as he shuffles his feet and kicks pebbles against the curb.

"Why are you following me?"

He turns around to look at his friends still inside the car.

"I said, Why are you following me?" she enunciates, exaggerating each syllable.

"Why are you following me?" he repeats, mocking her accent. His friends chuckle. He looks at them again and then

at my mother. He begins making stupid sounds to mimic a fake
Asian language. The boys in the car begin to laugh so hard they're
clutching their sides.

I brace myself as I see my mother's eyes bulging, her nostrils
flaring. She's in fight mode, not about to back down. She takes
a step closer to the boy and cranes her neck up at him, her fists
clenched on her hips. Her face is about six inches from his when
she screams, "You leave me and my children alone! Do you hear
me?" The volume of her voice startles them out of their laughter.
"You get the hell out of here right now! If I ever see you again I
swear I will *kill* you."

The stalker doesn't attempt to talk back or make fun of her a
second time. He just gets back in his car and drives away.

Three years later, my mother will get fed up with being grateful and begin to call out all the shitty things that people do to
her. She'll name the experience of being followed, harassed, persecuted. *Everyone in this town is out to get me.* At first it will seem
entirely rational, completely grounded in reality. Not crazy talk.
Not schizophrenia.

1986

IT'S THE SUMMER before my sophomore year of
high school and the boy I've had a crush on for a year invites me
over to his house. I'd been hanging around him and his friends
my entire freshman year, thinking that they were part of the
cool alternative crowd. Finally, he noticed me! Practically every
moment between the invitation and the date, I obsess over what
to wear and fantasize about him falling in love with me.

I arrive at his house swimming in anticipation and sporting

a new magenta tube skirt. Ten minutes later he's asking me to "get baked." He pulls out a pipe and a bag of weed. My first time smoking. "Take another hit, Gracie," he says again and again, putting the pipe in my mouth until I'm too stoned to move, barely able to speak. He kisses me. I'm too incapacitated to kiss back. The Beatles are playing in the background. *Michelle, ma belle.* My first kiss. He takes his pants off and tells me to suck his cock. I try to speak and manage the words, "Not yet." I'm too incapacitated to fight back.

Years later, I will learn that the pot was laced with embalming fluid.

As soon as I get home, my mother calls out, "Grace-ya, come talk to me!" I'm still high and terrified that she'll know what I've been doing. She looks at me affectionately, takes my hand, and calls me Soon-hee, her old-fashioned Korean name for me that means the "most innocent girl." "Soon-hee-ya, you are my innocent girl, aren't you?" I feel spooked that she's saying this to me now, at this particular moment. More than anything I'm consumed with guilt and shame.

Years later, I will understand that innocence was another thing that she wished so dearly for me to have precisely because it had been denied to her. My guilt and shame will turn to rage.

My sophomore year begins a month later. I'm at tennis practice hitting balls against the wall while I wait my turn to drill serves on the far court. It's a perfect late summer day—blue skies, 75 degrees, the kind of weather that reminds you that you're connected to something larger, that heartache passes. I listen to the pop and swish of the balls' movements and let the rhythm soothe me.

Three of the boy's friends appear out of nowhere and surround me, cornering me against the wall. They jeer, "I heard Dan fucked your mouth." One of them grabs my racket and the other two pin me to the ground. The boy with the racket hits me between the legs with the handle, pumps it up and down, to simulate a rape. *They seemed to be having a very good time.* "It's true what they say about Oriental girls," he shouts. *Indelible in the hippocampus is the laughter—their uproarious laughter . . . their having fun at my expense.*[3] They disperse once the joke gets old.

I look up, and no one—not the coach or any of the other girls—seems to have noticed the assault that happened in plain sight. I try to locate Jenny, and then spot her on the far court, too distant to have seen clearly. But the coach, the only adult present, is on the court closest to me with seven or eight girls. None of them so much as glances at me, even as I struggle to get up off the ground, brush the dirt off my uniform, and hobble to pick up my racket that the boys tossed against the fence. I wonder if they're choosing not to see, because that's the kind of thing that happens in Chehalis.

Later that fall: a scene of my impulsive near suicide at age fifteen. A fight with my parents that started over something trivial. Me, traumatized by my first sexual experience, the sexual violence I can't yet name. I release my anguish with a loud guttural cry and run across the kitchen toward the knife block. "I'm going to kill myself!" I yell as I grab the chef's knife. My father wrests it out of my hand, my mother stands back and gasps. I collapse on the floor in tears.

"I hate this town!" I scream at my father. "Why did you bring me here?"

He looks shocked. "Would it have been better if I'd left you in Korea?"

"Korea? What's Korea got to do with any of this?" I shout. "Why couldn't we have lived in Seattle?"

I am so mired in my personal hell that I can't see that my mother's hell is burning hotter.

In a few weeks, I'll discover that she's been hallucinating, and no one in my family will believe me. It'll be another thing that almost makes me crack, but I'll hang on long enough to get out of Chehalis. And she will encourage me to get out. One day as I'm studying for the PSATs, she will approach me at the kitchen table, set plates of fruit and jjin bbang in front of me, and comb my hair with her fingers. "Huh-huh. Chakhada! Study hard and go to best college, far away. There is nothing for you in a place like this."

Twenty, thirty years later, I'll look back on 1986 as the year my mother began to die.

New York City, 2016

IT'S THE NIGHT of the presidential election, and as I ride the subway home from Manhattan to Brooklyn, Jenny texts me from Seattle: "What the fuck is happening?"

"Unusually large turnout of rural white voters," I text back.

"Oh lord," she replies.

In the days ahead, friends and colleagues in my little blue bubble of New York City will ask, "Who are all these people that voted for him?"

My simmering rage about the bullies and rapists and xenophobes from my childhood, all the injustices my mother faced, will boil over once again. One small thing I'll be grateful for is that she'll never have to see a Trump presidency. My mother, now eight years dead.

Jenny and I exchange a few more texts about the rural uprising and the horror that is upon us. "Hold your babies close," she says. What else can we do but try to survive?

In the wake of the 2016 election, I began reading *Our Most Trou-bling Madness: Case Studies in Schizophrenia across Cultures.* In T. M. Luhrmann's introduction, she makes a compelling argument that the set of experiences we refer to as "schizophrenia" is as much a social disease as it is biological. Luhrmann outlines several social risk factors that have been so widely evidenced by the research that they're now indisputable, and my mother's case ticks off five out of six boxes. Three of them had always been associated with poor mental health outcomes: social adversity during childhood, low socioeconomic status, and physical or sexual trauma. But the other two are less obvious from the outside: immigration and being a person of color in a white neighborhood.

My mother didn't have to be schizophrenic.

I always knew it in my bones, but could never legitimately make a case for it without the science to prove it.

The risk increases with what is called "ethnic density": the incidence of schizophrenia among nonwhite people rises as their presence in the neighborhood begins to fall.[4]

I thought about Chehalis, the seat of Lewis County, where 65 percent of voters cast their ballots for Donald Trump, where not much had changed since 1972 when my Korean family moved there.

The number of immigrants and people of color grew from three to several hundred, most of them coming from Mexico, but the town as a whole remains about 87 percent white and Christian.

In the 1990s, on my occasional visits home from college, I heard rumors of Asian and Mexican people being beaten or killed in hate crimes and former classmates becoming neo-Nazis. Despite the nineties rhetoric of multiculturalism, it seemed that racist sentiments were on the rise as more immigrants moved to Chehalis over the next three decades. The Uncle Sam billboard would reflect this renewed xenophobia: *Is it immigration or an invasion?*

In 2010 the City Council adopted a new official nickname out of fear of the "local media using the nickname The Friendly City in a contrary way if negative news about Chehalis were to come to light."[5] Now it is called "The Rose City."

In 2016 Chehalis's neighboring "twin city" of Centralia made it on a top-ten list of places with the most KKK members per capita, but the KKK had long been active in Lewis County. In 1924 Chehalis hosted a regional gathering of as many as seventy thousand Klansmen rallying at the fairgrounds. When the *Daily Chronicle* interviewed Grand Wizard David Duke in 1976 and asked about his plans to open a chapter in Chehalis, he responded that there were already members in the area.[6]

After Trump took office and amplified the voices of white supremacy, the billboard made another one of its highly controversial, news-breaking statements: *Freedom Is Dangerous! Slavery Is Peaceful!*

In Chehalis, *we were never meant to survive.*

PART II

The double function of the mouth—both in processing food into digestible matter and in producing sense— sutures that space to the domestic and civic production of language, to storytelling.

—*KYLA WAZANA TOMPKINS*, Racial Indigestion

4. UMMA

Chehalis, Washington, 1976

"WHAT DO YOU WANT to be when you grow up?" I was five years old the first time I can remember my mother asking me about my career aspirations. The high, clear pitch of her voice sounded like glasses clinking together, a sign that she wanted to coax something out of you. She knelt down, her long hair sweeping the linoleum, and looked at me with expectant brown eyes. "Huh, Grace-ya?" She held a smile for a few seconds before her dimples receded into the roundness of her cheeks.

"A cook." As soon as the words flew out of my mouth, I knew I had made a colossal mistake.

"Aaawhaaaaat?!" She leaped to her feet and loomed over me. Her nostrils flared, her face turned red, and she huffed the correct answer in short staccatos. "You can be. A Doctor. Lawyer. Or professor."

I doubt that I really wanted to be a cook then, or ever gave my future much thought, but as young children tend to do, I imagined myself doing the very things I saw adults do. My mother was always cooking, but for her, it was an obligation, not a profession.

If I had been a bit older, I might have realized that she had been recently obsessed with a song I made up whose refrain went, "*I wish I were a pencil leader, pencil leader, pencil leader.*" I sang it in a slow mournful tone, and sometimes exchanged the word "leader" for "eater." No matter, my mother interpreted it to mean that I would someday become a great scholar and told everyone she knew that I had documented my intentions through song. When she talked on the phone with relatives, the quick clip of Gyeongsang saturi, my family's regional Korean dialect, would be interrupted by the slowly enunciated English words "I wish I were a pencil leader." She switched back to Korean and there was a lilt in her voice. It was the sound of my mother smiling. When visitors came to the house, she told them about my master oeuvre and asked me to sing it. The song was accompanied by artwork—pictures of pencils that I had drawn with pencils—and she proudly displayed the drawings too.

It was foretold that I would become an academic. On a child's first birthday in Korea, objects are laid in front of her that predict her future. If she grabs the noodles, she will have a long life. If she grabs the coins, she will be rich. And if she grabs the pencils, she will become a scholar. In my adult life I would joke with my Korean friends that my mother had rigged the game by setting out three piles of pencils. *You will be greaaat scholar one day, Grace-ya.* She carefully injected this message into the substrate of my dreams. It was my destiny.

"A cook? What kind of answer is that?" she muttered to my father.

He urged her to calm down and said something that would later clue me in to their cultural difference. He was born of an Irish Canadian mother and an English American father, and twenty-two years older than my mother. He never missed an issue of *Forbes* or *National Geographic*, and was a devotee of PBS. "She's not talking about becoming a fry cook," he said. "She's talking about becoming a Julia Child."

"Ajuliawhat?"

"Julia Child. She's the most respected cook in America. Her television program—"

"I *don't* care! She is not going to be a cook!" Whenever my mother yelled, her whole body shook. Three and a half years of living in the United States had not converted her to the idea that cooking was an admirable profession, regardless of whether or not one did it on television. Cooking was the business of house-wives and the working class—two categories that had largely determined my mother's status in life. The funny thing is that she must have been cooking when this incident erupted because a knife suddenly appears in my memory.

She returned her gaze to me and gripped the knife handle until her knuckles turned white and shook it to the beat of her words. "Grace, you can be *anything* in the world. And you. Want. To be. A cook?" Tears threatened to break through her anger. "No. You will *not* be a cook. You will *never*. Be. A cook." She stormed off to the other side of our six-room bungalow, having crushed my culinary dreams.

The parents of my childhood memory were about as different as two people could be—my mother was daring and vivacious, my father fearful and wizened—but they were drawn to each other by the economic and geopolitical events that charted their respective paths, and both of them suffered from a generalized dissatisfaction with the way their lives had turned out.

My father had once aspired to be a farmer, having raised pigs throughout his youth. He began to study agricultural science at Washington State University in 1937, but this was during the Great Depression, when he could neither afford to finish college nor make a living as a farmer. Life's twists and turns led him down other avenues, first as a butcher, then as a mason. In the 1960s, he finally landed in the US Merchant Marines, which provided him with the best and steadiest income that a man of his education and abilities could hope for. It also offered travel opportunities to exotic locales like Korea, where he met my mother. My paternal grandfather disappeared a year after my father's birth, leaving my grandmother Grace to be a single mother for the next ten years until she remarried. My father's attraction to my mother was as much about healing the wounds of his past as it was about her, and in fact, he once told me so when I asked him why he had married her. "She was all alone with your brother. I wanted to give that boy a proper home," he said, nearly in tears.

My mother's career trajectory was not so obvious, partly because she could never openly talk about her life circumstances and partly because women in the 1970s, and particularly Korean women, were not supposed to have careers. They might have had jobs, but not careers.

Both of my parents rose up from childhood destitution into the relative comfort of the middle class, and although it made life easier, it did not make them happy. Whereas my father grumbled openly, my mother only hinted that she wanted something more. When my father spoke of his unfulfilled longings, he knew that men in their late fifties rarely got second chances. My mother, on the other hand, was still young enough to wish that she could "be someone."

One day, when I was five or six, something happened that made me understand that she had aspirations too. I was in the kitchen watching her chop a mound of garlic cloves into a fine paste in a matter of seconds. She packed it into a pint-size mason jar, stored it away in the fridge, and started on her next task. It seemed to me that she performed a magical feat each time she picked up a knife. She then took out a bag of apples and a paring knife and peeled the apples in one swift motion, keeping the entire peel intact—a whole bag in less time than it took to sing a song. She liked to sing when she cooked, usually songs she learned from the American movies she watched in Korea during the 1960s. I had never considered her singing as anything more than a habit, but this time I noticed that her voice emitted a deep, powerful resonance. She belted out the words "*Que sera sera. Whatever will be, will be. The future's not ours to see. Que sera sera.*" Her body swayed as if she were performing for some imagined audience and, in that moment, I could see her on stage.

"Wow, Mama. You're a good singer."

"Everyone used to tell me what pretty voice I have. I could be professional, you know."

"Why aren't you?"

"Why aren't I? Hah! Because I have to take care of *you*, Mangshitori."

"Mangshitori" was a Japanese-inflected, Koreanized version of the word *monster*, one of many linguistic oddities that were the products of my mother's first language being Japanese, her second being Korean, and her third, English.

Though I sensed longing in my mother's words about her unrealized singing career, it wasn't quite regret. It would be more than a decade before I understood that her greatest wish was not to be a singer, but an educated person.

During the fall of my senior year of high school, as I was filling out my application for Brown University, my father inadvertently revealed one of my mother's secrets. He found an error on the application.

"Your mother didn't go to high school."

"Yeah, she did."

My father shook his head and sighed. "Dammit, why is she lying about that? She only finished junior high," he said.

I still didn't believe him, so I walked down the hall, from his study into the kitchen, where she was preparing dinner. "Mom, didn't you graduate from high school?" I asked. "Dad's saying that you didn't."

"Go on. Tell her," said my father, who had followed me and was now standing in the doorway.

My mother whipped her head around and glared at him. "Why you have to say that?" she hissed.

"They're asking for it on her application to Brown, for Christ's sake! How was I supposed to know you were hiding it from her?"

"So it's true?" I asked, bewildered that she had been lying to me about it my whole life.

My mother didn't say a word. She just fixed her gaze on the wall, her eyes full of fury.

"Mom?" Her only response was to slink away to her bedroom and hide there for the rest of the night.

While the boys in my mother's family had been granted the privilege of going to high school and college, my mother learned early on that the role of girls was to serve men and make sacrifices for their families. And she did serve and sacrifice, but she also wanted something more. And if this something more was not going to be hers, she wanted to make sure it would be mine. It would take me a lifetime to figure this out—that my success could be her vindication, that my education could be her second chance.

My mother's seemingly mundane question—"What do you want to be when you grow up?"—arrived sometime during the summer of 1976, around the eve of my entry into kindergarten. She had been preparing for a scenario in which her daughter was destined for academic stardom. Otherwise, how could I have provoked such a strong reaction? Primed by my songwriting quips about leading pencils, the wheels of my mother's fantasy must have been churning at full speed. Earlier that summer we had taken a road trip to California, and when we visited the San Diego Zoo, I remembered the names of several obscure animals.

"Look! There's a dik-dik. It's like a little tiny antelope."

"Hwaaa!" my mother said, exhaling the sound that Koreans use to express wonder. "How do you know that?"

"I read about it in my wildlife cards."

"You see," my father said as he patted my head, "I knew you'd enjoy them, honey."

Encouraged by my parents' reaction, I searched for more opportunities to show off my newfound zoological knowledge. "There's a capybara! It's the largest rodent in the world." My mother stopped in her tracks and studied my face, as if she were examining some curiosity. Her eyes widened and her tone became solemn and deliberate. "Hwaaaaa . . . The girl is a genius." My brother probably rolled his eyes and groaned, something I distinctly remember him doing in response to my mother's doting. I, on the other hand, was still small enough for her to mold without resistance.

We returned from summer vacation and I started school, carrying my mother's expectations. She put me on the bus, and as I watched her figure fade into the distance, the neighborhood bully that would later chase me into a ditch sat next to me and said, "Your mommy is never coming back for you." Before my first day of school even started, the blond bully had sniffed me out as her victim. Maybe it was my fear that the bully's words would come true combined with my regret over having disappointed my mother, but something drove me to do well in school so that I could please her. Between my strangeness and my competence, I quickly developed a persona in this kindergarten microcosm of rural America. I became the model student. The alien. The Asian. I studied hard, and as a result, I restored my mother's faith that I had a brilliant future in academia.

The story of my becoming a scholar—of my kindergarten tribulations and my mother's Herculean efforts to create favorable conditions for my growth—is not an easy narrative. I can only make sense of it in fragments stitched together, and a few clear snapshots that hold the pieces together. At the age of five,

I learned that telling your mother you wanted to be a cook was such devastating news that it could make the trees in the backyard tremble at the sound of her outrage. These trees—the flowering plums, the sugar maples, the dogwoods, the oaks—were close companions to which I had attributed mystical powers. Ten years later, when my mother's mind became florid, they would become the source of her hallucinations.

Flash forward another twenty years or so, and you can glimpse the outcome of the first memorable conflict I ever had with my mother when I was five, layered with the emotional residues of watching her fall to pieces. By the age of thirty-three, I had spent eighteen years witnessing her struggles with schizophrenia, and managing my own psychic roller coaster of hope and despair. The entirety of my adult life had been shaped by my mother's mental agony and my desire to make her want to live. So at the age of thirty-three, I became the person she had once dreamed of becoming. I had acquired various letters after my name, most important of which were PhD. But to her dismay, I also held a certificate in pastry arts from a culinary institute.

I had been building up my own baking business until I got an offer for a tenure-track position as a sociology professor at the City University of New York. The tenure track consumed all my time. I stopped baking, barely had time to cook for myself, but in my mother's view, that was all excellent news because there was no greater honor than to be called "Professor." She once told me, "If I were you, I would be the happiest person in the world." But she wasn't me, and I wasn't that happy. Yet I continued down that path because I was driven by a need to repay the debt owed to her.

There was my personal debt of knowing that her singular motivation had always been to give her children a life of opportunity, but there were also societal debts—American society's debt to the immigrants who make their food, clean their toilets, raise their children; Korean society's debt to the droves of young

UMMA
71

women who put their bodies and sexual labor on the front lines
of national security, to whom no one would ever speak the words
"thank you for your service."[1] In neither case were the debtees
treated with gratitude. Instead, the debtors would make them
into the cause of society's ills, the very things that needed to
be eradicated. I was driven by the inescapable feeling that the
societal debt owed to my mother was crushing me, and the only
way to lighten the burden would be to repay some of it myself.
By becoming the "great scholar" she dreamed I would be, I might
help her find some redemption. By studying her life and trying to
make sense of it, I might find some too.

At thirty-seven, I became a tenured professor and published
my first book about the ghosts of the Korean War—a book
that was inspired by and dedicated to my mother. I had started
researching and writing it as a way of trying to answer the questions that no one else was willing to answer for me.

During the first few weeks after I turned in my manuscript to
the press, when I'd go visit her in New Jersey, she would pull a
book from my bag, gaze wondrously at the cover, and ask, "Is this
your book?"

"No," I'd laugh. "The production process takes a long time."

But something else happened when I was thirty-seven, two
days after I had gotten the cover design and fantasized about
being able to show it to her. "Look, Mom," I had planned to say.
"*This* is my book."

March 9, 2008

IT WAS AROUND four o'clock on a Sunday afternoon. I returned to my home in Prospect Heights, Brooklyn,

after taking my College of Staten Island students to meet with members of a Liberian church as part of our immigration class. My phone rang and I knew something was wrong the moment I saw my brother's name on the screen. "Shit," I muttered to myself. What's going on? I couldn't remember the last time he had called me for anything other than an emergency.

"Hello?"

"Were you here yesterday? Did you see Mom?" The urgency in his voice and the very fact that I was talking to him on the phone caught me off guard.

"Uh, I don't remember. Maybe . . . wait, no . . . I was there last weekend. Why?" My limbs grew heavy, the way they always did when someone confronted me. My mind was spinning all kinds of different scenarios about what was the matter, yet none of them was as horrible as the truth.

"Grace, Mom passed away."

A searing sensation engulfed my body, the feeling of muscle melting off bone. I struggled to stay upright as the conversation continued. I began to frenetically pace around my one-room studio apartment, trying to flee from the news of my mother's death. My brother's words became garbled sounds, and my own words, repeated every few seconds, were like vultures circling above me. "No. It's not true . . ."

When?

How?

We never did figure out the answers to these questions. All we knew was where. She died in her living room, and this we knew because her body lay lifeless on the floor, curled up on the fluffy cream-colored rug between the couch and the glass-top coffee table.

After the call, I picked up Yoyo, my little gray tabby, and pressed my face into his fur. I became all too aware that I lived alone, that so much of my life had revolved around my mother, and now she was gone. Who did I have now? My father had died ten years earlier, my brother and I had been growing apart for years, and my life on the tenure track was so demanding that I had been unable to commit to a romantic relationship since a big breakup in 2004, four years prior. My mother was the person I loved most in the world, had always loved more than anyone. Who could I turn to for solace? I called Hosu and Rafael, my closest friends in New York, but neither of them answered. My instinct was to keep running in circles in that tiny apartment until the sensation of being in my body returned. When it did, I could feel my limbs shaking, my stomach trying to push up bile. Stay calm. Just find someone to keep you from falling apart, I kept telling myself. But other thoughts intruded: What if I had gone to see her yesterday? Maybe I could I have saved her from dying.

I spent the next few hours alternating between trying to get in touch with my friends and collapsing into the sound of my voice wailing "Umma," the Korean word for *Mama*. I hadn't called her that since I was a young child, but "Umma" was what cried out from my gut. The minutes moved like glaciers while I waited to make contact with someone, anyone. I finally found an ex-lover on Gchat. "Hi, James. Can you do me a favor?" I asked. "Can you please spend the night with me? I'm not interested in sex. I can't be alone right now. My mother just died."

This became one of my coping mechanisms over the following weeks: invite exes to spend the night, seek warmth and comfort in their bodies, use them as barriers against the depths of grief that threatened to drown me. They obliged, and for that I was grateful. But when Aura stroked my hair and said in the most tender voice, "Oh, Grace. You need to be babied. Let me baby you," I softened into the curves of her body and realized that I was looking for more than a wall against my feelings. I wanted to find my mother's touch again.

On the nights when no one was available to hold me, I walked across Flatbush Avenue to one of the budget Chinese spas that had recently opened along Fifth Avenue in Park Slope. "I'd like a one-hour massage, please. From a woman." In the dark and lavender-scented massage room, I could imagine that this Asian woman who was kneading the pain out of my body was my mother, who used to rub my back as I fell asleep at night and squeeze my legs as I awoke in the morning. I'd close my eyes and slip deeper into the dream that she was there with me. Umma. In the flesh. And not only was she still alive, she was the young mother of my childhood, her mind still intact, her spirit full of wonder. The mother I had lost so long ago.

When I finally got in touch with Hosu and asked if she would come with me to meet my brother at the mortuary the next morning, she didn't hesitate to say yes.

Hosu and I boarded the 8:32 a.m. Northeast Corridor Line train from Penn Station, New York, to Princeton, New Jersey.

"She asked me for saengseon jeon last weekend," I said, showing her the package of egg-battered fish that I had picked up in Koreatown. I popped a piece of fish in my mouth and gagged on my tears. Hosu grabbed my hand firmly and held it most of the way. Although she was prepared to go with me every step of the way, we decided that it would be better for her to wait for me in a nearby café in Princeton as my brother and I took care of business.

In the funeral director's office, my brother answered nearly all the questions, except for the ones about my mother's birthplace and parents' names, which were required for the death certificate. He hesitated, perhaps trying to remember—it was uncommon for Korean children to ever hear their elders' names—and I seized the opportunity to speak. "She was born in Osaka, Japan." I then went on to spell out my grandparents' names. When it came time to make the arrangements, my brother was decisive. She would be cremated, ashes kept in a no-frills plastic box. The funeral home need not provide a service because my brother and his family opted to do something on their own. I was still too shell-shocked from the night before to know exactly what I wanted, but I knew it wasn't the same thing that my brother wanted. The two of us had very different relationships with our mother, and besides, I was an outsider to the family that he and his wife had created. The director must have sensed my dismay and said, "You know, sometimes we divide the ashes to allow family members to honor their departed loved one each in their own way. Would you like to do that?"

"Yes," I said, without so much as a pause.

"Yeah, sure," my brother shrugged.

Once we finished our paperwork, the funeral director asked if we wanted to see the body. "Uh, I already saw it. You go ahead," my brother said to me. I felt his trauma reverberate in his words. What must it have been like for him to walk into our mother's apartment expecting to see her alive, but then to find her dead on the floor?

I followed the man downstairs into a dim room where my mother's body was lying on a metal table. I could see from a distance that she was wearing her pale-green nylon pajamas, and one of her forearms was in the air, fingers spread slightly, and curved into a claw. He walked me to the table and said, "We found a bracelet on her. Maybe you want to remove it." It was on the arm that was raised. I pulled the gold bangle over her hand and had to push the fingers together slightly to get it off. The stiffness of her fingers and the feeling of her cold skin made it real. My mother was dead. I took a piece of fish out of my bag and said to the director, "I know this might seem weird, but could you send this with her when you cremate her? It's an offering."

"Yes, of course. Would you like a moment alone with her?"

I nodded and began to cry again as I laid the fish next to her. "I didn't forget, Mama. I brought you the saengseon jeon." I repressed my horror and forced myself to caress her cold gray forehead. "I'm so sorry. I'm so sorry," I sobbed. Even as I was repeating the words like a mantra, I wondered if she could understand what I was apologizing for, or if I myself could articulate it. I was sorry that her life had been full of struggle, that she lived and died alone, that we were sending her body into the fire with nothing more than a piece of cold fish to usher her into the next world. Yet my regret was also much larger than any of these things. I kept saying the words until they stopped, like a windup clock whose ticking had run out. "I'm so sorry. I'm so sorry . . ."

Outside in the parking lot, my brother was sitting in his black-and-white Jeep Cherokee with the engine on, his hulking figure slightly shrunken behind the wheel. Despite his six-foot-two frame, he looked like a lost little boy. I got into the passenger side, and we drove in silence to the café where Hosu was waiting for me. Silence had become the norm between my brother and me over the years, neither of us making much of an attempt at either small talk or meaningful conversation, but this was different. With Mom gone, when will I ever see him again? I thought to myself. What if this is the last time? The café was only a few blocks away, and my time with him quickly ran out. My body began to tremble as I forced the sound of my voice to break through the silence. Even as I opened my mouth, I wasn't sure what I was going to say. I only knew that we were both hurting, and that maybe I should say to him what I myself would have wanted to hear. "I want you to know . . ." My voice was quaking. "I appreciate everything you did for Mom." He began to shake his head and blink tears away from his amber-brown eyes. I don't remember if he answered with any words, but his gestures gave form to my feelings. Whatever we might have done for her, it wasn't nearly enough.

When I got home that afternoon, FedEx rang my doorbell to deliver the copyedited manuscript of my book. For years I had been writing about the things that made up the social context of my mother's life in Korea, things she never talked about: the Korean War, civilian life under US militarism and South Korean dictatorship, and all the overt or subtle, yet always systematic, forms of violence against women and girls. I had taken on this project not out of pure intellectual curiosity but because I needed to know what happened to my mother. Or to be more precise, what might have happened to her. What things might have led her to begin hearing voices when I was fifteen? To become a shut-in when I was twenty-three? To spend the rest of her life with virtually no fresh air, sunlight, or human contact? How was it possible that she fell from being the active, vibrant mother of my childhood to the troubled, reclusive mother of my adulthood? And why did no one outside of my family care? I imagined her in every scenario that I wrote about, and wondered if that might have been the thing that pushed her over the edge. My mother was the figurative ghost of my book, and she began haunting me in a new way once she was actually dead. She was no longer the ghost of her own secret past, but the lost mother of my childhood, whispering, *Grace-ya, remember me?*

The minutiae of my childhood started to come into focus, and in particular, the details of my first year of school and all the things she did then to chart out my future. The picture came to me in pieces, one of which arrived on my first night back to school, when I was teaching my Food, Self, and Society class.

I walked in and scanned the room of thirty students, and as usual, only five or six looked alert, while the rest slumped in their chairs. Some were already sleeping.

I opened the class by writing a quote on the board: *Food*

everywhere is not just about eating, and eating (at least among humans)
is never simply a biological process.[2]

"Okay, keep this quote in mind as we begin the discussion.
Tonight we're talking about a piece called 'Japanese Mothers and
Obentos: The Lunch-Box as ideological state apparatus' by Anne
Allison.[3] Allison is borrowing the term 'ideological state appara-
tus' from the philosopher Louis Althusser. Does anyone remem-
ber what that means?"

After a pause, a young Black man in the back raised his hand
and said, "It's when you think you're doing something of your
own free will, but you're really doing it because you have to."

"Good! You've touched on how the ISA functions. Now
here's the definition: it's an institution designed to regulate
norms through cultural beliefs and practices rather than brute
force. A 'state apparatus,' like the police or military, regulates
society through force. An 'ideological state apparatus,' like the
media or school, regulates it through ideas. Just like you said, as
soon as you internalize the idea as your own, you don't notice
that someone else wants you to do it," I said as I scribbled notes
on the board. "So now, why does Allison say that the lunch box
is an ISA?"

A tanned twentysomething raised her hand and said, "This
story kind of surprised me."

"Why is that?" I asked.

"Because it didn't have anything to do with food."

Jesus Christ. I silently groaned and wished that I could take a
permanent bereavement leave. "Okay, let's remember the quote
on the board. 'Food' is more complicated than we might think.
This *does* have something to do with food," I said with as much
patience as I could muster.

"What these mothers do for their children, it's amazing," said
Tanya, a plump middle-aged white woman with short gray hair.
"They spent so much time making their kids' lunches that they

couldn't even work outside the home." She sounded wistful. After twenty years of playing the traditional role of wife and mother, Tanya was finally in college, and she was hungry for knowledge. The Tanyas made teaching worthwhile and, on this particular night, bearable. Without my mother, I started to feel like no one cared that I was a professor.

"Why do you think the mothers put so much time into their kids' lunches?" I asked. "Did their five-year-old children care whether the food looked perfect?"

"Because they love their children," said one of the struggling students.

"Sure, but why else? Remember that the institution of the school is invested in the way the mothers make the obento boxes. Allison's suggesting that it only *seems* like it's done out of love, when it might have more to do with politics."

"They were becoming education mothers," said an immigrant student.

"Yes!" I said, relieved that at least a few students had done the reading. "The kyoiku mama, the 'education mother,' whose sole purpose in life is to dedicate herself to her child's school success. So what's the link to the obento? Remember that Allison makes a very important point: the school's biggest emphasis in terms of the child's potential was not on homework, or something obviously associated with school, but on eating. On *food*. Such a huge effort on the part of the mothers only makes sense if the obento has some larger meaning. Right?"

My mind wandered to the email Tanya had written me a week earlier, offering her condolences: *I could tell how much your mother meant to you. It was obvious in the way that you talked about her.* Until I read those words I hadn't realized how much I spoke about her in class, or the extent to which my food course was yet another way of paying homage to her, nor had I realized how important the foods she cooked and ate were to her survival.

"The obento is what holds the key to the child's transition from home to school. It's the child's symbolic entry into citizenship," I continued as I walked around the room. "And that's why the state is so invested in the rules of the obento. A child's early relationship to food helps determine her future, and it's the *mother* who makes this happen. The mother who is making the obento that the child is excited to eat at school. The mother who puts so much time and effort into the obento that she'll inspire her young child to be a good student."

At that moment I became hyperaware that my own mother once believed that my academic future was riding on her culinary efforts. The time that she dedicated to food preparation rivaled that of the Japanese mothers, but the difference was that the school system in which I grew up had little stake in my mother's meal preparation. In that sense, my mother reclaimed the power of the proverbial obento and subjected it to her own will. I had always known that my mother's cooking transcended familial duty, or a desire to nurture, or a need to satisfy hunger or delight the senses. It was motivated by all of these things, yet there was also something more powerful lurking beneath the surface. She used it to generate income and live in relative peace as a foreigner in a rural town that did not welcome strangers, though I doubt any of these things registered with her. If you had asked her what cooking meant to her, she probably would have said, "It was just something I had to do."

I wanted to share these insights with my students and tell them how my mother used to cook as if our lives depended on it, but the lump in my throat hurt too much. The woman whose very body once fed me, whose body I was once a part of, was now a pile of ashes. I swallowed hard and pointed to the quote on the board and said, "So you see, food isn't just about eating."

After class, Sani, a cherub-faced Arab student, offered me a ride back to Brooklyn. We made small talk until we merged onto the Staten Island Expressway, and then she said it: "I'm sorry about your mother, Professor."

"Thank you. It was really sudden. I don't know what it means, but part of me thinks that she was trying to let me go. I spent so many years taking care of her, and I wonder if this was her way of giving me permission to go ahead and live my own life."

"Wow. What you're saying is amazing. I can't believe it," she said, her big brown eyes getting bigger. I wasn't sure which part she was amazed by, but I was grateful that she didn't shy away from talking about my loss. I surprised myself with my candor, but Sani had been driving me to Bay Ridge every week, and had confided her own struggles with me during the car ride. She was a twenty-one-year-old mother of a toddler and was determined to stay in school "to set a good example," and her family in Palestine had recently lost their home to a Jewish settlement, a cruel reality that she had been trying to make peace with all semester. I suppose it was my turn to open up to her.

I became quiet and introspective as we crossed the Verrazano Bridge, the massive towers and long steel cables mesmerizing me. I remembered the day when I had driven my mother from New Jersey to my old apartment in Queens. I told her that it was my favorite bridge, but she was not impressed. "Hmph. This bridge needs a new coat of paint, pretty badly," she had said. I wondered if she had seen it at night, lit up like strings of Christmas lights, might she have been able to see its beauty instead of its flaws?

Sani dropped me off at Eighty-Sixth Street. I shivered as I got out of the car, descended into the subway station, and took the R train back to my empty apartment.

The late winter freeze made my brother's garage feel like a walk-in refrigerator on the day I went back to New Jersey to sort through her belongings. He had already moved her stuff from the apartment upstairs into the garage. "I figured it would be easier for you this way," he said.

I began randomly unpacking the two dozen or so contractor bags and found things I hadn't seen in decades—the lacy night-gowns and satin slippers I used to try on whenever I could sneak into her bedroom closet, the ornate garments she sewed in her attic workshop, the perfumed soaps she had been saving for some special occasion that never arrived, the silver faux-fur jacket she wore only once, to the wedding of the logging tycoon whose house she used to clean until she fell from a second-story win-dow while washing it. Seeing the jacket sparked my memory of the day the accident happened. I was three or four and she had taken me to work with her.

"Stay right here near the window, so I can see you, Grace-ya?" she said, setting me up to play with some toys on the other side of the window. "Mama is going to be right here the whole time, okay? Make sure you can see me. Promise Mama that you don't go any farther than that."

I did as I was told and played quietly next to the window as she washed it from the outside. We made faces at each other through the glass, and in that instant the ladder tipped backward, and I watched as she disappeared from my sight. We were both temporarily paralyzed—she was injured, and I was keeping my promise to her that I wouldn't move.

In the next bag I unpacked was the old taupe-colored purse, but it didn't stir me in the same way because she carried it with her up until the end, on the rare occasions we took her out. But then I looked inside. There was a handkerchief and her wallet, neither of which seemed out of the ordinary at first. The hand-kerchief was stained with little puddles of mascara that belied my mother's persona as a tough woman. I had given her the wal-let for Christmas in 1993. It contained a long-expired driver's license and a parking ticket from a mental health center dated

May 1994, fourteen years before she died. It was the last time she had ever driven a car or gone outside on her own. I couldn't help but wonder about the connection between the tear-stained handkerchief and the document of her last foray into the world as a semifunctional person. I could barely stand the weight of these things, the tokens of my mother's shattered life.

But the last item I found inspired warmth as much as it did sadness. Inside the purse was nestled a small heavy bundle wrapped in several layers of fabric. I unraveled three long pieces of turquoise silk to uncover another bundle, wrapped in white tissue paper, inside which was yet another cloth cradling her most treasured jewelry. Among these pieces was a tiny gold bracelet that had once been mine. It was a delicate, narrow cuff with two little bells dangling from the center and clusters of flowers engraved on either side. Following the Korean custom of honoring a child's first birthday with gifts of gold, my mother had given it to me when I turned one. That bracelet used to be one of my most beloved objects when I was a girl, but I had forgotten about it until that moment.

Over the next hour, I packed as many of her belongings as I could fit into the back of my friend Rose's car and left the rest in the garage. "I'm leaving now!" I shouted as I knocked on my brother's back door. He came outside holding a black plastic box containing my half of the ashes, handed them to me, and said goodbye.

I got into the passenger seat of the car and set the box down between my feet, hugging it with my calves. "I can't believe this is all that's left of her," I said to Rose.

"I know. The feeling is surreal because you just want to"—she shook her head—"you just want to hug them, but they're gone."

When I got home, I placed my mother's ashes on the windowsill next to my bed, hung the frilly nightgowns on the clothesline that stretched across the sleep alcove of my studio apartment, and laid her favorite robe on my mattress. The sight of the robe suddenly angered me. I had seen her in it on so many recent occasions, but there it was, empty and lifeless. I screamed as I dumped the contents of the other bags onto the floor and grabbed her bra and a few random pieces to stuff inside the robe. I formed the robe into the shape of a woman, breasts and all, and lay down next to it, and buried my head into its shoulder. I smelled my mother's scent still on the robe, and another wave of grief pummeled me. I cried out uncontrollably, "Umma! Umma! Umma!" and dug my fingers into the makeshift effigy. "Umma, come back! Umma!"

As if she heard my call, a deluge of childhood memories washed over me. That's how I started to remember kindergarten.

It was still dark in my bedroom. It must have been near dawn but the mornings were gray and cold in the Pacific Northwest and no sunlight filtered in through my window. I slowly emerged from the fog of sleep to my mother's syrupy voice. I felt her hands grip my legs and gently squeeze to get the circulation going. Groggy but awake, I started to become aware of her massaging my legs and singing that it was time to get up. She quickly pulled back the covers and before there was a chance for me to feel the chill of morning air, she lifted me onto her back, wrapped me in a heated blanket, carried me into the kitchen, and gently placed me in a chair at the table. She kept the lights dimmed until my eyes adjusted and then gradually brightened the room. In front of me she placed a fragrant bowl of miyeok-guk with a scoop of rice in it. The seaweed soup was warm and briny, with little bits of beef and enough sesame oil to make it taste rich. It was one of my favorite foods and usually served on birthdays, so it felt like a special occasion. I was enjoying it so much that whatever anxiety I might have had about my first day of school dissipated.

This morning ritual continued my entire first year of school.

Every day she'd carry me from my bed to the kitchen table to serve me my favorite foods, even chocolate layer cake with chocolate icing, which I used to call "birthday cake." While I was eating, she'd heat my clothes in the dryer and bake my outerwear in the oven. Usually her timing was spot on, but when the shoelaces started getting crispy and others started noticing the burnt edges of my winter coat, I began to wonder if I seemed strange. Regardless, my mother's efforts paid off. I went to school with little or no resistance and I performed well. And yet, this was not enough for her. She needed insurance.

So she hatched a plan to throw an end-of-the-year cocktail party for the staff of the town's elementary, middle, and high schools. It was the first party she had ever hosted in the United States and she treated it as if it were the most important thing she would ever do. She spent days studying recipes in ladies' magazines, shopping for ingredients, and picturing exactly how she wanted everything to look. One day we drove to the Bon Marché to look for fancy service ware and later to a fabric store where we picked out material to make dresses. My mother was learning to sew and this was the perfect opportunity to practice her new skills. She selected a sleek velvet fabric in mottled brown and gold and a metallic lace trim studded with amber jewels for the neckline. For me, she chose white satin with grosgrain ribbon and tiny pink rosettes. When we got home, she ran up to the attic, and after an intense few hours, emerged in a low-cut ankle-length gown with ruching at the shoulders. She was five feet five—statuesque for a Korean woman of her time. The dress elongated her frame and flattered her miniature hourglass shape. "Hwaaa," she said as she admired herself in the mirror. "Don't I look pretty?"

On the day of the party, my mother was focused on the mass production of food. Every square inch of counter space was covered with thousands of hors d'oeuvres—water chestnuts wrapped in bacon, roasted mushroom caps stuffed with sweet Italian sausage and garlicky bread crumbs, bite-size bits of Korean barbecued beef, crudités carved into the shape of flowers and goldfish, fruit cut into fans, each one speared with a frilly toothpick and carefully arranged on small crystal platters. My parents, who never drank liquor, created a liquor cabinet just for the occasion. My father was there mostly in a supporting role, and as a man who sailed on a boat half the year, this was his usual role in our family. He cooed when my mother changed into her new dress and gold sandals. Her high heels and curled hair piled on top of her head added another five inches to her height, making her as tall as my father. She looked like some gilded goddess poised to walk down a red carpet. By contrast, my father looked quite plain. He wore something that didn't stand out, probably a clean, ironed, button-down shirt and a pair of creased dress pants, probably in neutral colors. Maybe he used a little Brylcreem on his thinning salt-and-pepper hair or dabbed a few drops of Aqua Velva on his strong wide jaw, the one vestige of his handsomeness that remained untouched by age. I think my brother was there, too, but I have no clear memory of him.

The first guests to arrive were my kindergarten teacher, Mrs. Jensson, looking the way she always did for school—mousy brown hair combed straight, cotton blouse and knee-length skirt. Her husband, Mr. Jensson, was dressed as plainly as my father. My velvet-and-lamé-clad mother greeted them and ushered them into a house that smelled like bacon and sesame oil. Other school staff arrived, and she practiced her most polite cocktail-party English. "Please come in." "Won't you take a seat?" "Do have some more." She laughed and smiled and served up an endless array of delicacies, working the crowd with a platter in each hand. When her guests were sufficiently drunk, she broke out the bulgogi skewers and said, "Want to try some Korean food? You never tried anything delicious as this one." By the end of the night, the crowd was thoroughly intoxicated. She had dazzled my current teachers and principals—as well as my future teachers and principals—with a generous supply of food and drink, served with a dash of flirtation.

This was perhaps the first time that she flipped the script; this was her territory, and she was now the host rather than the stranger, showing her guests how to properly welcome newcomers. My mother's magnanimity, her delicious food, her seductive charm, were all self-devised political tools to get what she needed, and maybe these tools had always been part of her arsenal, going back to her days as a club hostess in Korea. In this case, what she needed was to give her children an advantage in school. I couldn't yet see how shrewd she was, but my father would remind me every few years of her intellect. "You know where you got your smarts from, don't ya? Not from me!"

The party was such a success that it became an annual event. Though my mother had made it clear that cooking was not an acceptable profession for me, she unwittingly showed me how powerful it was. None of the adults would ever forget me.

When she was alive the only memory that stood out about kindergarten was that of the blond bully conjuring the specter of my mother's permanent absence, and once that absence became real, these other things surfaced. I sensed the phantom image of my young mother's hands gently shaking me. My body remembered our routine: the singing, the leg massages, the getting wrapped in heated blankets and transported to a dimly lit kitchen where breakfasts felt like birthdays.

I looked out at the piles of old clothes I had dumped onto the floor of my studio apartment, and there was the bejeweled velvet gown.

Grace-ya, remember me?

In her death, she was the sweetest of ghosts.

5. KIMCHI BLUES

*Unscientific studies conclude that if you were to ask
ten Koreans, "What is the one thing you cannot live
without?" at least seven of them would say* kimchi.

—THE ECONOMIST, *October 4, 2010*

*When my family was gone, I ate kimchi ... I might not
have survive without it.*

—My mother's war story

New York City, 2008

A WEEK AFTER MY MOTHER DIED, I stopped at a
grocery store in Manhattan's Koreatown and bought a jar of kimchi. I didn't give it much thought at first. It was just an instinct.
Stopping at that market on my way to Penn Station, where I'd
catch the Northeast Corridor line to her house, had become a
weekly habit during the ten years that she lived in New Jersey.

When I left the store that day, I meant to get on the downtown
Q train that would take me home, but instead I walked right past
it and had almost arrived at Penn Station before I remembered
that my mother had died. I stopped in the middle of the side-
walk on Thirty-Second Street, blocking the flow of foot traffic
as throngs of tourists and commuters pushed past me. I peered

into my shopping bag at the jar of kimchi and watched dark spots spread across the brown paper where my tears hit the bag. Why did I buy this? She's not here to eat this with me. I don't even like kimchi that much.

The kimchi sat in my fridge for weeks, swimming in a sea of garlic and chili, its odors slowly permeating all my other foods as it fermented. Everything I ate vaguely tasted of it, reminding me that my mother was gone.

The first time I opened the tall glass jar, the smell hit me so hard that waves of grief rose up through my chest and into my throat until my body gave into its weight, and I was sobbing over the kitchen sink.

Every couple of days I forced myself to eat some kimchi with my rice or ramen, tasting its transformation from the garlicky crunch of fresh cabbage to the pungent tang of soft ripe kimchi—the whole life cycle on my palate. By the time I ate my way through the jar, something shifted in my consciousness, and I went back to Han Ah Reum to buy some more. I contemplated the orderly rows of kimchi in all their varieties—garlic chive, oyster, radish, cucumber, scallion, and the classic napa cabbage— before selecting a quart of the classic mat kimchi.

"Remember," I said to myself. This time I knew full well she was dead.

It wasn't until I was assigned the family tree project at the age of nine, the same age as my mother when she became a refugee, that I began to understand that she had survived a war. She didn't utter another word about the war for at least ten years, and my curiosity about all the things left unsaid was a seed in my unconscious.

In the absence of her storytelling, I dedicated years of my adult life to researching civilian experiences. Some of the survivors who were children at the time came out a generation later to tell horrific tales of seeking refuge under piles of corpses during ground attacks, wading through rivers of the dead to search for their parents' remains, and watching helplessly as the people around them got dismembered by bombs. My mother couldn't bear to talk about the things she might have witnessed. The first time she ever volunteered a memory of the war, she told me a story about kimchi.

As the battle lines moved southward, families were forced to flee their homes. People were starving, but they got by on foraging and looting the homes and fields of other displaced families. Occasionally, they received gifts of food from American soldiers.

I was never really sure if I understood the facts of my mother's experience or if she herself remembered them correctly, but once she told me that when they were on the run, moving with hordes of other refugees, she became separated from her family. Somehow, she made her way back to her family's home, and then she remembered the big earthenware jars of kimchi that my grandmother had buried in the backyard. There was also some rice left in the pantry.

She dug up a jar, set aside a ration of kimchi and boiled a pot of rice, eating just enough to quell her hunger but not so much as to squander the kimchi. At the age of nine, my mother carried on like this week after week while she waited for her family to return. *That kimchi kept me alive for almost three seasons. I might not have survive without it.*

After the war, the places that offered the best hope for survival were American military bases, because that's where wealth was concentrated in Korea. And so my mother went there, her longing for America carefully cultivated by the social and historical context in which she came of age. She was captivated by the images of the United States that she saw in the movies and came to associate all things American with luxury. She did not anticipate that, in a country of such riches, she might one day starve.

The first part of the story is that of deprivation that began with the physical absence of Korean food.[1]

Our first port of entry to the United States in 1972 was Seattle, which then hosted a modest Korean population, enough to warrant a grocery store that carried Asian products. We only lived there a couple of months before moving. The story I heard years later was that my mother spent most of her days in Seattle homesick and crying. Maybe that's why my father thought it would be better for us to move to Chehalis. Maybe he imagined that the presence of his friends and relatives might ease my mother's transition. Indeed, some of them did welcome her with a parade of creamy tuna casseroles, lime Jell-O mixed with canned fruit cocktail and cottage cheese, snickerdoodles and homemade lemonade. The gestures were kind, but these exotic foods were not exactly an antidote to her homesickness.

The biggest shock was the food. Suddenly, every meal became a painful reminder of having left home.[2]

Shortly after our arrival in Chehalis, my father shipped out again, his work schedule alternating three months at home, three months at sea. When he was sailing the Pacific he was reachable only on the few days when he was on land, and so my mother was left behind in a new country, to navigate the pitfalls of her immigrant life with two kids to take care of. But what if she needed care too? Not once do I remember one of my father's relatives coming to visit us when he was away, although I don't know how much the presence of his family ever could have made up for the absence of hers.

I wonder if my father ever considered what it would be like for her in Chehalis when he wasn't there. He probably thought

that at least it would be better than Korea. That anything would
be better than Korea.

*Craving for Korean food was accompanied by homesickness and a loneli-
ness that resulted from the absence of other Koreans in their lives.*[3]

For the first few years of our life in America, my mother tried
to maintain a connection to Korea, taking us to Busan each summer, where my brother showed me all his old haunts. Though I
remember other kids teasing us for being twigki ainoko, a Korean
Japanese racial slur for "half white," my early childhood memories of Korea were among my fondest. We were surrounded by
family, Halmeoni and Imo lavishing us with treats and affection,
my brother still young enough to want to play with me.

At the end of our summers, my mother would pack suitcases
full of food and fib her way through customs at Sea–Tac International Airport. If she packed a bagful of dried anchovies, little
yellow melons, doenjang, and red peppers, it could still go unde-
tected despite the scent of fish and fermented soy paste. Kimchi,
on the other hand, was too sensitive to warm temperatures, too
likely to leak its juice inside the bag, too noxious in its odor to
safely carry on a nine-hour flight and sneak past customs agents.
The most difficult food to smuggle from Korea was also the most
important to the Korean palate. It's not as if my mother didn't
want to try, and maybe at some point she did. But the improper
transport of kimchi was a risky endeavor. Therefore, she settled
on bringing back gallon bags of gochu-garu and several jars of
preserved brine shrimp to make kimchi at home.

My father vowed to supply her with the fresh ingredients and
a whole refrigerator dedicated just to kimchi. The problem, however, was that there was not a single head of Korean cabbage to be
found anywhere in the rural Pacific Northwest during the 1970s,
and my father didn't know the difference between American cabbage and baechu.

The moment when she first received my father's generous gift of American cabbages, indignation spread across her face.

"What is this? This isn't real cabbage." Her voice grew panicky. "Oh no . . . oh no! What I'm going to do now?" In the next moment, she directed her rage toward my father. "What I'm supposed to do with this? Huh?" Then, more calmly, she turned the head over and over in her hands, inspecting it with incredulity. "Hwaaa . . . What American people can do with this, I have no idea."

The vegetable that Americans know as cabbage was an inferior specimen and wholly inadequate for making kimchi. Or so I inferred from my mother's rant. Once she recovered from this bitter disappointment, she set out to source the "real" cabbage, which Americans call "napa cabbage." She would drive to Seattle to look for it and did this on a semiregular basis. Sometimes she'd "het the jackpot" and come home with several cases of baechu, having bought out the store's whole supply. On less fortuitous occasions, all she could find was bok choy. It was not the same, but it was still better than nothing. In other words, it was better than American cabbage.

Women like my mother were the first link in the chain of Korean migration. These women, who were seldom acknowledged by other Koreans because of the stigma of having "mixed flesh with foreigners," sponsored relatives who were fleeing poverty or the string of military dictatorships that ruled South Korea after the war or the dangers of having family ties to North Korea. Almost all of these immigrants came because they had a sister, cousin, aunt, daughter, or niece who married an American and thus enabled them to do so. By the 1980s a significant Korean population was living in the United States, but the women who led the way endured extraordinary hardships as outsiders in both their host country and their families.

My father's family, too, was wary of my mother. Little by little, she chipped away at their fear by learning to cook their familiar foods and hosting all-American Thanksgiving dinners in which green Jell-O concoctions made an appearance on the table. The next day, when the American guests were gone, she would serve the leftover turkey with doenjang and kimchi.

My mother's experience of being marginalized within the new American family was not as extreme as that of other inter-married Korean women. According to Ji-Yeon Yuh's oral histories with Korean "military brides," Korean women who married American soldiers were expected to cook American food and therefore, to reproduce their husbands' cultures in the kitchen, often at the expense of their own. Husbands and in-laws typically found Korean food to be too foreign and smelly, so they discouraged—and sometimes forbade—the women from eating the strange food at home. Even the children of these marriages sometimes refused to identify with Korean food, and by exten-sion, rejected their mothers' cultures. In the absence of Korean food, the women found pale substitutes for kimchi in American pickles, made gochu-jang with heels of bread and Italian pepper flakes, rationed tiny morsels of real Korean banchan to last the duration of a whole bowl of rice.

Many of the women couldn't stomach the greasy starch-laden dishes that Americans favored. *Korean military brides who immi-grated to the United States in the post–World War II decades of the 1950s and 1960s, a time when the proverbial land of plenty was basking in unprecedented economic wealth, told me that "here, there was nothing to eat."* [4] *Not only did the absence of Korean food intensify their feel-ings of homesickness and loneliness, but it also caused physical problems: American food was so unpalatable that eating was difficult and hunger was a constant companion.* [5] They became malnourished and under-weight, depressed and anxious. Both body and spirit withered away.

To survive, some kept Korean food in their kitchens, if they could find it, but resorted to eating it on the sly—hiding secret stashes of Korean products and cooking it when no one was around to complain about the smell. The ones who had access to Korean food hosted underground meetings to feed the women who were not allowed to eat in their own homes. These women felt estranged from their American families and therefore did not think of their houses as their homes. At the same time, they could not return to Korea and became desperately homesick. And so communities developed around resurrecting the lives of women forced to assimilate so violently that they felt homeless.

At the safe houses, they ate kimchi and miyeok-guk together and shared stories of Korea. One of them explained that Korean food was more than just food: the experience of finally tasting the spicy, garlicky, fermented flavors of Korea was akin to being stranded in the desert and then taking your first sip of water. It was a narrow escape from a slow death. For a moment, some of these women found their way back home.

My mother once knew that experience of feeling lost for lack of Korean food, yet there was no one in Chehalis who could guide her to a familiar place. Instead, she became the very guide she wished she'd had.

As new Koreans started trickling into Chehalis, my mother took each of them under her wing. The first was named Kyeong, and she was married to an American. They had a daughter, Ellie, who was a year younger than me. Ellie's mom was also younger than mine, which made my mom her unni, or "older sister." Upon their first meeting, my mother greeted her with a jar of homemade kimchi and they soon became cooking companions.

The arrival of another Korean woman to my hometown meant that my mother expanded her Korean cooking repertoire. Many of the ingredients were hard to come by, so she led seaside foraging expeditions to look for them, and Ellie and I went along for the ride. We made bouquets out of driftwood and dug holes in the sand while our mothers filled ten-gallon buckets with clams and seaweed and the little oily fishes that Americans did not regard as food. They made chewy seaweed salads and fried smelts, and served them with rice and kimchi. These gatherings kept Ellie's mom afloat for a little while, but ultimately she could not stand being isolated from a Korean community, so Ellie and her family moved to Tacoma, which hosted the second largest Korean population in the state.

As a child, I never imagined that it was so hard on my mother to have limited access to Korean food, because there had always been American foods she enjoyed. She loved hamburgers and hot dogs, and any kind of meat, foods that had colonized the collective taste buds of South Korea during the American occupation and war. Despite liking these foods, she needed something more. For a Korean person, rural America was a food desert.

The gravity of what she must have felt only registered for me a few years before she died, when I told her that Hosu's friend Jandi was visiting from Korea and I had invited them both over for dinner.

"What are you cooking? Don't cook American food," she urged.

"I was thinking of making a coq au vin. It's a French dish. Chicken cooked in wine," I said.

"French, American. Same thing! Don't cook any Western food!"

"But she might like to try something new."

"I am telling you, she is not going to like it."

"You don't even know her!"

"Oh no, Grace. Koreans cannot eat that kind of food. It's making her sick. Cook Korean food."

A couple hours later, when the topic of my upcoming dinner

had long passed, my mother brought it up again. "Make Jandi some Korean food, okay?"

Her concern for my guest triggered a memory of a day from my childhood, when I was eight or nine years old and my mother discovered an Asian supermarket only thirty miles from our house. She came back with two hundred pounds of rice, the trunk stuffed to the brim with dried soybeans, gochu-garu, fish sauce, oyster sauce, brine shrimp, and fresh bean sprouts, and enough baechu to fill the backseat of the car.

"Thank the dickens I can eat rice and kimchi for a looooong time now!" she said.

Food, Korean food . . . I think about it, I dream about it, in my dreams there is no Korean food, or I am eating Korean food, or Korean food appears. This is what I dream about. When I first came . . . it was terrible, I wanted so badly to eat [Korean] food, it was terrible. Oh, I suffered very very much.[6]

The year after Ellie and her family left, there was Kay.

When Kay and her little brother arrived at my school, the teachers didn't know what to do. They had no capacity to help immigrant kids transition to life in America, so the school personnel came to me. They put Kay in my first-grade classroom and expected us to become lunch buddies, and we did.

Kay and her brother were not ordinary immigrants, because they came alone, at the ages of five and six. Kay told me the story of how they had gotten here. Her mother took them to the market and said, "Hold each other's hands tight, tight, and do not let go. Stay right here until I come back." They waited in the middle of the busy market, gripping each other's hands, letting go only to wipe the sweat from their palms. At nightfall, a man from an orphanage found the children, soiled and hungry, but still clutching each other per their mother's instructions. He took them to the orphanage, and a few weeks later, put the children on a plane

and sent them to Chehalis to be adopted by the Anderson family.
I would later learn that Kay's experience was not unique, and
many Korean adoptees that came to the United States during that
era were old enough to remember the families and homes they
had lost in Korea.

To welcome Kay and her brother, my school decided to
organize a "culture day" so that students from "different" cultures could showcase aspects of their heritage. In other words,
Kay and I were asked to go around to different classrooms as
guest speakers. She dressed up in hanbok—long undergarments
of hemp fabric beneath a wide-sleeved blouse and voluminous
skirt—and explained that it was the traditional dress of Korea. I
didn't have hanbok, only gomu-shin, the rubber shoes that were
shaped like canoes, but they no longer fit me, nor did I want to
wear them for fear of being teased. My teachers were not particularly interested in having me dress up anyway. What they really
wanted from me was my mother's cooking. She knew better
than to serve kimchi to a bunch of American kids, so instead she
made japchae, a colorful mix of clear noodles, spinach, and strips
of carrots, zucchini, beef, and egg seasoned in sesame oil and
garlic.

Kay gave a speech about her hanbok and fielded questions
about being an adoptee, recounting every detail of her abandonment, then my mother plated the japchae and passed it around
to the children.

"Ewww. They're made of worms!" one of them shouted.

"They are potato starch noodles," my mother shot back.
"Okay? Potato, potato."

I stood in the back silently watching a bloom of crimson
spread across my mother's face as she repressed her anger at the
wild accusation. We three Koreans continued to prance around
the school like that—Kay in her hanbok, my mother carrying a
tray of japchae, and me offering nothing in particular except the

presence of my racialized self. And despite putting our ethnicity on display, the kids continued to call us Chinese or Japanese.

My mother knew about Kay long before I met her in my first-grade class. She had never formally met the Andersons, but everyone knew my mother by reputation. She was known as "the Oriental" or "the Chinese Lady" and the only person in town who could speak Korean. Now, all of a sudden, her language difference was a valuable commodity.

The adoption agency had probably given Mr. and Mrs. Anderson a how-to guide: *Children are often upset at leaving everything familiar to them. If your child appears upset, just smile and cuddle him a little. Soon he will join the ranks of other happy American children. And all these problems will solve themselves . . . Korean children are eager to please and most will learn quickly.* [7]

But when Kay and Jason broke into a crying fit that could not be soothed, my mother was called in to evaluate the situation. She returned home clucking her teeth. No one needed to ask her what had happened because she launched into the story for anyone who would listen:

"Mrs. Anderson was fermenting some cabbage, you see, and the poor children thought it was kimchi . . . but it was sauerkraut." She held their disappointment in her heart for a moment and exhaled, "Aigu, dap-dap-eu-rah!" The weight of her emotions had become too much to bear. "Dap-dap-eu-rah!" she repeated, her voice swelling with the sound of tears. It was the first time I had ever seen my mother cry.

Then she collected herself and did the only reasonable thing one could do in this situation. She went to the kitchen and took some baechu out of the refrigerator, mixed a bath of warm water and salt in a huge metal mixing bowl, laid a cutting board on the floor, and got to work. She squatted down, quartered the heads of cabbage, and slid them into the brine. Next she pounded a fine paste of garlic with the handle of her knife, poured a stream of gochu-garu into another bowl, added brine shrimp, sugar, rice flour, and the garlic paste. She took the big ceramic jars down from the attic in anticipation of fermenting the kimchi. A few hours later, she rinsed the cabbage, added it to the bowl of chili mixture along with chopped scallions, and mixed it all up with her bare hands. She packed the seasoned leaves into the jars, and put them back in the attic to ferment.

Nothing could change the fact that Kay and Jason had been suddenly plucked from Korea and given a new family in Chehalis that could neither speak their language nor understand their culture, but my mother decided that never again would they have to go without kimchi. She immediately recognized them as mouths to feed, and for a brief moment, she became the Korean mother these children had lost.

I was always struck by her tenderness toward them, and as I learned more about my mother's past, I wondered how much of it had been a projection of her own loss, and whether she was the mother or the child in that projection. Did the presence of these scared, sad children trigger memories of the time when she was a quasi-orphan, forced to fend for herself in the midst of war, or did it cut to the heart of her alienation in America?

Well into my life as a researcher, and particularly through my collaborative work with Hosu, I would learn that the prototypical Korean birthmother looked a lot like my mother—the camptown woman of the 1950s and 1960s—and then I'd remember her complaining that the birth control pills she used to take hadn't worked. The look on her face when she said it was one of regret and horror, feelings that she never outwardly expressed about my brother or me. I couldn't help but wonder if there had been another child she had relinquished. The most unspeakable of all her secrets. Did the Anderson children conjure up the specter of a third child, airdropped into some middle American home, who was crying for her and longing for the taste of kimchi?

My mother visited the Andersons often and occasionally invited them over for a Korean dinner. But a few years later, when they adopted another Korean child, there came a breaking point.

The new girl was almost seventeen, and she was the only one of the children who retained her Korean name, maybe because the parents knew it was too late for her to adopt a new identity, or maybe because it sounded ambiguous enough to be American—Mina. Or if my mother's theory was correct, it was because their true intention had never been to make her part of the family.

"They don't want another child! They want a maid!" my mother cried. Again, she felt this child's suffering deeply.

I never knew what exactly transpired between her and the Anderson family, but the arrival of the seventeen-year-old Mina marked my mother's complete disengagement from them.

Mina, Kay, Jason, Kyeong, Ellie—all the Koreans who arrived after us—were either adoptees or from mixed race families like my own. We were joined by our common legacy as militarized subjects, having been borne out of the same murderous conditions of US intervention and war, the same sexist and imperialist social policies that fractured families in Korea. We were all bound by the discourse that said that the American family/nation rescued us.

My mother ruptured that discourse when she voiced her disgust with the Andersons. She wanted nothing more to do with people who exploited a girl for her labor and disguised it as charity.

A scene similar to that of Kay's arrival played out in my fourth-grade classroom. This time it was a boy, a bit older than me. He was so bewildered that he ran around the room in circles, peeing his pants. A male teacher from another class was chasing him and yelling at him to sit down. The school did not have a translator, so the teacher looked at me, and said, "You! Please. Tell him to sit down."

"Anjda," I said.

The boy stopped and studied me, then slowly sat down. "Hanguk saram-iya?"

"Umma Hanguk," I said in my broken Korean. "Busan gohyang."

He smiled and sat still for a while.

I told my mother about the new boy when I got home from school, and she prepared a fresh batch of kimchi.

Whenever a Korean child or wife arrived to her new American family, my mother was there to welcome her in their native tongue. She held a jar of kimchi in her hands and said, "Hammeokja." *Let's eat together.*

She offered kimchi as a balm for their dislocations because she understood that the everyday acts of eating and cooking preserved a connection to the people and places that one left behind. By inserting herself into the scene of induction, my mother also gave presence to the Korean kinship ties that had been lost or erased. And thus, in another, more subtle way, she ruptured the discourse that the American family/nation was our savior, to whom we owed everything.

I don't think she ever intended for her kimchi to be a kind of resistance, but there was something about making and sharing kimchi that made her feel alive, that made her fight to keep on living in the face of murderous conditions.

The final recipient of my mother's kimchi was me. When I left home to go to college three thousand miles away, she gifted me a rice cooker and a quart jar of kimchi. She wrapped the jar in multiple layers of plastic bags for me to put in my suitcase, but I initially rejected it because I didn't want it stinking up my clothes.

"Grace, just take it," she said. "These American college people don't know how to feed Asian kids. Just take it so I don't have to worry about you."

She knew that I'd have access to unlimited food at the campus dining hall, so her concern wasn't just about me getting enough to eat. For my mother, kimchi represented survival, and she believed that it would get me through whatever challenges life might throw my way.

A few years later, when I got my first apartment, I asked for her recipe so that I could be empowered to have it at all times. For years I'd been begging her to teach me to cook Korean food, but she always refused, claiming that it was a "waste of time" and that I should be studying instead. Yet she gave me the kimchi recipe without hesitation. If there was one thing from my family's culinary history she wanted me to hold on to, it was this.

One night, shortly after my mother's death, I lay in bed doubting my capacity to live in a world without her. The pain of her being suddenly gone, and of knowing how much her existence had been consumed by suffering, was so intense that I wished for my own death as relief. I began to drift away, and a scene from my early childhood flashed beneath the surface of sleep:

I am seated in a high chair, watching my mother. She stands at the kitchen sink, in a loose cotton jumper—sleeveless and short, in lavender pink—her long hair free, her feet bare. My mother's delicate hands are under a running faucet, rinsing a soft leaf of fermented cabbage until every flake of chili washes away. She tears the leaf into small strips with her fingers, first lengthwise, then pinching with the nails of her thumb and forefinger, she cuts the strips crosswise. I can see her slim nut-brown hands in great detail—her fingers long and tapered, the quicks of her nails reaching the edges of her fingers. They work swiftly to remove the heat from the kimchi. She brings the little pieces to me and feeds me with her hands. "Not too spicy, Grace-ya?" she asks. I eat. "Oh, kimchi jal mung-neh! Good girl!" She is smiling, pleased that I am developing a taste for kimchi.

As I became more lucid, the image remained and I knew with all my senses that it was not a dream. It was my earliest memory of eating, and my earliest memory of my mother. I closed my eyes to be with her again, to see the look of comfort on her face as her hands poised to feed me, to hear her say, "Ja. Kimchi deo mu-ra. Grace-ya, we are survivors. You can endure anything."

6. MADAME MUSHROOM

Chehalis, Washington, 1979

WHEN I WAS ABOUT SEVEN OR EIGHT, my mother developed an addiction to foraging. From the stories my father told me about her penchant for all-night gambling in Korea, I knew that she had an addictive personality and a bit of a wild streak. "You should have seen your mother go. She could outlast every damn one of them," my father would say, his pale cheeks blushing as he recalled my mother's blackjack binges. "Boy, she was a pro." He said all this as a warning to me when I invited her to play Old Maid.

I remember that restless side of her too—of her constantly wanting to infuse a little excitement into our humdrum rural American life by raising the stakes. She made wagers on the most mundane things, like guessing the number of seeds inside a tangerine or competing to see who could peel the longest continuous strip from an apple. These were minor diversions of no consequence, but whenever there was anything real at stake, you couldn't help also feeling the rush of my mother's adrenaline. She always exuded an unnatural confidence that she could win, and once she was in the game, she'd stay till the bitter end.

Chehalis was made up of three distinct landscapes. The residential and commercial area, known as "the city," was buttressed by sprawling farmlands on one side—"the country." On the other side of the city was lush, green wilderness, a combination of secondary-growth forest and patches of land still untouched by the burgeoning timber industry. While there was a lot of movement across the "city/country" border as "city" folk went to visit relatives or purchase produce straight from the farm, it was not as common in that time and place to see people search for food in the wild. Although the forest had once fed the Chehalis people and the white settlers who displaced them, by the 1970s there was a clear distinction: the farmland was for growing food, and the forest was for growing timber.

Both of my parents came from agrarian roots, but my father was much more intimate with the farm. He got his first lesson in steering a plough horse when he was a toddler, and started raising pigs when he was fifteen. For my mother, the wilderness held much more allure. When she was a child in Korea, when all the farmlands had been destroyed, hunting and foraging in the mountains was one of the things that had kept her family alive. The forest provided nourishment, not just during the war, but throughout all of Korea's culinary history.

My mother had found other wild food sources in the Pacific Northwest—the rocky beaches of Puget Sound were abundant with seaweed and fish, but she always ignored the posted warning signs about penalties for overfishing. She got in trouble with the law for depleting the smelt population, and despite a hefty fine, couldn't stop herself from doing it again. After the second citation, she stopped going back. "What's the use if I can't get a lot?" she said. There was no law against picking seaweed, but the coast was an hour drive away while the forest was right there on the outskirts of town.

After years of struggling to get by in Chehalis, of trying to follow the rules and play the good wife, my mother's spirit needed something more. Maybe she could no longer resist the little voices in her head that told her to cross over to the other side—to that uncivilized and uninhabited place—to see what she might find.

The first time she went into the woods, she snatched up a few stray plants that she had eaten in Korea, like wild onions or burdock, without any grand plans beyond that night's dinner. But my mother knew a gold mine when she saw one. Once she discovered that this forested area was fertile ground for foraging, it didn't take long for her to become hooked. The forest was the one place in Chehalis that called her. It felt familiar, and at the same time, was rich with discovery.

By the time my mother started foraging, she was working full-time and single-parenting half-time, whenever my father was out to sea. Her first paid job in Chehalis had been to clean the house of the logging magnate who lived in the next town over. She made one dollar an hour—slightly less than half the minimum wage in the mid-1970s, and after she fell off the ladder washing his windows—an accident that left her with chronic back pain for the rest of her life—she told the millionaire to find another maid. That summer when we went to Korea, she cut her waist-length hair short and sold it. Upon our return to Chehalis, she got a full-time job working the graveyard shift, from 11:00 p.m. to 7:00 a.m., at a juvenile detention facility called Green Hill, where she stayed for the duration of her working life.

One night early on during her tenure at Green Hill, as my brother and I were sleeping on the red-and-green floral mat we had brought back from Korea, she came into our room, turned on a dim light, and woke me up. She kneeled down next to me and whispered, "Grace-ya, promise me something. Don't tell anyone that I'm going to work at night or they will take you away from me." Though I didn't understand what she was talking about at the time, I could feel her fear. I nodded, and she stroked my hair with her slender hand.

In my adult life, I would remember this moment as I learned about the case of Chong Sun France, a Korean immigrant woman and former sex worker whose young child died when she left him alone at night. France's husband had abandoned her and their children after bringing them to North Carolina. Tasked with the responsibility of supporting her family, she got a job working in a nightclub. She made the decision to leave her children alone while she went to work, and one early morning she came home to find that her son had been crushed to death by a dresser. She took the blame for her child's death, as any mother might do, but she phrased it in a distinctly Korean-mother kind of way: *I killed him! I killed him!*

She wailed the words over and over again to the police. This admission of guilt, combined with her heavy accent, immigrant status, and history as a sex worker, got her convicted of murder in the second degree and sentenced to twenty years in prison.

I saw my own mother in France and felt grateful that nothing bad had ever happened when my brother and I were alone at night. He was twelve when she started working the graveyard shift, and although she probably felt that he was mature enough to handle being the babysitter during our sleeping hours, she must have lived with constant anxiety. If one of us had gotten hurt, would she have gone to prison? And where was my father's culpability in this? He knew she was working, and in fact, helped her to find the job. Although he made a good income as a merchant marine, he didn't give her access to his money, and instead left her an allowance during his monthslong absences. According to my mother, my father was a "cheapskate" and a "scrooge" because it wasn't nearly enough to take care of a family. According to my father, she could make do if only she tried harder and gave up the things that he deemed unnecessary. Regardless, my mother felt compelled to go out and earn her own money, and my father agreed to the plan.

I was never sure what exactly she did at Green Hill, though she told me that she was a counselor. I wondered why they needed a counselor when people were sleeping. Once, after she told me about a fight that she broke up between two of the detainees by hitting one of them with a folding chair, I thought to myself that she must have been a security guard, but then again, she didn't dress like a security guard. She styled her new short hair with a curling iron and put on fancy ruffled blouses, dress pants, and high heels to go to work.

It was a few years into working this job that her forest outings began. She would get home from work between 7:05 and 7:10 in the morning, send us off to school, change her clothes, and then head out into the wilderness. On some days when I got home from school, she still hadn't slept. I would find her sitting on the kitchen floor, surrounded by little mountains of greenery. Dinner was on the table by 6:00 p.m. and always featured whatever she had gathered from the forest that morning. And then she slept for three or four hours before getting up to go to work again.

The focus of her early foraging expeditions was to find things that were not readily available in grocery stores. In the springtime she gathered fiddlehead ferns, or gosari, a popular ingredient that one might find today as a side dish in a Korean restaurant or on top of a sizzling bowl of bibimbap. As some intrepid forager must have discovered generations ago, raw fiddleheads are toxic to humans and must be treated carefully before they can be eaten. The Korean method of preparing gosari for human consumption involves sun-drying them first, and therefore my mother spent a lot of time on the roof of our house. The nights and mornings were misty, and it rained often, so she'd have to tend to the plants twice daily. She spread them out over big white sheets at midday and then gathered them up again before nightfall.

"Why is your mom always walking around on the roof?" one of the kids in the neighborhood asked me once.

"She's drying ferns," I said, embarrassed because I knew it didn't make any sense to someone who didn't eat gosari.

Equally alarming to the people in my town was the sight of my mother picking dandelion leaves on the side of the road, in big open fields, along the railroad tracks, everywhere except for other people's yards. She made that exception not out of respect for private property but because Americans considered dandelions weeds and sprayed them with herbicide. My mother was popping up in all kinds of unusual places, and her foreign ways made her seem like the town crazy.

Most people in Chehalis got their food from the grocery store, or else they drove out to the country, or grew things in their backyards. Some people hunted deer and picked gooseberries or crab apples that had crept onto their property, but otherwise, the wilderness was not on many people's radar as a major food source. It was a time when modern convenience foods had captured the imaginations of Americans (microwavable plastic pouches that turned into meals with the press of a button, just-add-water-and-chill instant cheesecakes). Industry was well on its way to displacing nature as the maker of our food. Though many people were still connected to the farm, they seemed to have forgotten that the wilderness could also feed us. My mother was about to change all that, however.

Midsummer 1979

IT'S 7:OO A.M. and the air is slightly damp, the sun not yet searing. My mother returns home from work, changes out of her dress clothes into jeans, a T-shirt, and tennis shoes, packs a water cooler and a bucket into the car, and ventures out into the forest. She's ripe with anticipation, but doesn't know exactly what she's looking for. As she makes a clearing in the brush, her sleeve catches on a sharp sticker. She tries to free herself, then notices a cluster of tiny red fruit hanging just below the plant's palm-shaped leaves. She takes a closer look and sees the hidden gems in a gamut of red and purple hues. The small berries are growing on strong, thorny stalks that jut out at forty-five-degree angles. The plants are tall, and she has to force her way through the thicket to get to the ripe fruit inside. Only a smattering of them are ready to be picked. The rest are beckoning her return.

Later, she will come home with scratches all over her arms and face, juice-stained fingers, and a small bowlful of blackberries. Her eyes will be full of excitement, her voice breathless, as she says, "I think I het the jackpot."

Blackberries became my mother's singular obsession. They were difficult to harvest, but the very challenge of it seemed to fuel her desire to pick them. The day after her initial discovery, she went back to that spot in the forest, equipped with large containers and long sleeves to protect her arms from the tangle of thorns. She returned home with five gallons of blackberries, intoxicated from the bounty. The next day it was seven, then ten, fourteen, twenty, each day breaking the previous day's record. Literally overnight, the kitchen became filled with wild blackberries and all manner of blackberry products that got distributed to friends, relatives, and enemies.

At first she did it for the satisfaction of knowing that she could feed everyone around her, mingled with the thrill of the hunt. But once she started, my mother could not stop. Her hands had become tattooed with hundreds of tiny purple lines, where the blackberry juice had seeped into scratch marks on her skin. Soon

there were far too many blackberries for one family and its associates to consume. On some days the kitchen was so completely
dedicated to processing the blackberries that I was forbidden to
set foot in it. Even if I had wanted to, there was no floor space left
through which I could have walked. There would be an assembly
line set up on the floor with giant metal tubs of just-picked blackberries on one side, a big basin of water in the middle, and fresh
tubs for the washed berries on the other side. After the berries
were cleaned, she would lay them out gently on sheet pans lined
with paper towels and pack them into Ziploc bags that she put
away in the fridge or freezer.

After a few days like this, there was no room left to store
any fresh food other than blackberries. The kitchen was literally
overflowing. And that's when it struck her. As she squatted on
the kitchen floor, transferring some cleaned berries into a gallon
Ziploc bag, she decided that it was time to start selling. Having
schooled herself well in the ways of American women and their
love of baking and canning, she found a business opportunity in
our economically depressed town. She bought two industrial
freezers and put an ad in the local paper: *Small wild blackberries.
Fresh or frozen. $13 a gallon.*

Within a few weeks, our house became the busiest regional
hub of blackberry traffic, and my family renamed summer
"Blackberry Season." New customers came every day, and my
mother greeted them with, "You want small wild blackberries?
All right then. You come to the right place." Her purple hands
gestured for them to enter.

This was the moment of her ascent, when she had something
of value that others clamored for, that was exclusively hers to
trade. In Marxist terms, she owned both the product and the
means of production. In psychic terms, she had the capacity to
feed the very community that had treated her as a second-class
citizen, to rise above the fray and be the gracious one.

If my mother hadn't already been a recognizable character in Chehalis, she certainly became one then. Her celebrity grew as people from neighboring towns came to our kitchen to buy wild blackberries, as well as value-added products like blackberry pies and jams. Word spread and soon she became known as "the Blackberry Lady" instead of "the Chinese Lady." People all over town greeted me with "Say, aren't you the Blackberry Lady's girl?"

Once her new reputation set in, she worked even harder to keep up with demand. When one blackberry patch was picked clean, she would have to start the search over again. There were days when the forest was unyielding, prompting her to come home and snort with disgust, "I barely filled up one gallon today!"

Her disappointment drove her deeper into the woods to uncover the vines heaviest with fruit. The deeper she went, the more dangerous her hunts became. She encountered hostiles—bears competing for the same berries, or white men with rifles who didn't look too kindly upon foreigners encroaching upon their hunting grounds. But my mother was not intimidated. She bought herself a .38 Special to let the hunters know that she had leveled the playing field. Nothing was going to stop her.

That summer changed my mother. She no longer depended on her femininity to get attention or make a profit. Working in the woods meant that she had to shed her frilly dresses and heels, and start dressing like a lumberjack. As much as she had once represented my ideal of feminine beauty, she also came to embody masculine strength. By this point, she had replaced my father as the masculine parental figure. He had become a frail old man in my eyes when, a year earlier, he had had a heart attack. I had found him splayed out and unresponsive on his bedroom floor, my mother shaking him furiously and screaming at me to call an ambulance. When I was on the phone with 911, amid the desperate cries of a vulnerable would-be widow, I thought I heard her anger break through. *Don! Don! Don't leave me, you sonofabitch!* If there was any chance that he might abandon her in his wretched little town, then she'd better start making a place for herself in it. Perhaps it was the specter of my father as a dead man that gave rise to my mother as the fearless, gun-toting Blackberry Lady.

Blackberry Season, 1980

THE NEXT SUMMER, I begged my mother to take me with her to the forest, but she refused on the grounds that I'd slow her down.

"Please, can I go with you?"

"You're going to whine and meow, and then I have to worry about you. What a nuisance!"

"Please, Mama. Pleeeease! I promise I won't bother you."

"Why you wanna go so bad? You are not going to like it."

I couldn't understand that blackberry picking was *work*. Hot. Labor intensive. Treacherous. And a big source of my mother's income. But I persisted until she gave in. Just as she predicted, the combination of summer heat, hilly terrain, and brambles was so grueling that I needed her to take care of me. We stopped frequently so that I could sit in the shade and sip on ice water from her cooler, and then we headed home a good two hours early.

"Aigu! Grace-ya. I told you! No more blackberry picking for you."

A couple weeks later, when my father came home from work for the summer and decided he wanted to spend Blackberry Season by my mother's side, she put up a similar protest.

"I'm going with you from now on," he declared.

"Oh no you don't! It's too hard for you."

"Nonsense!"

"Oooh yeah. You don't know what it is like."

"Balls!"

"What if it's putting too much stress on your heart?"

"I don't want you out there alone anymore. You're a woman! It's dangerous."

"Darnit! Why you bugging me? I can take care of myself! I been doing it, aren't I?"

They volleyed like this for several minutes before my mother resigned herself to bringing him along. Though she had become the stronger of the two, he could not admit it.

On the third or fourth day of my father's company, my mother came home early. She plopped down in the plush swivel chair in our living room and scowled with her arms crossed. I approached with trepidation and asked her what was the matter.

"It's your father," she snapped.

"What did he do?"

She shook her head and didn't answer.

"What happened?"

"Your father's heart stopped today."

"What? Where is he?" I asked, my voice beginning to quiver.

"I had to take him to the hospital." She got out of the chair, went to her bedroom, and slammed the door. I couldn't tell what she was angrier about—that he almost left her widowed again or that she lost a perfectly good day of blackberry picking that she could never get back.

My father had his first heart attack when I was seven, his second when I was nine, and his third when I was fifteen, so there were a good five years when his life didn't hang in the balance. During those five years when my father was not on the verge of death, my mother focused her energy on her business activities. During Blackberry Season, she was at the top of her game, but like all seasons, it, too, waned. And then a similar pattern emerged with mushrooms.

In *The Omnivore's Dilemma*, Michael Pollan muses on the "mushroom hunter" as a special brand of forager. The endeavor of harvesting wild mushrooms is called "hunting" rather than "foraging" or "picking" to denote the courage and skill involved in the act of distinguishing the edible from the poisonous. One wrong turn—mistaking a false chanterelle for a chanterelle, for example—could result in the mushroom hunter's sudden demise. The other challenge that faces the hunter is that mushrooms camouflage themselves against the forest floor, so it takes a well-trained human eye to spot them.

After experiencing blackberry withdrawal at the end of the summer, my mother realized that the fall was prime time to begin her search for mushrooms. In the damp, cool climate of the Pacific Northwest, mushrooms grew during many seasons. She first thought of mushroom hunting as something that could sustain her until next Blackberry Season, but as it turned out, mushrooms became more than just a temporary fix. Though my father had warned her about the dangers of poisonous mushrooms, she was again undaunted. Having already familiarized herself with the forest, all she needed to do was give herself a crash course in mycology. For $14.95, she bought an encyclopedic book called *The Mushroom Hunter's Field Guide*, and despite her limited literacy in English and the dense academic nature of the book, she studied it cover to cover, several times over. When put to the test, she seemed to have a sixth sense for spotting mushrooms. In a split second she could coax a mushroom out of its hiding place and catalog it as either delicious or dangerous. If we happened upon a mushroom that was toxic, she blurted out ominous warnings.

"Oh no no no! Don't touch that! It's make you sick!" She

spoke with just as much excitement about the edible mushrooms. "Yaaaa! Porcini! I het the jackpot!"

Mushroom hunting did not involve the same level of physical exertion as blackberry picking—there were no sharp thorns or thickets to navigate, no blazing sun—so my mother allowed me to accompany her on a few excursions. I loved being enveloped by ancient, moss-covered trees and the earthy smell of damp leaves. We were the only two people in the forest. She an explorer and I her sidekick, traveling through a mystical universe of undiscovered species.

My mother's enthusiasm for mushrooms was infectious, and without even realizing it, I learned to categorize them according to growing season, the type of tree with which they grew, and best culinary uses. There were fall mushrooms and spring mushrooms. Meaty mushrooms and dainty mushrooms. Half the year our dinners featured some variety of fresh mushroom: hedgehogs, chanterelles, lobsters, chicken of the woods, which indeed tasted just like chicken. By the time I was ten, I became an expert on gourmet mushrooms, though this was before I had any concept of "gourmet." It was the early 1980s, when words like "foodie" and "locavore" were not a part of anyone's vocabulary, yet my mother was on the cusp of an emerging market for wild mushrooms.

She sold them to a distributor called Madame Mushroom that supplied restaurants and specialty stores throughout the Pacific Northwest. Once, she picked me up from school on her way to sell, and we drove down some winding dirt paths to Madame Mushroom's roadside stand. It was a rare treat to be privy to my mother's negotiations. There was a group of other hunters there selling their wares, but my mother's exceeded theirs tenfold. I looked around and could see a clear demarcation line between the pros and the hobbyists, with my mother on one side and everyone else on the other. Whomever it was that dared to call herself "Madame Mushroom" could not have kept up that identity without my mother's supply. After that trip, I knew who the real Madame Mushroom was. My mother. The Blackberry Lady by summer, Madame Mushroom by fall.

I don't know how she did it, but somehow she singlehandedly supplied the whole town, and later the whole region, with wild produce. She did it for six or seven years while also keeping her night job, and maybe, at the root of it, she didn't want to see the people around her ever be hungry again.

There was never a moment of my childhood when the kitchen wasn't completely stocked. Though she sold most of her harvest, her rule was that a portion of it went first to our family. Around the time she began foraging, my father built an extension of our house, with another pantry. Behind the industrial freezers full of blackberries was a set of deep shelves, about ten by ten feet, filled with the fruits of my parents' labor. The shelves were tightly packed with rows of mason jars, two shelves each of blackberry jam and wild mushrooms. The rest were filled with the things my father grew in his one-acre garden—corn, beans, tomatoes—and the stone fruit they had picked together at local orchards. Never have I seen as much food in one kitchen as I did in my childhood home.

It took me a long time to realize that my mother's level of productivity was extraordinary, that most people cannot work at the speed at which she worked, or live for years on so little sleep. As a child I was always in awe of her ability to do so many things well. To me, she was some butch forest goddess, earth mother, and breadwinner all wrapped in one, sort of like the woman from the perfume commercial who could bring home the bacon and fry it up in a pan. I couldn't see the darkness that was brewing on the heels of her meteoric rise as a professional forager.

New Jersey Transit, 2001

ON ONE OF THOSE rare but "absolutely necessary" occasions that my mother allowed herself to go outside, we traveled together by train from New Jersey to New York. As we passed through the more scenic portions of the industrial Northeast Corridor, I watched her eyes grow wide as she looked out the window. Her face twitched as she was transfixed on something outside.

"What do you see out there, Mom?"

"Suk. So much suk."

"What's that?"

"Those plants, you see?" She pointed, but from the moving train, all I could see was a blur of green.

"What do they look like?"

"I don't know what you call in English." She held out her index finger and squeezed the tip with the thumb and index finger of her other hand. "Leaves about this big, that got the silver color, kind of whitish color underneath. They're everywhere! Oh god! They make the best soup."

Her focus didn't waver the whole train ride, and every stop or two, she glanced at the door wondering if she had enough time to pick some suk before the train pulled away. After fifteen years, I saw the belated manifestations of my mother's foraging withdrawals. The suk was taunting her to come outside. She had caught a glimpse of what the Northeast wilds had to offer, yet was powerless to taste it.

For weeks she talked about her cravings for suk and the missed opportunity to pick it. But in time, she conceded, and things returned to the way they had been before she knew what grew outside the train window.

Princeton, New Jersey, 2006

MORE SEASONS PASSED, and I became her regular cook as cooking became something she could no longer do herself. She didn't like it if I spent too much time or money on the meals, but on holidays, she gave me permission to splurge. "Okay, we get the best cut of meat because Christmas only comes once a year," she would say. It became our tradition to prepare a beef tenderloin, and I usually made a red wine sauce to go with it, but one year I bought wild mushrooms instead, for old times' sake. As soon as I opened the door of her apartment that Christmas Eve, I made the announcement.

"Mom! I'm cooking mushrooms to go with the roast!"

"Oh, really? What kind of mushrooms you get?"

"Chanterelles!"

"Chanterelles, huh? How much you pay for that?"

"Oh, it was really expensive. You probably don't want to know." I was always reluctant to tell her how much things cost, but I could never lie to her. "Whole Foods sells them for forty dollars a pound."

"Forty dollars a pound?! Hwaaa!"

"It was overpriced. I know. But it's a holiday."

"Forty dollars a pound! I used to pick *thousands* of pounds of those! You remember?"

"Was it really that much?"

"Oh, easily!" She seemed put off by my question. "Maybe even more than thousands. *Tens* of thousands."

The memory struck a bittersweet chord. By that time, we were in year twelve of her life as a shut-in.

"Remember how I cooked for you?" she asked. "I used to cook 'em with bacon and onions and put it over rice. You kids just loved it."

"Yeah, that was really good. You were a great cook."

"Forty dollars a pound!" She began to get agitated. "Hah! They are not even that special. Not like porcini. Now those are good. But chanterelles? For forty dollars a pound?"

"Mom, don't worry about it. Let's just enjoy the dinner."

"I can't believe it." She shook her head and sighed. "I could make so much money now."

More seasons passed and the number of years she stayed indoors surpassed the number of years she lived unfettered, when the natural world was her domain. I wondered if, after all that time, her sense memory of the forest had grown dim, if her wild streak had finally faded away. Every once in a while, after the first spring rains, I'd see a familiar look of hunger in her eyes as she'd look out the window and study the trees in the distance. In the Northeast, conifers were sparse, but there were lots of elms, whose death gave life to some of the most delicate mushrooms. My mother would whisper their names in tandem with her breath, the sounds barely audible.

Morel. Oyster. Inky cap.

She'd imagine a horizon beyond the walls of her house and muse out loud, "What do you suppose is out there?"

PART III

Schizophrenia is the story of how poverty, violence and being on the wrong side of power drive us mad.

—*T. M. LUHRMANN*, Our Most Troubling Madness

7. SCHIZOPHRENOGENESIS

People who are humiliated and abused and bullied are more likely to fall ill. People who are born poor or live poor are more likely to fall ill. People with dark skins are more likely to fall ill in white-skinned neighborhoods ... when life beats people up, they are at more risk for developing psychosis.[1]

SCHIZOPHRENOGENESIS = schizophrenic + genesis: the production of schizophrenia. Sometimes refers to the onset of schizophrenia, sometimes to the causes. The story of the mind's cleaving. The story of being on the wrong side of power.

Chehalis, Washington, 1986

THE GROUND IS LITTERED with rotting fruit, little purple bodies seeping sweet, dark blood into the dust. No longer fit for pies, they have become wine for bees.

At the site of one of my mother's usual blackberry patches, the smell of decay wafts in the late summer breeze. The rains will come soon, and a blanket of pine and fir and deciduous leaves of all kinds will cover the dead berries. Nearby, an oak or elm will

fall ill, and its withering body will nourish new life—perhaps
a cluster of healing maitake will rise up at the tree's trunk. My
mother will not be there to find them this year.

The seasons will turn again, and the winter will be unchar-
acteristically cold for the temperate Pacific Northwest. The sun
will not come out for weeks at a time, and my mother will find
new ways to spend her time indoors. Sometimes she will spend
it taking care of my sick father, nursing him through his third
and fourth heart attacks, but more often, she will be drawn to
our new remote-controlled television. She will sit on the beige
sectional with her feet propped up, looking for hidden messages
in *Wheel of Fortune* and *The Joker's Wild*. She will look for clues
beyond the obvious—in the cadence of Pat Sajak's voice, in the
flick of a wrist or the speed of a wheel, in the pattern of jokers
and devils, and in the repetition of all of these things.

Spring will come again, but she will not go out to search for
mushrooms or fiddleheads, nor will she look for blackberries in
the summer. She will not go out into the wilderness ever again.

The year I turned fifteen, the world grew dark as my mother
became sick, my father became sicker, and our kitchen grew
sparse. My sense of stability or instability had always been implicated in my mother's well-being, and when she foraged, family
life felt solid. But somehow I hardly noticed when she suddenly
stopped going out into the woods. Her abandonment of the thing
she most loved should have been a warning that she was developing what Western medical discourse calls "mental illness,"
what Koreans might describe as a "pained spirit." Whatever you
choose to call it, it took me a whole year to see that it was con-
suming her.

Her illness wasn't obvious at first because it was overshadowed by my father's, which was recognizable in a way that mental
illness never is. In 1986 he had his third heart attack.

It was my sophomore year of high school, a mild fall day maybe in late September or early October, and my mother came to pick me up from tennis practice so we could go to the hospital. My coach, who had been invested in my family ever since my brother emerged as the town tennis star seven years earlier, approached her to raise concerns about my performance.

"I've noticed that Grace is having trouble concentrating," he said. "She needs to step it up." At six feet eight, he was well over a foot taller than my mother and me, literally talking down to us.

This was shortly after the three boys interrupted practice to pretend rape and mock me in front of the whole team. My mother knew nothing about the incident, so she offered a different explanation.

"You see, Grace is sad girl lately because her father had a heart attack."

"Mom!" I said under my breath, mortified that she exposed something so personal.

"No, no. It's okay," the coach assured me before he turned his attention back to my mother.

I felt embarrassed that I was embarrassed, as if I was a bad daughter for not putting my grief on display.

The two adults continued to talk about my father's condition as I bounced the racket against my calf and watched a cumulus cloud float in the sky. I became flooded with visions of his first heart attack: I am seven, visiting my father in the intensive-care unit. "Grace-ya, tell Abeoji what you got for him," my mother says about the violets I insisted that we buy. My tongue is leaden and useless, but I manage to extend my hands and hold a pot up in front of his face. *What's the matter? Cat got your tongue*, I expect him to say, but he can't talk either. He mouths the words "Thank you, honey." A creaking sound has replaced his voice.

My dread grew as I remembered those violets under the harsh

white lights of the hospital room, my father's face extra pale,
like the color of pie dough, from having had his chest cut open.
The faint smell of flowers mixed with the stench of death and
antiseptic.

I couldn't bear the thought of going to the hospital again. All
I wanted was to finish tennis practice, then hang out with Jenny
and listen to the Cure and talk about boys. Sometimes we talked
about big philosophical questions too. "God isn't a man in the
sky," she once said as we lay on the lawn of our high school, gaz-
ing toward the heavens. "God *is* the sky. And the clouds, and the
trees, and you and me."

My awareness drifted back to the present moment, back to
my tennis coach wishing my father a quick recovery. I spotted
Jenny's bouncy blond curls on the other side of the courts and
waved goodbye.

"Gaja," my mother said. "Let's go."

We got in the car and went to the hospital to see my father,
and again, I sat in a chair beside his bed and stared at him without
speaking.

My father was once again the patient, my mother the nurse.
Their now-familiar roles. She always made sure to follow the
doctor's orders, planning menus around what he wanted to eat
but adjusting it whenever the doctor told him to cut back on
sodium and saturated fat or add more fiber, serving "soysage" and
tofu ice cream long before plant-based protein was a thing. She
constantly fretted over his heart and tried to keep him out of
physically demanding situations. She worked two jobs so as not
to spend too much of *his* money, and still, she kept the house
spotless and comfortable. Her third shift.

She had never before faltered on her care duties, but what
could she do when the doctor advised him to reduce his stress?
My parents' very relationship was stressful. My mother's discon-

tent and overwork bursting the seams of her emotional labor. My father always reacting to her provocations.

The only thing he knew to do was retire from his job as a merchant marine captain, but his retirement created new stressors. Mainly, they were money and my mother.

Retirement ushered in a new era of my parents' conflict. It was the first time since they met that they spent more than three months at a time together. Leaving his job as a ship captain with an all-male crew at his beck and call to be home with an angsty teenage daughter and spitfire wife—two women he could not control—must have been a hard transition. In his poor health, he wanted to be the center of attention at all times, and my mother, who had become increasingly independent of him over the years, would not have given him that even if she'd been capable of it. Each day he grew slightly more bitter, and it made me wonder whether distance had been the glue holding my parents together for all those years.

Household bickering became a constant, and one of them was always threatening to divorce the other. I spent a lot of time in my room, trying to shut out my parents and their problems. Once, despite having the volume of Siouxsie and the Banshees' "Happy House" cranked up to drown out their fighting, I still heard my mother yell, "When Grace goes away to college, I'm leaving you!"

It was too much. I ran out and screamed, "Just get a divorce now so I don't have to listen to this anymore!" My outburst stunned them into temporary submission, ending the fight, but I was under no illusion that I had any real power to change things.

They had been spending more time together, not just because my father had stopped working, but because my mother had suddenly quit foraging and was home more too. It didn't take long before he began complaining that he wished he could go back to sea, that she would be the death of him.

My parents' marriage had always been volatile and sometimes violent. The most indelible fight in my memory happened when I was very young—the same height as my father's leg, which must have made me two, maybe three. Perhaps he thought that I was too young to be able to remember. Indeed, I had repressed the event for well over a decade, until one day he teased my mother for being part elephant because of the ivory in her nose.

"Why do you have ivory in your nose?" I laughed. She did not look amused.

"It got broken and they fix it with ivory," she mumbled, averting her eyes. I could feel her fuming some mix of resentment and shame, and I knew not to ask how it got broken.

And then the memory came rushing back.

My parents are yelling at each other in the dining room, and it quickly escalates into my father hitting her. I howl and beg him to stop, but he hits her again. I run to him, throw my arms around his leg, and stand on top of his foot, thinking that I can hold him down long enough for my mother to run away. He drags me along as he corners her. I can't see what's happening because my face is buried in his thigh, but then I hear the cracking sound of bone against bone, her screaming. I sink my teeth into his leg, and he shakes me off with such a forceful kick that it sends me flying against the dining room chairs. He doesn't even look in my direction, but maybe it's because I don't cry. Unfettered, he starts in again on my mother. The sight of him beating her fills me with such terror that I feel no pain in my body. I pick myself up and attack his leg again.

I write this now as the mother of a young child and can barely fathom how deep my father's passion must have been for him to not see what he had done to me, what he was doing to me. Or that this was a seed that he had planted. I tried to talk to him about it when I was in my twenties, but he was flabbergasted that I had even questioned it. "But she deserved it!" he insisted, throwing his hands up in the air.

I can remember neither how the fight started or ended nor the physical injuries left in its wake, and I'm uncertain of whether this fight was the cause of my mother's broken nose. The only things I'm certain of are those fragments burned into my mind: the screams, the punching sounds, the dining room chairs. Above all, I remember clinging to my father's leg as if my life depended on it.

The fight I witnessed when I was a toddler was not the only time he had been violent toward her, but as he got older and weaker, my mother became a formidable opponent. Once, when I was in eighth grade, she took one of the same dining room chairs that I had fallen against and hit my father with it. I wasn't there to witness this particular fight, but I walked in on them just as things were simmering down. My father was in the bathroom, fumbling through one of the cabinets, then opening a box of Band-Aids with his trembling hands. His glasses had snapped in half and the jagged metal frame had cut the bridge of his nose.

"That'll teach you to mess with me, you no-good sonofabitch," my mother spat from the hallway.

"Your mother hit me with a chair!" he said to me as I stared dumbfounded at the two of them.

In the days that followed these episodes, my parents carried on as if nothing had happened. Their fights were storms that punctuated stretches of dreary weather.

But as my father's health deteriorated, I became more sympathetic toward him, and by the time I was in high school, I often took his side. It had become challenging to live with my mother.

She was often agitated, obsessing about certain people in town and their "nosiness" into her affairs, often worrying that her coworkers at Green Hill or our neighbors were spreading rumors about our family. This was nothing new, because we had long been the subject of gossip, but then her suspicions would grow into an elaborate pyramid of potential enemies. Anyone within six degrees of separation from someone she mistrusted could come under her scrutiny; anyone within two was automatically blacklisted. Soon, entire geographic regions would be the hotbed of malicious activity.

One day, I was talking to one of my friends on the phone in our kitchen and I heard the slight rustle of someone picking up the other phone in my parents' bedroom. My mother's voice interrupted the conversation with a stern but measured, "Hang up. Hang up the phone right now." And I did, out of embarrassment.

"Jesus, Mom! What did you do that for?"

"You cannot talk to that Julie anymore. She's one of the bad people."

"What are you talking about?"

"She lives in Adna, doesn't she?"

"So?"

"Don't you know, Grace?" She sounded exasperated by my naivete. "All people from that town want to hurt us."

"Oh my god!" I yelled as I burst into tears and ran to my room.

For months, she'd been telling my father that people were watching her, talking about her behind her back, or openly confronting her. I can't remember if he ever tried to do anything about it or just dismissed it as her "nonsense."

March 24, 1986

Dad,

Hi! How are you doing? I'm doing all right . . . Mom wanted to write to you but she's been busy. She's working for Mrs. Murdock doing yard work. She has really been driving me crazy with all her Green Hill nonsense. Maybe it isn't nonsense but she's taking it way out of proportion. Any person that is nice to me she thinks is actually trying to *harm me. She has ruined my social life. A good social life is important, not <u>just</u> grades, especially at my age. I think you can understand that better than Mom can. Well, I don't have much more to say. I just wanted to say hello to my dear father. Mom sends her love. I love you, too, even if sometimes we don't get along. I don't know what I would do without you.*

Love Always, Grace

In 2016 I found this letter addressed to my father in Guam, the last place he was stationed before retirement. It's the only concrete piece of evidence I have of what transpired that year, and it contradicted my memory, which told me that her paranoia had started in the fall.

I don't remember if my father ever responded to the letter, nor do I remember writing it in the first place, but what I see now is that my words were an appeal for help. In March 1986, I had already internalized my mother's complaints as "nonsense," and yet, I also had a flicker of doubt that maybe she was telling the truth.

There was something real in her protest, not just the ravings of a lunatic. How many times had women who told the truth been muzzled with the label of madness? This is a question I would come to ask myself time and again once I became a graduate student in New York.

The first time I can remember articulating what I wanted my adult life to look like, it was 1984. Rebecca Brown, a then up-and-coming writer from Seattle who had just published her first book, came to my junior high school to do a creative-writing workshop. She approached my desk to ask me what my aspirations were, and without skipping a beat, I told her that I wanted to live in New York. "You would fit right in there!" she replied.

Although I wasn't sure what she meant, I took it as a compli-
ment. I wasn't sure what *I* meant either, except that New York
was the polar opposite of Chehalis. New York was a big city full
of possibility, full of different kinds of people.

By 1986 I had a much more concrete idea of what exactly
I wanted to run away from. It wasn't just my parents, but the
whole town. The narrow-minded people who hated everything
that I loved, everything that I was. The people whose mission was
to spread their hate. At fifteen, I didn't yet know how well organized they were, or that the same people were at the epicenter of
my mother's torment.

Besides her coworkers at Green Hill, the other group that gave
my mother the most grief was the John Birch Society, a radical right-wing organization founded in 1958 and named after
an American who had been killed by the Chinese at the end of
World War II. Their mission was to fight the Cold War by weed-
ing out communism at home. In their view, desegregation, civil
rights, and any sort of social welfare or social-justice work were
all part of a communist plot to weaken America. They warned
their followers of government conspiracies and put scare quotes
around words such as "human rights."

But few people in the American mainstream took the JBS
seriously. In 1961 the *New York Times* dismissed them as part of
the "lunatic fringe," and in 1963 Bob Dylan wrote a scathingly
satirical song, "Talkin' John Birch Paranoid Blues." By the 1970s,
they seemed to have faded out of American politics. Yet in places
like Chehalis, they were still alive and well when my family lived
there, supplying the Hamilton Farm sign with many of its slogans.

My mother often speculated about which of our neighbors
and associates were Birchers. Even at the time I didn't think
there was anything unreasonable about her wariness, since it
was a well-known fact that they wanted to purge the town of

immigrants, particularly the ones who had come from communist parts of the world. There was a point at which white people in rural Washington State began to recognize Korea as a country separate from China and Japan. The question began to shift from "Are you Chinese or Japanese?" to "Are you from North or South Korea?" Either question was loaded when coming from a Bircher. *Look out you Commies!*[2]

I moved to New York to pursue my graduate studies when I was twenty-five, and I never encountered anyone there of my generation who had heard of the John Birch Society. It felt like I had moved far, far away from the hateful, paranoid politics of my upbringing. But by the mid-2010s, news articles began to pop up in progressive media outlets about the group's resurgence. Some articles warned of its growing influence in the Republican Party and the dangers it could pose to American democracy if not taken seriously, while others argued that the damage had already been done, that they had already spread their roots far and wide enough through conservative America. One observer noted that Trump's election was evidence of the group's lasting impact on American politics.

In 2018 the JBS website would say of the so-called migrant caravan, "This is an invasion, and it is NOT a 'human right.'" The article would urge its readers to call the president to demand a wall, a militarized border, an end to asylum.

In quiet rural communities such as Chehalis, their stealth operations to smoke out commies paid off. The Birchers' agenda would become national law. *Yee-hoo, I'm a real John Bircher now!*[3]

Although my parents seemed more and more irritated by each other's presence, they still had some residue of loyalty toward one another, and my father urged my mother to quit her job because she was always coming home from work distressed.

She did quit Green Hill, and without that job or foraging, her life suddenly became sedentary. She began watching television, something she rarely had the time or inclination to do before, and I thought at first that some leisure would do her good. She was especially drawn to *Wheel of Fortune*, and would talk to herself in a quiet but animated voice about the puzzles, sometimes just guessing the hidden words and sometimes questioning the meaning behind them. *Why they say that, I wonder?* She would pause as if listening, her eyes intensely focused on the screen. *What do you mean by that?*

There were other times when it seemed like she was talking to a presence that wasn't really there—a few words and phrases whispered to household objects. I wavered back and forth between worrying that she had a psychological problem and telling myself that we all talk to ourselves sometimes. But my mother wasn't just talking. She seemed to be arguing with someone under her breath, sometimes getting so worked up that she couldn't focus on the person that was actually there talking to her.

One day, on our way to go shopping, we stopped to make a deposit at the bank. We pulled up to the drive-through, and a pretty blond teller greeted us with a bubbly "How are you all doing today?"

"Fine. Thank you. And you?" said my mother.

"Oh, can't complain. How's Don been feeling?"

My mother furrowed her brow and glared at the teller. "You stop talking about my husband."

The woman was taken aback. "Oh, I—"

"That is none of your business," my mother snapped, her eyes wild. "Why are you always nosing around and sniffing around my family? What do you want with us?"

"Mom, stop," I pleaded. She fixed her eyes on the girl a while longer, who now looked petrified, then drove away.

"Why did you do that? She didn't do anything!"

"Didn't you hear what she said about your father?"

"Huh? That's just what people say when they're making small talk. God, Mom! What's wrong with you?"

At the time I thought that she must have believed that the young blond had designs on my sixty-seven-year-old father, but now I think that it's far more likely that my mother's brain probably translated the words "How's Don been feeling?" into something entirely different: *Is it true that Don has another family in the Philippines? You're a fool to believe he'd be loyal to you. Don is leaking secrets to the Russians. He's told Gorbachev about your brother in North Korea. North Korea . . . You'd better watch out, 'cause the Birchers have you in their sights.*

Increasingly, the rumors she believed people were spreading about us involved high-profile politicians. I learned this when I found her dressed in a powder-blue pantsuit, racing around the house looking for her car keys.

"Mom, what's the matter?"

"I have to go for important meeting! I'm going to be late!"

"What meeting?"

She stopped for a minute and gave me a solemn look. "Grace, I have to tell you something."

"What?" My heart started to pound.

"People are saying bad things about our family and I have to go clear it up."

"What kinds of bad things?" I felt frozen, like I was being chased in a nightmare but my legs wouldn't move.

"They are saying that your brother is child of Booth Gardner."

"What? That doesn't make any sense!" Although I knew that people speculated about our parentage, the idea of my mother having had an affair with the governor was a stretch of anyone's imagination.

"I know. Who would spread such nasty rumor? You know,

Grace, it is not true. I never do anything like that to your father."
Her explanation became even more incoherent because my
brother wasn't even my father's biological child. He had been
born five years before my parents met.

"Mom, that's crazy. Who would say something like that?"

"These people want to ruin our family! I have to go meet with
Booth now so he can clear my name. He's waiting for me!" She
scurried out of the house and disappeared for the next two hours.

Did she really make an appointment with the governor? Was
it even possible to do that if you were just a regular person? What
if she just showed up there, demanding to see him? Would they
call security and lock her up? When she returned she said that
the meeting had gone well and there was nothing more to worry
about. I could no longer deny that there was something wrong
with my mother.

At first I looked for "logical explanations"—the things people tell
themselves to suppress their instincts. My father had been attrib-
uting her erratic behavior to menopause, but he probably held an
antiquated view that *"madness" associated with "the change of life" was
not madness at all—not a serious affliction to be taken seriously—but
a women's malady.*[4]

It was still decades before researchers had learned that the
drop in estrogen that accompanies menopause might in fact be
a trigger for schizophrenia, or that estrogen therapy could be an
effective treatment.[5] I knew as little about menopause at the age
of fifteen as I did about schizophrenia, so at first I followed my
father's lead that it was "just menopause."

Or maybe the culprit was grief. My grandmother had died
several months earlier, after having lived in the United States for
almost five years with my cousin Jinho, the grandson she had
raised after he became orphaned during the war, and his wife Sun.

During those years, we spent most Saturday nights at

Halmeoni's place in Oregon, where we ate everything out of bowls: rice in one bowl, soup in another, little bowls of kimchi and seasoned greens, a shallow bowl for stewed fish or jangjorim, the smallest bowls reserved for sauces. At the end of the meal, the leftovers were kept in their bowls and covered with stiff square cloths that Halmeoni had brought with her from Korea.

Even in 1980, when my grandmother first migrated, she already seemed ancient. She was born in 1900—before the Japanese invaded Korea, before industrialization, or any such a notion as two Koreas split along ideological lines. She wore her long white hair tied in a knot and fastened with a wooden stick, and she dressed in traditional hanbok and gomu-shin. Spine curved from a lifetime of carrying bundles on her head and children on her back, Halmeoni stood at four feet ten, a veritable little old lady.

She never caught up to the idea of a modernized Korea and was even less inclined to learn the ways of modern America, although she did love cornflakes doused in sugar-sweetened half-and-half and delighted in the spectacle of *World Wide Wrestling*. After dinner she would call me over to the TV—"Geu-re-ya! Reh-seu-ring bwa-ra!"—as she sat on the edge of her floor cushion with the corners of her mouth turned upward in a toothless smile. At the precise moment that the fake blood started to pour, she would clap her hands and shout, "Aigu, yalgu-jida!" *How bizarre and thrilling!*

On Sunday mornings, as my mother and I prepared to return to Chehalis, Halmeoni and I would watch our family's food-exchange ritual unfold: my mother offering a trunkful of fresh produce she had picked along with her blackberry pies and jams, Jinho and Sun countering with a cooler full of fish, both parties refusing to accept before finally giving in. "Aigu, Jinho-ya! Deugara!" my mother would yell in our family's regional dialect, to end the standoff. *Go back inside!*

It would take years for me to realize how much those weekend visits made me feel like I belonged to a family, and that they
did even more so for my mother.

My grandmother's jesa was held at a Korean church in Portland that she and my cousins used to attend. There was an altar
with a larger-than-life headshot of Halmeoni, her tawny skin
flecked with dark-brown sunspots, her lips and eyelids drooping
under the weight of eighty-five hard years. In front of the picture was a mother-of-pearl table filled with piles of fruit, rice
cakes, mandu, pajeon, and dozens of other foods that Sun and
my mother had prepared. The smell of incense wafted through
the air. I didn't know the other people there, but they walked to
the front one by one and bowed before the picture of my grandmother. My mother cried through the whole ceremony—a deep,
guttural wail that filled the entire space of the church, loud and
long enough to mourn legions of the dead.

*Schizophrenia can occur when a life crisis or some great, tragic dis-
appointment incites its emergence. . . . Initial breakdowns are typically
insidious, appearing at first to be minimal, but leading to grave effect.*[6]

One night, on the cusp of sleep, I felt a strange presence in my
room. I opened my eyes to see a small shadowy figure standing
at the foot of the bed. "There are demons in the house," it said. I
was scared, but as my eyes focused, I saw that it was Halmeoni.
She was wearing white hanbok with a knitted sunshine-yellow
vest over it. A bright energy radiated from her, and she spoke
in a silent language. "Mah-mi is sick. Take care of her for me.
Huh, Geu-re-ya?" When she called my name, Geu-re-ya, I could
feel her wrinkled little hand pat my foot. I tried to answer,
but by the time the words reached my tongue, she was already
gone.

The next morning I told my mother. "I saw Halmae-ya in
front of my bed last night. I'm not sure if it was real or a dream."

"You did? Oh, I want to see her too." She sighed, "Dap-dap-eu-rah. She loved you so much."

In the days after my mother's supposed meeting with the governor, I remembered the dream and her response to it, and took it to mean that she wanted me to carry out Halmeoni's wishes. I was afraid to talk to anyone about it, so I took matters into my own hands. Anyway, Halmeoni had appointed *me* my mother's caretaker. No one else was supposed to do it.

Each day during lunch recess, I escaped my friends to go to the school library and hid among the stacks to read the twelfth-grade psychology textbook and clinical diagnostic manuals. I can't remember if I ever talked to Jenny about it, though I most certainly kept my research a secret from my family until I had armed myself with enough knowledge about mental illness to make a credible claim.

DIAGNOSTIC CRITERIA FOR A SCHIZOPHRENIC DISORDER

A. *At least one of the following during a phase of illness:*
   — *bizarre delusions (content is patently absurd and has no possible basis in fact) . . .*
   — *delusions with persecutory or jealous content if accompanied by hallucinations . . .*
   — *auditory hallucinations . . .*
   — *markedly illogical thinking . . .*
B. *Deterioration from a previous level of functioning in such areas as work, social relations, and self-care.*
C. *Duration: Continuous signs of the illness for at least six months . . .*[7]

Every book I read said more or less the same thing, and I became convinced that my mother was schizophrenic. But the books that could help me understand *why* she had become schizophrenic weren't in my high school library. Some of them hadn't even been written yet.

In 1986 the dominant thinking in psychiatry was that schizophrenia was a random and strictly biological phenomenon, a malfunction of the brain caused by genetics and treated with medical intervention, the "bio-bio-bio" paradigm.[8] Neither cause nor treatment could be found in the social.

The biomedical model of the 1980s was a complete reversal of the psychoanalytic model of the 1960s, which located the cause of schizophrenia in a person's childhood and their reaction to the mother's inadequate affection. "The schizophrenogenic mother." While the bio-bio-bio paradigm stopped blaming mothers, it also sent the message that if you had the gene for it, schizophrenia would be a foregone conclusion. Society had zero responsibility.

It would take thirty years for the research to swing back in the other direction to say, "We now have direct evidence that people are more likely to fall ill with schizophrenia in some social settings than in others . . . that something about the social world gets under our skin."[9]

When my brother came home for the holidays that year, I asked to speak privately with him and my father in the office. The atmosphere in the room grew tense as they waited for me to speak. "I think there's something wrong with Mom," I began, then broke down sobbing. I could no longer remember the words I had prepared about how I'd been reading the *DSM* and could match up every one of her odd behaviors with the symptoms of schizophrenia. I skipped the whole speech and blurted out, "She's paranoid schizophrenic!"

The men in my family unleashed their denials in unison.

"What? That's not true!" my brother barked.

"How could you say something like that about your mother? You're a goddamn liar!" said my father.

My heart splintered when he hurled his accusation at me, not just because I wanted to defend my character but because I desperately wished that he was right. I was fifteen years old and had no idea what else to do.

I wonder how I would have reacted to the news had I not been the one to first witness her unraveling, if I had been the older child who had just graduated from college, to be told by a much younger sibling that your mother had lost her mind, and not just to any mental illness, but to the most stigmatized kind of crazy there was. I probably wouldn't have believed it either.

But what was my father's excuse? He had seen the changes in her behavior, and nine months earlier I had written him letting him know that things were getting worse. Maybe his denial was driven by the fear that my mother would vanish into her delusions leaving only the shell of a wife. Maybe he needed to believe that she would keep on taking care of him until his last breath.

Without the support of anyone in my family, I decided to seek professional help by going to the local mental health center to speak with a counselor. The man who called me into his office was young and white, probably in his midtwenties. At fifteen, I didn't know to question his age or experience. People in their twenties seemed so wise to me. I felt incapacitated by my own confused feelings because I worried that I was somehow betraying my family by speaking with a stranger about private matters, but I told myself that this was the right thing—the only thing—to do. I was hopeful that the meeting would have a happy ending and that I would soon get my mother back.

"So, what brings you here today?" the counselor asked.

I was afraid that my nervousness would make me unintelligible, but it had the opposite effect. I was articulate and assertive. "I think my mother is paranoid schizophrenic. I checked out some books from my high school library and everything matches."

"What are her symptoms?"

"She thinks that people are following her, and that Ronald Reagan has our phones tapped. She thinks that one of my friends is involved in a government conspiracy. She watches *Wheel of Fortune* and thinks that the puzzles are sending her secret messages."

"You're right. That does sound a lot like schizophrenia . . . How old is she?"

"Forty-five," I said. The counselor fidgeted as I waited for him to say more. He was quiet, as if he didn't know what to do next.

"So? How do I help her?" I asked.

"Unfortunately, unless she consents to treatment, there's nothing you can do. The only way you can have her committed is if she hurts someone."

"You mean the police could make her get help?"

"Yes, but . . . even then, I'm not sure that it would do much."

"But why not?"

"Schizophrenia is a very serious illness."

I was confused by the counselor's response. "Well, isn't that all the more reason to do something about it?"

"Your mother is forty-five. I'm afraid it's too late now."

"What? What do you mean?"

"Maybe if you had caught it earlier we might have been able to treat it. I'm sorry."

"How is that possible? Aren't you here to help people? Why won't you help me?"

Anger and disappointment roiled inside of me and formed a tight knot that throbbed in my chest. The man's words sounded so complacent that I wanted to twist his arm until it snapped like a dry twig, make him scream until he showed some authentic remorse. I narrowed my eyes into slits as tears streaked black eyeliner down my face.

"So that's it? Now I go home and just deal with it? I have to just live with it? Forever?"

"I'm sorry, but there's nothing we can do for your mother."

The expert had just told me that my mother's life was in the dustbin and not worth trying to save. It was my first experience with the mental health system, and I had no frame of reference with which to evaluate the advice I had gotten or to understand that the counselor might have been operating on the assumption that my mother had developed schizophrenia in her twenties, which was typical among men. The belief in psychiatry was that the longer one waits to start treatment, the poorer the outcome, and maybe he thought that my mother's symptoms had gone untreated for twenty years. The conventional wisdom on schizophrenia had been, has always been, based on men's experience.

While the age of onset for men peaks in the late teens to early twenties, for women it is after twenty-five.[10] Among women, there is also a second peak, starting at the age of forty-five and typically coinciding with menopause, but this would not be recognized by researchers until 1993 and would never make it into the mainstream.[11]

"Youth has been a diagnostic criterion for schizophrenia for a hundred years, including within the pages of the *DSM*, where schizophrenia has sometimes included an age limit: As recently as the 1980s, a person could not be tagged schizophrenic if he or she was older than 40."[12] As recently as 2020, popular websites such as WebMD claimed that "people rarely develop schizophrenia before they're twelve or after they're forty."[13] Beliefs about schizophrenia contradicted the reality that a forty-five-year-old woman could experience its onset.

Decades later I would look back at this moment as the origin of my han—the untranslatable Korean word that refers to "unresolved resentment against injustice," "a blockage . . . that's tangled up and cannot be untied," or "knotted grief."[14] Han *not only refers to a consciousness of ongoing trauma and a lack of resolution, but also the* means *to its own resolution.*[15]

In the days following my visit to the mental health center, a cho-
rus of voices invaded my head, all shouting at once and competing for my attention:

She's paranoid schizophrenic.

   How could you say something like that about your mother?

      *Don't you know, Grace? All people from that town want to
      hurt us.*

Mah-mi is sick. Take care of her for me. Huh, Geu-re-ya?

   The only way you can have her committed is if she hurts someone.

      She's paranoid schizophrenic.

         You're a goddamn liar.

She's paranoid schizophrenic.

   I'm afraid it's too late now.

      Huh, Geu-re-ya?

And then my mother and I got into a fight. It was probably
sparked by one of our usual conflicts, that she thought I wasn't
studying enough or that one of my friends was a spy, and I seized
it as an opportunity to help her. The voices were still screaming
at me, this time telling me I needed to escalate the fight so that
I could prove that my mother was a danger. I said something to
provoke her into hitting me, something that she couldn't possibly
have seen coming. She slapped me hard enough to leave a red
mark on my face, and I picked up the phone and called the police.
The only way you can have her committed is if she hurts someone.

The police came to arrest her, but somehow I didn't think
it would come to that. I thought I could just explain to them
that I wanted her to get psychiatric help, and they would tell
her that she had to do it. The shame and anger that spread across
her face when they cuffed her silenced every last thought in my
head.

At the police station I told them what the counselor at the
mental health center had said and begged them to send her to the
hospital instead of keeping her in jail. "Sorry, honey. It doesn't

work that way. I wish we could help your mom, but there's nothing we can do for her." It was the second time I had heard those words from an authority figure: *There's nothing we can do.*

My memory of the rest of that night is blacked out except for the things my mother and father said once she was released. "What kind of a girl puts her own mother in jail?" she said. "You're persona non grata in this house," he said.

My last-ditch effort had been a complete failure.

I spent the rest of high school learning to live with my mother's schizophrenia. I lost myself in music and literature and boys, smoked pot, and sought daily refuge at Jenny's house.

Despite her voices and the vast amount of energy she spent battling the Birchers and Ronald Reagan, my mother was still somewhat functional, so everyone in my household managed to pretend that we were a normal family. In time we learned to forget the terrible thing I did to her, and the way the voices compelled me to do it. Indeed, there were moments when she was her old self enough for me to believe that she had recovered. Sometimes she would pull herself away from the TV long enough to spend the day picking strawberries at the U-Pick and the next day making jam, or cook up a feast for no occasion. Sometimes she would say the kind of motherly things she used to say before the government put surveillance devices in her head. *I never had chance to study, but you do. Grace-ya, keep studying hard and you can do anything. You have such bright future ahead of you.*

Perhaps that's why I didn't hesitate to go to college three thousand miles away, because my father broke down crying on the day I got my acceptance from Brown University, his hands shaking as he read and reread the letter, because my mother drank a glass of champagne for the first time in her life and danced around the living room, because I knew what an earth-shattering event it was for both of my unpedigreed parents. I had known for as long as I was conscious of my mother's desires that she dreamed of me joining the Ivy League.

I felt overwhelming pride that I had been admitted, which was only amplified by my parents' joy. Most of all, I felt the ache of my own desires. I wanted to transcend the confinement of my miserable little town and my mother's delusions. The world was huge again, and I would emerge from the dark days of my adolescence into another spring, and life would start anew.

Yet the distance that going away to college gave me, and being in the world of ideas and critical thinking would eventually lead me to search for the causes of my mother's schizophrenia. With each new revelation, my han became more tangled up in hers, collected more emotional residue, and gave more force to my life's decisions. As I worked to untangle our han, the loosened threads led me back to 1986, when at age fifteen I first saw my mother through the lens of disposability, when I first got the notion that she had been cheated out of her own life and left to wander the earth as a ghost.

Thirty-two years later I would still be trying to untie the knot.

New York City, 2018

I AM TEACHING an undergraduate class on the sociology of mental illness, giving a lecture on the demise of community mental health, which was conceived of as the more humane and effective alternative to institutionalizing the mentally ill. John F. Kennedy, my mother's first American hero, signed the Community Mental Health Act in 1963, but the investment in community-based mental health was never enough to serve all the people who needed it. When Reagan took office in 1981, he began to cut federal spending on mental health services until only 11 percent of the original budget remained.[16]

In the middle of the lecture a thought hits me. She always said that Reagan was trying to take her down, and maybe she was right after all.

Community mental health facilities became so woefully underfunded that they intentionally let people with the most severe mental illnesses fall through the cracks; the sickest people were the ones who used up the most resources.

There's nothing we can do for your mother.

In the absence of real mental health care, people with mental illnesses were shuttled into prisons or left on the streets to fend for themselves. According to Allen Frances, it is for these reasons that the United States is the worst place in the world to have a serious mental illness.[17]

Two weeks later, I'll be leading a discussion with my students about the case of Nakesha Williams, a young, gifted, and Black woman whose mental health spiraled downward until she ended up homeless on the streets of New York City and eventually died while sitting on a bench at the corner of Fifth Avenue and Forty-Sixth Street.[18] One of my students will say that the story gripped her because it began when Nakesha was a college student, that the same thing could happen to any one of them in the class. "In all the stories we've read the person is fine until something triggers their crazy. Maybe it was the sexual abuse that triggered her crazy."

After that class, I will think again about my mother. Was there anything else that happened in 1986, some stone I left unturned? Have I become so attached to the narrative I've constructed that I can't see what's right in front of me? I will close my eyes and let all the pieces of the story fall away, and Green Hill will be left standing.

Memories will flash up.

I am ten or eleven, asking if I can see where she works. My curiosity sends her into a panic. "No, no, no!" she shouts. "You don't know what kind of bad things going on in there! You can never go to that place! You hear me?" At the time I thought it was because she didn't want me to go near the juveniles.

I am fifteen and she has just come home from work, visibly upset, talking with my father in their bedroom. The door closed. Her voice shrill. My father urging her to keep it down. My mother's complaints about Green Hill have begun to change from "what they are saying about us" to "what they are doing to me."

I will dive deeper into my memory for some clue of what might have happened there. What egregious thing did they do to her? Unable to come up with anything tangible, I will search the internet for pictures of the place to jog my memory. The first click will reveal the image of the sprawling compound that is located off of I-5, just before Exit 76. Between the edge of the lawn and the razor-wire fence is a line of poplar trees standing at attention. Even when I was little, I thought they looked like soldiers or a firing squad. With the next click, I will find the "bad things going on in there."

Rampant Sexual Abuse at the Green Hill School in Chehalis.[19]

In 2018 plaintiffs filed a lawsuit against Green Hill, alleging that they had been repeatedly raped when they were incarcerated there, as minors. "For years, a culture of sexual misconduct existed at Green Hill School. . . . Retaliation and suppression of complaints were common. . . . [S]upervisory staff actively condoned the abuse and protected the abusers."[20] "At least six or more children at the school [were] being abused by staff, [and that was] the tip of the iceberg."[21] "One victim state[d] that he tried to call the Prison Rape Elimination Act (PREA) hotline but was prevented from using the phone."[22] The investigation also revealed that the boys witnessed sexual misconduct of staff toward each other.[23]

There was a paper trail of abuse that went back to 2009, when the cook, Deanna Witters, pleaded guilty to assaulting the children and received a thirty-day jail sentence in exchange for the names of five other abusive staff members, none of whom was charged or asked to resign. "It's the culture out there," she said. "It happens all the time."[24] In another case, a male employee, Everett Fairchild, was accused of sexually assaulting a female coworker in 2007.[25] When asked to respond to the scandals in 2007 and 2009, Green Hill's superintendent brushed it off: "When a facility has 250 employees, bad things are bound to happen."[26]

How long had these bad things been happening? The period of time in which victims had the courage to take their abusers to court dated back to 2007, but it must have been going on for much longer. Each witness, whether employee or detainee, described sexual assault as pervasive and deeply rooted in the culture of the institution.

Witters was thirty and Fairchild twenty-six in 1986 when my mother was coming home from work every morning distraught about the "bad people at Green Hill." Could they have been there, abusing the boys, assaulting the other staff, while my mother was told to keep her mouth shut? If not them, then someone else? I try to imagine her in this kind of environment and wonder what horrors she witnessed, what might have been done to her, what vile acts she might have been invited to do. I imagine the interaction of this trauma with her past in the camptown and our ambiguous family history with Japanese colonization and militarized sexual slavery.

Maybe it was the sexual abuse that triggered her crazy.

Another strand of the knot will come loose. Eleven years spent working in the dead of night at a place that systematically violated minors and kept this abuse an organized secret.

Something about the social world gets under the skin, but that something cannot be reduced to any one thing. It is the horror of Green Hill, but it is also the strident anti-immigrant rhetoric that says *This is an invasion, and it is NOT a "human right,"* the damaging Cold War that my mother faced on both sides of the Pacific. It is my father believing that *she deserved it*. It is the loss of my halmeoni, my mother's first home.

Thirty-two years after my mother went mad, I will have disentangled the threads enough to see where each one leads, to see that the thing that triggered her crazy was the knot itself.

8. BROWN

October 23, 1989

Hi, Mommy and Daddy!

Does this look like me on the front? I don't know what possessed me to get a Halloween card. I guess I just thought it was cute. And it's only fair to let you know that I charged this card the same time I got some notebooks! I hope you don't mind.

I want you to know that I feel very fortunate to have parents like you. I think of one of my friends here, Elena, who can't afford to buy a coat, or Chris, whose parents won't pay for him to go to school at all, and I don't know what I did to deserve to be here. Well, thank you.

Oh, if you didn't already hear, Brown finally won a football game, against Cornell, 28–7 or something like that!

HAPPY HALLOWEEN FROM YOUR LITTLE GHOUL.

See you in less than two months!

Love, Grace

During my first semester at Brown I felt a sense of lightness in which my spirit could soar beyond the physical boundaries of my body into a world without limits. While college gave me a taste of adulthood, more important was that being there allowed me to be a child, to look at the world with wonder. And the distance from my parents allowed me some moments of forgetting; it made me see only the good in them.

Although I had been nervous about the transition from my rural public high school to an Ivy League university, my curiosity proved stronger than my fear, and so I held my own in the classroom. I wasn't a stellar student in that context, but I was competent, and that was good enough.

I was surprised to find that I thrived socially in college in a way I'd never thought possible. Growing up in Chehalis, I had always been shy and somewhat of a loner, with Jenny as my one true friend. Upon my arrival at Brown, I became enamored with my new classmates because their lives were so interesting and radically different from mine: they were from cities or suburbs, had gone to high schools that were bigger than my entire hometown, or had been educated in small international schools in France and Switzerland. They were of ethnic and racial backgrounds I had never encountered growing up; I had never met a Jewish, Italian, or South Asian person, or a Latinx person who didn't have Mexican roots, and I had never known anyone to be openly gay. In my hometown, if you were even perceived as gay, you'd better be prepared to get the shit kicked out of you, as Jenny's boyfriend had learned the previous summer, when the two of them were walking down the street holding hands, and he was beaten to a pulp by a group of guys in cowboy boots. There was a reason why kids in Chehalis called cowboy boots and the people who wore them "shitkickers." It didn't matter that Jenny and her boyfriend were a straight couple. To them, he was still a fag.

I was swimming in oxytocin those first months at Brown, making fast friendships with just about anyone who would let me in, though the friends that lasted were similar to me in that they were immigrants or students of color or kids from families that had to sacrifice something for them to be in the Ivy League. Jaquetta was my best friend from my freshman dorm. She was a drop-dead gorgeous Black girl and a classically trained pianist from Connecticut with an elegant, Afrocentric style. Her idol was Nina Simone, and we would dance around her room to "My Baby Just Cares for Me" or sit and brood to "Four Women" while smoking clove cigarettes. Sandra was another one of my best friends, whom I had met in an environmental studies class and later traveled with in Brazil. She was the youngest of four kids in a close-knit Brazilian family from Newark and she was also stunning, with her sea-green eyes and beach-brown skin. Unlike many of the other students, we were not "legacies." We were in the first generation of our families to attend college, and kids like us made up a small minority of the student population. Being around them made me feel like I was part of a special group— we were powerful, beautiful underdogs, and together we would rise up.

Among our classmates were the sons and daughters of the rich and famous—the children of Diana Ross, Ted Turner, and Marlon Brando were all in my graduating class, as was the grandson of Haile Selassie, and the heir to the Getty oil fortune. I met students whose parents were high-powered politicians, well-known members of the literati, foreign dignitaries, and Fortune 500 CEOs. They owned yachts and various country homes, grew up with gardeners and drivers, and casually used the words "summer" and "winter" as verbs.

There were social classes at Brown that I had never heard of, such as "old money" and "new money." For members of both classes, the cost of a plane ticket would have been a negligible sum, but for my parents it was an extravagance. I was the only student I met during my time there who had enrolled without ever having seen the campus. It could have been that my parents just lacked the cultural capital to know that you were supposed to visit a college before deciding to go there. Brown had been my top choice because of the way they touted pluralism and diversity in their recruitment literature. It was the only school I had applied to, so I certainly wasn't going to study elsewhere. What would have been the point of visiting? I had even received a formal invitation to attend "Third World Weekend" for admitted students of color to visit the campus, but my father had been offended by the term "third world." "Don't they know that Korea's not a third world country anymore?" He was as baffled as he was miffed.

I had applied for early admission to Brown in October 1988, and when my acceptance letter arrived in December, my father bought himself a gift from the Brown bookstore catalog. It was a vintage poster of the first annual Tournament of the Roses, a 1916 football game between Brown University and Washington State University, where he had studied agricultural science for three semesters before he ran out of money and had to hitch a ride home in the back of a flatbed truck.

The poster represented the completion of his unfinished college legacy, and somehow my going to Brown had been written in the stars at the meeting of our two colleges in 1916—three years before my father was born. I imagine that he would have told me something like that if he could have gotten the words out, but instead he just pointed at the poster and nodded his head. His lip quivered for a moment before he said in his gravelly voice, "It's a damn good Christmas present."

His other present was the defibrillator he got implanted in his chest after his heart stopped on Christmas Day.

In October 1989 the university planned three days of activities for visiting parents of first-year students, which they called "Parents' Weekend." I pressured my parents to come because I didn't want to be known as the only kid whose parents weren't there. They gave in but decided to make a six-thousand-mile round-trip drive from Washington State to Rhode Island instead of flying. Twelve hours after they hit the road, I got a call from my mother.

"Grace-ya. I'm sorry."

"What's the matter?"

"Your father's heart is acting up again."

"Oh no! Is he okay?"

"I think so, but he's not going to make it for all that long trip. We are already in Idaho but he says we need to go to the hospital."

I felt guilty that I had been the reason for their epic road trip, but there was hardly time to process the information before my mother hung up the phone. As Parents' Weekend rolled around, I couldn't help but feel sorry for myself, like I was an orphan in the midst of children whose parents were by their side, while mine were in a hospital somewhere in Coeur d'Alene.

I didn't realize then how much things were about to change. My mother was still, in her own way, taking care of my father, still acting like a mother. Still calling me on the phone. Still saying "I'm sorry." I took for granted these tiny maternal gestures that she was still capable of.

My parents didn't get divorced as soon as I left for college as they had threatened, but their lives did become increasingly disparate. My mother spent most of her days sitting on the beige sectional watching TV, and she slept there at night too. My father stayed in his office, slept in the bedroom, and went out to visit his shopkeeper friends or his cousin Buck's pig ranch. During my visits home freshman year, I alternated between their two separate spheres of inside and outside, bringing them together only at dinnertime.

My mother was still going out once in a while; she did yard work and grocery shopping, and once or twice a week she'd volunteer for the United Way or the Special Olympics, something she began to do after quitting Green Hill. Generally speaking, she could make her way out of the house whenever the situation demanded it, as it did when my father got fed up and left her.

November 20, 1990

Hi Dad,

Sorry it's taken me so long to write. I've been extremely busy lately . . . I'm so happy to be able to spend a few days without classes and without having to go to bed at 2:00 and get up at 7:00.

I think I know what I want for Christmas. I got this catalog in the mail with things I like in it. I'm enclosing the order form and pictures of two pairs of earrings but don't get both pairs. You can sort of surprise me this way. What do you want or need?

You don't have to worry about not seeing me when I'm home. If Mom doesn't mind, I'd like to spend Christmas Eve at home and Christmas Day (or part of it, at least) with you in Raymond. I'm sure I'll visit you a couple more times. Even though I'm only going to be home for two and a half weeks, it's more time than I know what to do with in Chehalis. See you soon.

Love, Grace

By Christmas of my sophomore year, my father initiated my parents' first separation and had moved in with his cousin in Raymond, a fishing town even smaller than Chehalis. We had the house to ourselves on Christmas, sharing it only with the cousin's two Siamese cats. The space was small and cluttered with extraneous housewares like horse figurines, throw pillows with chunky crocheted covers, and candy bowls of peppermint ribbons.

"How is it living here?" I asked.

"It's all right. Can't complain. It sure as hell beats living with your mother."

He opened the fridge, took out a plate of ham, and heated it in the microwave.

"Are you hungry?" he asked as he lifted the lid of a simmering pot. The scent of sugary baked beans filled the room. "Your father's not much of a cook, but I tried to fix it up with some garlic and spices."

We set the small dining table for two and ate leftover ham and baked beans from a can. The humble meal we shared that night seemed more intimate than any of the meals we had eaten together at home. It was the first time he had ever cooked for me. The strangeness of the environment made my father more familiar to me, yet at the same time, the change of scenery revealed new things about him. His voice was soft, in a tone that sounded like gratitude.

After dinner he presented me with a pair of dangling silver earrings that looked like Tlingit totem poles: one of the pairs that I had asked for. I couldn't remember the last time he had attempted a surprise gift.

My mother had selected most of my gifts in the past, with the exception of my sixth birthday. I came home from school that day to find a Baldwin spinet piano in the living room and was so stunned that I could have gotten a present that big that I shouted, "This is the best birthday ever!" My father radiated pride. He dreamed that one day I would perform his favorite piece of classical music—Rachmaninov's Prelude in C-sharp minor—and I was diligent in my practice for nine years. I stopped playing the piano at age fifteen, when my interests began to wander in other directions and my mother went mad, but I did perform the Rachmaninov concerto for my final piano recital. My father watched me from the front row, his eyes glistening.

I opened the jewelry box, feigning anticipation. "Thanks, Daddy. I love them."

"You're welcome, honey. I'm glad you like them. Now, your birthday's coming up. Is there anything you want?"

"Well, I could use some kitchen stuff. I want to learn how to cook."

All of my prior college cooking experience had been executed with the use of three instruments: a microwave, a hot pot, and the rice cooker my mother had given me as a going-away present.

The next day we drove to a kitchen store at the local outlet mall. I picked out two metal mixing bowls, a whisk, two wooden spoons, and a spatula. The total rang in at around forty dollars, which was no small purchase for my father during his retirement, yet he asked me several times if there was anything else I needed. "No," I said. "That's enough to start."

When it was time for me to go back to my mother, he asked if he could take a picture of me. The next few times I visited him, that picture of me from Christmas 1990 was on his desk. In the photo, I am standing in his cousin's living room against a backdrop of barn-themed wallpaper and a synthetic Christmas tree, wearing a purple alpaca sweater that I had bought from some hippies at the student union that fall. The totem-pole earrings peek through my long black hair.

I barely remember my mother that Christmas or for much of that year. The most salient memory I have of being with her during sophomore year was when she came to visit me for Mother's Day weekend, the last vacation she would ever take. My brother flew her out to Rhode Island and drove himself up from New Jersey, and the two of them stayed at the downtown Omni Biltmore in a room that overlooked the city—all of it a Mother's Day gift from my brother. I was grateful to him for making it happen, and even more so now, realizing that a visit from Mom was something that he himself had never gotten when he was away at college.

How different this was from the travel she had experienced in the past. The family vacations of my childhood were road trips along the West Coast, where we slept in Motel 6s with vibrating beds and the scent of stale cigarettes. I only remember two trips: one to California in 1976 and another to British Columbia in

1980. In the years in between, the years after, were my father's broken promises, my mother's lamentations. *You never take me anywhere! All I do is work.* She wanted him to show her all the places that America was famous for: The Grand Canyon. Niagara Falls. Washington, DC. New York City. *So many years I live in this country and why I still never see anything?*

Maybe the Biltmore brought her a little closer to her American dream. "Hwaaa, I like this hotel," she said as she ran her fingers across the crisp white bedsheets. It must have been thrilling to experience business-class accommodations, to momentarily see herself as a person of high status.

It was thrilling for me, too, to have her there. After two years as the only student I knew whose family had never visited, I couldn't wait to introduce her and my brother to my friends. When we arrived at my dorm, they met two of my suitemates, but my closest friends were away visiting their own mothers that weekend. Seven years later, when Sandra, Jaquetta, and I were all living in New York, I would say to them, "It occurred to me that you must think I'm lying about having a mother because you've never met her and probably never will."

I spotted another friend in the courtyard outside my dorm and waved him over. "Hello. Nice to meet you," my mother said to him in a flat voice. I had gotten used to her affect and hardly noticed that she didn't make eye contact with him. I was simply relishing the joy and excitement of having her there to witness my college life. In that moment, I felt proud of her, prouder than I had felt in years. A few days later the friend would have only one thing to say about her: "Your mom is weird."

"What kind of thing is that to say?" I would snap back, unable to hide my hurt.

Instead of apologizing, he would reassert: "But she *is* weird."

Being away at college had made me forget what my mother looked like through the eyes of others.

There were no letters from me to my father in 1991.

If I had written to him after sophomore year, my words were not the kind he wanted to hang on to.

There were several moments when I could feel the fault lines forming between my father and me, but it was perhaps in my junior year that I first became aware of the cracks.

I had started a semester-long study-abroad program, but six weeks in, my travels were aborted. During one of my regularly scheduled phone calls home, my father told me that he was dying. "I really don't think I'm going to make it that much longer, Grace." So I flew back home expecting to find him on his deathbed but instead found him gardening in the front yard. Another miraculous recovery.

So I went back to Brown in the fall, and the fact that I had enrolled late meant that all the campus housing was full and I became one of the few juniors to live off-campus. For $250 a month, I shared an apartment with two senior girls in Fox Point, a sleepy Portuguese neighborhood that was a fifteen-minute walk from campus. We had the first floor of a two-story wooden house with a porch, and although the peeling mint-green paint on the exterior and the scratched floorboards inside made the house feel a little shabby, it also had a good deal of late Victorian charm—tin ceilings and decorative iron grates over the heating vents in the floor. For the first time in my life, I had a fully equipped kitchen of my own, and I finally put to use the mixing bowls that my father had gotten me for my birthday.

I bought Molly Katzen's *The Enchanted Broccoli Forest* and *Sundays at Moosewood Restaurant* cookbooks, and cooking became my new favorite method of escape. It was not a conscious escape, but rather something that allowed me to be immersed in the present of measuring and mixing and mincing, of tasting and fine-tuning my creation into a product that I could share with others. The level of concentration I put into cooking kept me from drifting off into daydreams or fretting over my parents' problems. My adult life would begin to flourish in the space of the kitchen, the foil to my family's disintegration.

My parents' first separation didn't last long. They were back together when I returned from Brazil, but my mother had become even more withdrawn.

She had stopped opening the curtains or turning on the lights. She just sat on the couch suspended in a state of perpetual darkness, with her feet reclined and knees bent, chin tucked into her chest and eyes half-closed. Despite two years of witnessing her gradually waste away on the couch, my father still believed that she was doing it to spite him.

"Your mother could go back to work if she wanted to. Hell, she can be like her old self if she really wanted to—take care of the house, cook dinner, keep me company. You know, like she used to. But she just doesn't want to, dammit."

The newly minted feminist in me reacted negatively to his expectations. "Why does she always have to cook and clean for you? Huh, Dad? You can do some of it yourself, you know!"

I neglected to consider his age or his ailing heart. Although I knew he had almost died four times, I still had no real concept of what it was to be old and in need of physical help. But the bottom line was that my mother could not snap out of her schizophrenia no matter how much he complained, so he told her that it was her turn to leave. This time, their separation turned into a divorce.

My mother got an apartment in Oregon to be near my cousin Jinho, whom I had always known to be one of her closest family members; he was five and my mother was nine when my grandmother adopted him.

I never questioned whether or not she was in good hands with Jinho and Sun. It wasn't until the following year that I learned that my cousins rarely saw her because she was reluctant to leave her apartment and had stopped answering the phone. They never found out that she was mentally ill, and probably wondered why she never wanted to see them. In Korean, there is almost no concept for mental illness, which I would be reminded of throughout my thirties whenever I tried to explain to my aunt why my mother never came with me to Korea. The closest I could get to a translation was "Mah-eum-i apa-yo." *Her spirit hurts.*

Once I knew what it felt like to not live with my parents, being around them again began to make *my* spirit hurt. My mother's was not the same kind of hurt. Mine motivated me to leave, while hers kept her chained to the couch.

The other unanticipated benefit of returning to Brown in the fall of 1991, besides the kitchen, was a new best friend. Rafael was getting a master's degree in Portuguese and Brazilian studies, my undergraduate major. He was Mexican American of Polish and Spanish descent, but he poked fun at the culture of identity politics on campus. "*I* identify as Chicana," he said, imitating one of our classmates. "What do *you* identify as?"

It was not easy to fit him into a box. He was also Jewish, gay, transnational (having grown up in Mexico, Brazil, and Texas), irreverent yet soft-spoken, and a self-described freak of nature. In elementary school he was asked to draw a picture of the animal that best represented him, and he chose a duck-billed platypus, one of the few mammals that lays eggs. His influence on my thinking propelled me to question the societal norms I had grown up with on an even deeper level. I had been questioning my sexuality for several months when I met him, but was too afraid to vocalize my feelings out of fear that my father would stop loving me. When I was in junior high and high school, during the early days of the AIDS crisis, my father had some choice words about "those goddamn degenerates" and warned me to steer clear of them. But my new friendship overpowered my fear. I had never felt more accepting of myself than when I was with Rafael.

Above all, Rafael showed me the importance of play and exuberance. We would sometimes smoke weed to heighten the pleasure of eating, then indulge our larica—the Portuguese word that Sandra had taught us for "the munchies." We trekked into neighborhoods beyond College Hill in search of exquisite treats like cheesecake sundaes, which we devoured between giggles. He taught me to dance salsa and shed my inhibitions in spades, as we danced late into the night, patronizing both Latin places like La Fragancia and gay clubs like Gerardo's. If cooking in my new kitchen grounded me, then dancing with my new friend released me. Being with him allowed me to exist in the moment, to liberate myself from the traumas of the past.

He meshed well with my other friends, especially Sandra, since they shared a connection to Brazil. I felt a sense of great accomplishment and relief that I had finally found a community, and not only was I a part of it, I was the "glue," according to Rafael. *You're always the one to bring people together.* Rafael became my chosen family. Decades later, my son would come to know him as Uncle Rafa.

More and more, my college experience was broadening my worldview in such a way that it became incompatible with my father's. It was not just my kinship with the "goddamn degenerates" that did it but also the subjects I had chosen to study.

My father was a blue-collar man with a strong intellectual streak. He was an avid reader of English literature and even nicknamed himself "the Ancient Mariner" after Samuel Taylor Coleridge's poem. His love of reading rubbed off on me, and I took comparative literature classes every semester. He had invested most of his hard-earned money in my education—not just for college but also in all the things that helped get me there: two years of private French lessons in junior high and two study-abroad trips to France in high school so that I could become a fluent reader of French.

When I got to Brown, I found that I was more drawn to literature from parts of the world that were unfamiliar to me—not France, but the Francophone world, places like Martinique and the Maghreb. As I learned Portuguese, I glimpsed the vistas of the Lusophone world too. And I studied Japanese literature in translation alongside African women writers such as Tsitsi Dangarembga and Mariama Bâ. I thought my father would have approved of this, because he had long nurtured my desire to see the world by bringing me trinkets from far-flung places like Singapore and Goa. But then again, they were trinkets, not literature.

"It's a damn shame they're not teaching you something else," he said after a few semesters of patiently waiting for me to take the kind of classes he thought I should be taking. By "something else," he meant the Western canon. He had been reading Allan Bloom's *The Closing of the American Mind* at the same time that I'd been reveling in the writings of people of color. I took it personally that he disapproved of my choices and dismissed the literary contributions of the authors I was reading. My studies and social experience at Brown allowed me to feel, for the first time, that I was good enough. I didn't have to be white or try to be white to have a voice.

"Western writers aren't superior," I told him. "It's just that people from the colonized world have been silenced for so long that you never got a chance to hear them. How would you even know how valuable they are?"

"Look at what happened to Africa and India after they became independent!" he said, shaking his head.

"What?" I was completely thrown off by the turn the conversation had just taken.

"Those people don't know how to govern themselves."

"*Those* people?" I worked to process what my father was saying. It wasn't just about literature anymore. "You mean you think they were better off colonized?"

"They used to say that the sun never sets on the British Empire," he said, his voice dripping with nostalgia. "And it was true, goddammit!"

As my father and I had these arguments, I came to realize that *I* was one of the Others he disdained. My friendships and romantic interests gravitated toward men and women who had ties to the "third world"—though, even among us, there was debate over whether or not this was an appropriate term. "Developing country" became the politically correct term that replaced "third world country," but "third world" was a more forceful reminder of unequal power relations between nations and peoples. It also included immigrant groups that might have originated in a colonizing country of Europe, but still lagged behind in terms of social and economic power. In Providence, Rhode Island, this included the Portuguese: a large linguistic minority community that was underrepresented at the Ivy League campus in its backyard, besides as janitors or cafeteria workers. I was coming into consciousness, beginning to understand myself as a colonized person.

My parents' divorce only lasted slightly longer than their first separation. They got married to each other again within the year. When I saw them after they got back together, I was so moved that I could barely stave off my tears. "How many grown kids get to congratulate their own parents for getting married?" My father just nodded, because he, too, was getting choked up. My mother was silent, her face unreadable. I prodded. "How do you feel, Mom? Aren't you happy?" She pursed her lips together and gave the slightest of nods. I took it to mean that things were better between them and they had renewed their vows to care for each other.

Again, I had forgotten. I had forgotten what it was like to live with my mother, what it was like for her to live with my father.

1992

Dear Don,

Thank you for your generous contribution to David Duke for President . . .

Nothing would ever be the same again between us after I found a letter on my father's desk from David Duke. In 1992 the *New York Times* had described Duke's followers as the "racial right,"[1] while the *Los Angeles Times* noted that, according to Duke, "American democracy is in danger because the growth of non-white, non-Christian ethnic groups is turning the nation into 'a Third World country.'"[2] It was this kind of rhetoric that appealed to his supporters. In the Republican primaries, Duke fared worse in Washington State than in any other state in which he was on the ballot. Only 1.16 percent of Washington Republicans voted for him, and among that percentage of voters was my father.

"Dad, what is this?" I said as I picked up the letter and blinked at it. I wanted to yell, "David Duke is a white supremacist!" but felt like I had just been punched in the stomach, so instead the words wheezed out of my mouth. Oblivious to my revulsion, he said that the United States was heading down the wrong path, and that David Duke was just the man to steer it back in the right direction. "It's what our country needs right now."

Childhood memories began to flood through my body. There were the usual ones of being a victim of racialized violence, the ones I could never really forget, but they were soon interrupted by a different memory in which I was the perpetrator.

I am three years old. Our paperboy, the only Black kid in town, arrives on his bike and I run to the screen door, delighted to see him. "Hi, N——!" I say, because I think that's his name. In an instant my mother pulls me away. "I'm so sorry," she says to the boy. "She doesn't know what that means. Oh, I am sorry. Please forgive her."

She grabs me by the shoulders and says, "Grace, you can never call anyone that."

"But that's what Daddy calls him," I say softly, a burning sensation I cannot yet name spreading through my body.

Reliving this scene in my mind filled me with horror and shame that my father had put that word in my mouth when I was too young to understand its dehumanizing power. How carelessly he tossed it about. *Eeny, meeny, miney, mo, catch a n— by the toe.*

I wondered if the boy remembered me after all those years, if the face of bigotry that he saw when he looked back on his life was that of a three-year-old Asian girl. And then an even more disturbing thought occurred to me: What if that boy was the same boy from my brother's high school, the one named Chris, who killed himself? The paperboy was about the same age as my brother, and Chris was the only Black teenager in my brother's high school. What if I had been some small link in the chain of events that led to Chris's death?

The memory triggered another, this one of my father calling my mother "Mongoloid."

I am ten or eleven. I am sitting at the kitchen table when my parents begin to argue. "Why you have to say something like that?" my mother says. "I told you to stop." He pushes back. "Well, you're part Mongol, ain't ya?" Then he makes a joke about me being the "baby Mongoloid." She becomes furious and yells, "How many times I gotta tell you stop using that word?" He is once again unapologetic and smirking. "But that's what it says on her birth certificate."

My hand clenched as I held the letter, crumpling the David Duke stationery. When the air returned to my lungs, I threw it at him and screamed with the entire force of my body, "Who do you think you're talking to? I'm your Asian daughter!"

My father stared and stuttered. "But—but—what are you talking about? You—you're not Black."

"I'm not white either!"

Having spent much of his adult life in Asia, my father had grown fond of Asians and was perhaps willfully blind to white supremacy's mission to keep all nonwhite races subordinated. Or maybe he had always viewed Asians as more palatable than other nonwhite people. After all, he did grow up at a time when the colonial hierarchy of the "family of man" structured Western thinking on race (e.g., "Mongoloids" rank below "Caucasoids" but above "Negroids"). He had probably internalized the belief that Asians were hardworking model minorities that had the potential to approximate whiteness, with a little help from people like him. My rejection of white identity must have made him feel like a failure.

He also didn't understand that racial domination doesn't just take the form of the white terrorist burning a cross in your front yard. It can also look like the man you live with, the man you love. The man who defends your birth country, the place where he found his wife. *Don't they know that Korea's not a third world country anymore?* But it sure was in the 1960s when he met my mother, at least by his definition.

Nor did he understand that his opportunities to travel to Asia had been a consequence of the deeply unequal and violent relationship between the American military and the countries they occupied. He spent time in the Philippines, Guam, Okinawa, and Korea because the American military had bases there, and as a member of the American military, he was given special privileges, such as official access to local women. Official access to my mother. But I didn't understand that yet either.

I walked away from him and tried to calm down, but something that my brother had said to me a few weeks earlier buzzed in my ear like a mosquito. "Dad's worried that you're going to date a Black guy." What fucking business is it of his who I date? I thought to myself, and with that, I charged back into his office.

"I heard that you're afraid of me dating a Black man. Well, would you feel better if it was a Black *woman*?" Although I had no dating prospects of any kind, my community was mostly Black and Brown, and increasingly queer. This hypothetical possibility was my way of telling him that, not only was I not his approximately white daughter, I was a goddamn degenerate to boot.

My father's face tightened into a scowl. "Does your mother know what you are?"

There was no time to waste. I had to tell her before he did, so I rushed into the living room, sat down on the couch next to her, and took a deep breath. "Mom, there's something I have to ask you."

"Wha?"

"Would you still love me if I liked women? I mean, romantically?"

Her eyes darted around the room for a few seconds, and she said in a calm, steady voice, "Oh. You are not one of those, are you?" But a moment later she patted my thigh. "Of course I still love you. Hmph! What kind of person don't love their own children?"

My father began sending me letters about my "degenerate lifestyle," which he initially signed "Love, Dad." Gradually his signoff changed to just "Dad" and then to no greeting or sign-off. At that point I stopped opening his letters.

The topic of my romantic life never came up again until a year after graduation, when I moved in with Cesar, a boyfriend that I'd end up living with for ten years. My brother would tell me, "Dad's okay with him being Mexican. He's just relieved that it's a man."

Though I couldn't forgive my father's bigotry when I was in college, later I would be able to see him within his social context. For most of his life, queer sexuality was treated as a moral defect, a crime, or a disease. It was illegal in Washington State until 1976, the *DSM* classified it as a psychiatric disorder until 1980, and it was grounds for barring an immigrant from entering the United States until 1990.

My father had been born a white male in America in 1919, just four years after Woodrow Wilson screened *The Birth of a Nation* in the White House as a cautionary tale of the perils of allowing Black people their freedom. And when my father was five years old, the KKK held one of its largest "super rallies" in Chehalis.[3] No doubt it was the biggest spectacle he ever could have seen, the town swarmed with seventy thousand cloaked and hooded Klansmen, a dozen of them for every inhabitant of Chehalis. Perhaps it was his equivalent of my bicentennial, a momentous occasion from early life that would shape his sense of self in the world.

He came of age when the sun never set on the British Empire, while my coming of age happened when people from formerly colonized parts of the world were populating college campuses and revising dominant accounts of history to include themselves in it. As postcolonial scholars of the time argued: the empire was writing back. Through this new prism of the experiences of women, the colonized, and the oppressed, I began to see the injustices my mother faced. I had witnessed many of them with my own eyes, but I still didn't know much about her past in Korea. All I knew for sure was that she had survived a war, had worked in some sort of a service job, and had been denied the opportunity to go to school. From what I had deduced, my mother had become her family's breadwinner at some point because her father had died and her brother had disappeared.

In a class on bilingual education, I learned about John Ogbu's theory of involuntary minorities—groups with the most subordinated status of all minorities because they became part of a society by force, such as Chicanos, Native Americans, or African Americans in the United States, or Koreans in Japan. Then came a revelation. I realized that the reason my mother had been born in Japan, and the reason she shut down whenever I asked her about it, was because her family, or at least her mother, had been forced laborers. I told Sandra about the epiphany, and she chuckled at what she thought was an arbitrary distinction. "What's the difference between forced labor and slavery?" I thought about her question. Was "forced labor" a euphemism or was it just a broader term that included various forms of slavery? It was deeply disturbing to think that my mother had been born into slavery of any form.

The longer I was at Brown and the more distance I had from my childhood, the more I put my parents under a microscope. I saw the way that the power dynamics in my family mirrored a larger dynamic of social inequality, and my father became the main object of my criticism. The very thing that he had worked so hard for—my first-class education—was also the thing that created a gulf between us so wide and deep that we could never again stand on common ground.

We had stopped talking until two weeks before my college graduation, when he called and said, "I'm ready to be conciliatory." But I wasn't.

I cried on the phone to my brother because I wanted more than anything for my mother to come to my graduation, even though I knew full well that she had become afraid of strangers and certainly couldn't tolerate a crowd.

"Can't you try to convince her?" I pleaded, not remembering that she hadn't made it to his college graduation either.

"Uh, I doubt it, but one of your parents wants to go." I felt conflicted and spent the next few days wavering back and forth between whether it would be worse to have my father at my graduation or to not have him there. Ultimately, I couldn't bear the thought of him coming while my mother stayed at home, huddled in the corner of her darkness.

So I went to my college graduation, an event that I once imagined would be the proudest moment of my parents' lives, without them there to witness it. I listened to the commencement speeches about what great heights I would achieve as a Brown grad and the exciting new life that awaited, but all I could feel was my parents' absence.

9. JANUARYSEVENTH

Providence, Rhode Island, 1994

WHAT I REMEMBER MOST about the year I turned twenty-three was the snow. It seemed to fall every few days that winter, sometimes by the foot, and although I'd been living in Providence for four years, I still hadn't gotten used to the "wind-chill factor" (a concept I had never heard of growing up) or the sensation of tiny pellets of ice whipping across my face. In Chehalis, it rarely got cold enough to snow, and if it did, the snow came in the form of a soft ephemeral dust that coated the landscape for a few hours in the morning before melting into the damp ground by midday.

After graduating from college, I moved to Smith Hill, a quaint neighborhood in Providence near the capitol building, where I lived on the top floor of a nineteenth-century carriage house that had been built on a slope. My awareness of the amount of snowfall that year was made more acute by my first car, a silver '87 Volkswagen Golf with standard transmission. Even a small accumulation made pulling up the driveway treacherous, and there was a constant ache in my arms and back from shoveling.

It's a curious thing that my memory takes me to snow, because there were far more important things to remember about that year, like the gnawing fear that I was never going to get my old mother back. On the eve of 1994, the fictions that had barely

held my family together came bursting apart and threatened to
break me along with them.

Sometime in late 1993, after my father announced that he was
done with her, my mother moved to a leafy suburban neighborhood about a mile from my brother's house in New Jersey.

My brother and his wife had been working up to the idea of
having her live near them for some time anyway, because my
mother needed more than my father could give her. I was grateful that they were going to take care of her, though I doubt I was
able to express it at the time. I had just graduated college and
yearned for the opportunity to pursue a career and romantic life,
while my brother and his wife were older and more stable. He
had a lucrative job as an investment banker; they had just bought
their first house and had their first child. Having my mother
there could fit into the bigger picture of their lives in a way that
it couldn't in mine. Besides, my brother was my mother's first-
born and her only son. Among Koreans, caring for elderly or
sick parents was the first son's responsibility. The adult daughter's responsibility was to loosen ties with her mother and forge
new ones with a mother-in-law. Although my sister-in-law was a
white woman from Arkansas, she'd been aware of these cultural
practices. That she was to act as my mother's daughter. That my
brother's authority would always eclipse mine.

"Your mother will do whatever he tells her to do," she'd say,
and this time he told Mom that she was coming to live in New
Jersey.

He also told her that she had to see a psychiatrist, and while
I thought it was a godsend that she might finally get some treatment, this development would also stir up the years of emotional
sediment about the situation—my frustration at not being able
to get help for her, my embarrassment about the police debacle.
The way my family had ostracized me for even daring to speak

the word "schizophrenic" made me believe that the only thing that could earn their forgiveness was my silence.

Somehow I managed to live with my mother's madness because she was still able to do basic things for herself. She could feed and groom herself, or talk on the phone if she knew it was me calling. *You give me a signal, okay? Let it ring twice and hang up, then you call right back.* I managed to live with it because, until my sister-in-law came along, no one else would admit that there was something terribly wrong, and I lacked the resources to deal with it myself.

I was a senior in high school the first time I remember my sister-in-law saying that my mother had "problems." It might have been during the same visit when, seated at our kitchen table, she and my brother casually announced that "by the way, we got married"—the words making my father's jaw go slack, my mother's eyes skitter.

Somehow this memory of my sister-in-law at our bright-white kitchen table, sitting under the glare and hum of fluorescent lights, morphs into another memory. The same scene but with a smaller cast, my mother and father absent. *I think your mom has problems.* Someone in her own family (an aunt?) had problems, too, she said. The knot in my chest tightened, then loosened ever so slightly as the words landed. Was this message for me more than it was for my brother? Was it to say that she could see what I'd been going through and that soon enough she would make my brother see too? Yes, my mother *had problems.* It was a euphemism spoken by someone whose place in my family was secure enough to speak what had always been unspeakable. Maybe an outsider was exactly what we needed to shake things up.

By the time I graduated from college, both my brother and his wife could say it plainly: *schizophrenic.*

Although my mother had already spent years staying more or

less confined to the house, increasingly to one room, leaving the house she knew for a different one on the opposite side of the country seemed to have opened some traumatic wounds of her wartime childhood and of fleeing her home.

Her new place was a one-bedroom apartment in a little wooden house surrounded by dense foliage. The trees shading the windows provided her some privacy, but the leaves were already turning, her camouflage dwindling by the day.

It was perhaps the second or third time I visited her when I first felt winter's quickening breath on my skin. The sky was gray and heavy with snow clouds, and night fell before she had even put on a pot of rice. We sat in her living room after eating, and the low, persistent wail of a siren interrupted the otherwise peaceful silence of our surroundings.

"Do you hear that, Grace?" she asked. "What do you suppose that is?"

"I don't know. Is it an ambulance?" I knew it wasn't, but I wanted to give her an answer. The noise seemed like it was being radioed in.

"Sounds like an air-raid siren," she said in an audible whisper.

"Have you heard it before?"

"Every day at the same time." She began wringing her hands.

I was glad to have been there to hear what she heard, so that her reports of air-raid sirens would not be filed away as another auditory hallucination, another crazy thing that she did or said.

Ten years later, while I was writing my doctoral dissertation, I would learn that the Korean War's staggering civilian death toll had primarily been caused by aerial bombing with napalm. The Americans' fire and fury decimating schools and orphanages, incinerating the flesh of screaming children.

During my next visit, I arrived to find my brother picking up broken glass in front of the entrance. My mother had been on her way to a psychiatric appointment, but she couldn't figure out how to unlock the front door. Then her key had gotten jammed, so she got a kitchen knife—the one she had used for as long as I could remember to crush garlic and slice bulgogi—and broke the glass out of the window to escape the house.

I wondered if she had heard the siren when it happened, if that piercing sound had burrowed into her mind and convinced her that this was an emergency. That she needed to LEAVE NOW.

"How am I supposed to explain this to the landlord?" my brother asked as he surveyed the wreckage.

I would leave it to him to figure out the lie. The truth was just too complicated.

At certain times each day, my mother would chant—something that my sister-in-law referred to as the "timing thing." At 1:07 she repeated "January seventh," my birthday, over and over again with the speed of an auctioneer, until the minute was up.

Januaryseventhjanuaryseventhjanuaryseventhjanuaryseventhjanuaryseventhjanuaryseventhjanuaryseventhjanuaryseventhjanuaryseventhjanuaryseventhjanuaryseventhjanuaryseventh . . .

She did the same for my brother's, but there was another time-date I didn't recognize: 9:45. She did not repeat it in the same way, but said it only once every twelve hours. I was frightened the first time I witnessed it because we had been in the middle of a mundane conversation, and suddenly she straightened her posture, pointed to the clock with one firm shake of her right index finger, and announced in a loud, arresting voice, "September forty-five!" And then, as if nothing had happened, she returned her attention back to me and finished her previous thought exactly where it had left off. I was always spooked by it, much more so than any of her other quirks. It didn't feel like these words and actions had just been generated by her mind, but rather, that there was some other presence in the room, a supernatural force that was using her body to speak.

The layers of meaning behind the "timing thing" would begin to unfold that year, and for years to come.

In September 1945 the United States occupied the southern half of the Korean peninsula, where they would:

— establish a new nation called "South Korea," with a hand-picked, Harvard-educated president;
— lay the groundwork for a "laboratory" in which new weapons of mass destruction would be tested on communists and groups of refugees that might be harboring them;
— build an infrastructure for "entertaining" the American troops that would remain there to this day.

In every memory I have of my mother's first months on the East Coast, I am cold. Chilled in her underheated apartment. Shivering in the driveway as my sister-in-law stops me from leaving so she can tell me something important, her words like incendiary bomblets scattered over my psyche, sometimes exploding long after impact.

Grace, your mom is doing this thing. This panicking thing.

Grace, your mom is getting worse.

Grace, your mom—there's something I need to tell you . . .

The day before New Year's Eve, she dropped the big bomb, its devastation swift and brutal. I had been staying with my mother over the holidays and was on my way to meet Sandra and Jaquetta at a mall in Philadelphia when my sister-in-law pulled up. She got out of her cream-colored station wagon and began unloading a delivery of groceries. She had taken on this responsibility of shopping for my mother while also caring for my infant niece. In retrospect, I see how the stress of a baby and my mother—two new arrivals with completely different needs—must have worn her to the bone.

"Are you leaving already?" she asked.

"I'm just going shopping for a New Year's Eve outfit, but I'll be back in a few hours."

Her face showed the strain of sleepless nights. "Grace, your mom—there's something I need to tell you . . ."

What now? I was feeling stressed by all her pronouncements, though I couldn't articulate exactly why, only that it made my helplessness in the face of my mother's illness all the more painful. What new development could have caused my sister-in-law to hesitate like that? Why the preface when she usually just spat out the words? There was nothing she could say about my mother's condition that would have come as a shock to me. I had already been through eight years of erratic behaviors, mood swings, and hallucinations. What could she possibly tell me that I didn't already know?

"Grace, your mother used to be a prostitute."

What is she talking about? My skin turned hot, barely able to contain the feelings of confusion bubbling beneath it. "How do you know that?" I can't remember if I actually vocalized this question, but she answered it nonetheless.

"Look, your brother remembers it. Go ask him. He remembers when she used to get dressed up." *Dressed up.* The clothing, a metonym for the profession.

My memory flickered with scenes of Halloween 1984 when Jenny and I had made a last-minute decision to go trick-or-treating. "Let's dress up as hookers," one of us said. We were thirteen-year-old girls beginning to explore our sexuality, and prostitutes were the only women we knew of who had the freedom to be overtly sexual. We hastily got dressed: caked-on makeup, teased hair, miniskirts, and fishnet tights that we had bought at Spencer's. As I was about to walk out that night, my mother blocked the doorway with her body and glared at me. "What d'you think you are supposed to be, huh?" Her scornful tone stung, and I feared that at any moment she might uncross her arms and slap me. My voice was meek, but I answered quickly. "A punk rocker." Even then I knew that she would kill me before she let me be a prostitute.

Of course she had wanted to stop me. I was glamorizing the very life that she had escaped and had tried to bury. But how could that be? How could that have been her life?

My head started to spin and I leaned against the open door of my car to hold myself up as my sister-in-law continued to talk. "He never told you because he wanted to spare you, but now you need to know. Your mom's getting worse."

Spare me? I wasn't sure if I was more disturbed by my mother's past or the fact that it had been kept a secret from me my whole life. Why was I the last to know?

And then I would twist my face up to hold in the tears, and my sister-in-law would try to console me by saying that it hadn't been that bad. "It was one of the nicer clubs. It wasn't like she was on the streets."

Even after the revelation, my brother never told me. He never could say the words that his wife spoke, nor could anyone else in my family say the word "prostitute."

When I asked him if it was true, he said, "How do you think she met your father?" as if I were stupid for not realizing it sooner.

When I asked my father about it, he broke down in tears and said, "Your mother did that as seldom as possible. She didn't want to do it. I got her out of there."

"But didn't you have something to do with her being there before you got her out of there?" My father just stared at me, dumbstruck. "You know," I said, "because you were one of her customers before you got her out of there? She couldn't have worked there without the customers. You know, supply and demand."

In September 1945 the United States acquired the "comfort

stations," a system of sexual slavery that had been set up by the Japanese imperial army, keeping both the facilities and the women who had been laboring there, turning them into the first brothels to service American soldiers in Korea. In the 1950s these brothels would draw a new crop of girls from the countryside, girls who sought to support themselves or provide for their families in the aftermath of the Korean War. By the 1960s the South Korean government would officially sponsor sexual services exclusively for US military personnel.

Before her mental illness drove her indoors, never again to be the object of another's desiring gaze, my mother had the beauty and allure of a celebrity—smoky black kohl smudged around her double-lidded eyes, always dressed to the nines. Her face was round and symmetrical with deep dimples and perfectly straight teeth, her complexion an even sandy brown—exotic, but not too brown for most white men. I could see how her attractiveness helped her make a living and survive during and after the war.

In the accounts of civilian experiences of the Korean War that I would research in graduate school, some of the variables that helped people survive were youth, femininity, and ability to communicate in English. Those three things meant that American soldiers were more inclined to help them, or to spare their lives during a massacre. Despite my mother's lack of formal education, she taught herself English, one word at a time from a dictionary, and tried to perfect it by watching a lot of American movies. She was beautiful, and she spoke English. My mother was determined to survive.

Shopping provided a momentary diversion from the avalanche of thoughts and feelings set into motion by my sister-in-law's disclosure, but when I came back to my mother's house later that night, the weight of her hidden history pressed down on me as soon as I walked through the door. I looked at her sitting quietly on the couch, doing her usual nothing.

"Do you want to see what I'm wearing tomorrow night?" I asked, trying to act as if nothing had changed.

"Yeah, let's see."

It was a long black skirt with a slit up the side and a long-sleeved black lace top. I modeled it for her, turning from side-to-side at the end of an imaginary runway.

"That's very attractive, Grace," she said. "Very attractive." I was relieved that she approved of the outfit.

"I'm going to a New Year's Eve party with Sandra and Jaquetta at SOB's. It's a Brazilian nightclub in New York."

"Nightclub? Be careful of what kind of things going on in there."

"Don't worry, Ma. It's just for dancing."

For the first time I understood my mother's alarm whenever I mentioned that I was going out to a club or bar. For her they were not merely places to socialize and let loose.

My sleep that night was fitful, and each time I lay awake, images of my mother as a prostitute intruded upon my thoughts. A Suzie Wong clinging to her white man. A lotus flower arm in arm with her GI John. No, I thought. Not my mother.

I tried to visualize the transaction—the exchange of sex for money, my mother in the back room of a nightclub—and imagined her feeling ashamed and afraid, but finding some inner strength to cope. When it happened, maybe she pretended to be a Hollywood actress in the role of an impassioned lover, or perhaps she found ways to dissociate by staring at some spot on the wall the way she did whenever she avoided my questions about what kind of work she did in Korea. Maybe her voices had been there all along, talking her through it until it was over.

I tried to stop the endless questions in my mind, the stream of images of my young mother—she would have been younger than me, maybe twenty or twenty-one—with some grunting American soldier on top of her, one after another.

No. Make it stop.

Later that night, after she had said goodnight and thought I was asleep, I heard her shuffle into the kitchen and chatter under her breath. I couldn't make out the words, but they were coming fast, as if she were speaking in tongues. Then I heard her gulping air.

"Ma, what's happening? Are you okay?" I called out toward the sounds.

She answered only by breathing louder and faster. I threw the covers back, got up off the couch, and walked into the kitchen. I squinted into the darkness and saw her holding on to the edge of the counter with both hands, rocking back and forth against it.

Then the heavy breathing, the chanting, the rocking, all of it stopped suddenly, and she became still. "Everything is fine. Go back to bed."

Varick Street was still relatively quiet when I met Sandra and Jaquetta at SOB's. We ordered three rum and cokes and sat at a table decorated with fake palm fronds. Normally the prospect of getting dressed up to go out, especially on New Year's, would have excited me, but there was a heaviness blanketing the celebration. My sorrow must have overpowered the electric energy of the party because one of them asked me what was wrong.

"Yesterday my sister-in-law told me that my mom was a prostitute in Korea."

Jaquetta gasped and covered her mouth, a reaction that mirrored the shock I was still feeling. But Sandra didn't seem the least bit surprised. She gave me a sympathetic look and said, "But you must have known. You must have known there was something else."

Huh? Even my friend knew before I did?

I can't remember how long we sat there like that, or if there was any further conversation about it, but I have some vague memory that I wanted to talk, to begin to sort out all my feelings of sadness and shame—shame that I would later come to interrogate and beat into submission through my research. If I had started to talk about it, I was probably interrupted by the promoter introducing the night's entertainment. It was an up-and-coming pop singer named Marc Anthony, donning basketball shoes and a Tweety Bird cap, and by the time he took the stage, the three of us were on our feet and dancing. He kept making eye contact with me as he sang and shimmied, prompting Jaquetta to shout over the music, "Hey, I think he likes you!" I tossed my head back and laughed. "Not my type!" Maybe it was the attention, or maybe it was the rum talking, but I told myself I was going to have fun. Fuck it! It's New Year's Eve, and we're ringing in 1994!

In 1994, eight years after I diagnosed my mother from a high school psychology textbook, she got an official psychiatric diagnosis of schizophrenia, and the doctor started her on medication. We thought that drugs were going to be the answer to all our problems because that's what the rhetoric of the time had been saying: that schizophrenia and other mental illnesses were simply chemical imbalances of the brain, corrected by feeding the brain the right cocktail of chemicals.

We waited for the drugs to work so that my mother could be normal again. Instead, her affect grew duller, and she complained more. *I don't like it. My hands are all the time shaking. My tongue feels swollen. The side of my face is numb.* She began to suffer from tardive dyskinesia, a condition of repetitive involuntary motion of the face and limbs. To treat her schizophrenia, she was given a new disease.

It was unthinkable at the time to allow her to go off her meds, because we had waited so long for her to get on them, and she had finally agreed. The public perception of schizophrenia was that it was a disease of violent aggression, and although I had never known her to be this way, the responsible thing to do was to keep her on the medication so that she wouldn't hurt others or herself.

I can't remember if the first drug my mother took was Haldol or Mellaril, but both of them came under intense scrutiny decades after they were first put on the market. Like most people in 1994, I was unaware of the critique that psychiatry was becoming a bedfellow of the prison-industrial complex—that drugs were being used as a form of carceral control or that mental illness was becoming increasingly criminalized. Sometimes the diagnosis came after the imprisonment, as a method of chemical incarceration. The trend of substituting incarceration for mental health care would continue until there were far more mentally ill people in prisons than in health care facilities. These bodies—primarily Black and Brown bodies, bodies inscribed with social illness—would become concentrated in large penal institutions. *The race issue has been like a stave driven into the American system of values, a stave so deeply imbedded in the American ethos as to render America a nation of ethical schizophrenics.*[1] By 2007 Los Angeles County Jail, Cook County Jail in Chicago, and Rikers Island in New York City would become the "three largest inpatient psychiatric facilities" in the United States.[2] In other words, the largest drug dispensaries, the new asylums.

In the late 1960s schizophrenia was in the midst of getting a radical makeover, from an affliction of white middle-class housewives and intellectual white men to a "protest psychosis" that befell angry Black men and others that suffered from "delusional anti-whiteness."[3] Haldol was being used as a chemical restraint to keep oppositional behavior in check, often prescribed to psychiatric detainees affiliated with the Black Power Movement. One of the first ads for Haldol depicted a Black man with a clenched fist, and the caption read, *Assaultive and belligerent? Cooperation often begins with Haldol.*[4]

Decades later, the research would show that the first generations of patients who were prescribed Haldol were given ten times the appropriate dosage, effectively turning them into zombies. The use of Mellaril was also challenged after research linked it to heart attacks and shortened lifespans of its users, and it was taken off the market in 2005.

In 1994 my mother was finally in treatment for her schizophrenia and was prescribed either Haldol or Mellaril. Even though all the signs would show that her mental state was getting more disturbed, we were told to keep waiting for the drugs to work.

And while we kept waiting, she kept speaking up about her growing mental discomfort. *This medication makes me feel like something is wrong.*

The voices of the mentally ill are equivalent to the miner's canary. Their stories are alerting us to the fact that something is wrong with psychiatry's overreliance on a biological model of suffering.[5]

I was back in Providence on January 7, 1994, my twenty-third birthday, and an on-and-off love interest had planned to take me out to dinner for my birthday. It was my first real date since graduating from college, and I was eagerly awaiting his arrival when big wet flakes started falling from the sky. There was already an inch on the ground by the time he rang the doorbell.

I buzzed him in and as he walked up the stairs and into the loft kitchen, he brushed the snow off his shoulders and said, "I was thinking we could stay in and order a pizza so we don't have to go out in the snow."

Order pizza? I couldn't hide my disappointment, and the

sadness I'd been carrying around with me since New Year's rose to the surface. I didn't want to cry in front of him, and especially not then, but there was no way to hold it in. I plopped down at the tiled kitchen table, rested my forehead in my hands, and began sobbing in great heaves. When I caught my breath, I said, "It's not just about the pizza. It's my mother. I found out that she used to be a prostitute."

He stood there in silence watching me cry for a minute, then started back toward the door.

"You're leaving?"

"I'm sorry." There was a chill in his voice. "That reminds me of things from my own past that are equally disturbing."

"But it's my birthday," I whimpered as he walked down the stairs and back out into the flurries.

I stared at the little puddle of dirty melted snow that his boots had left behind on my kitchen floor as I wiped my nose on the back of my sleeve. There was nothing I could do but crawl under my comforter and nestle deeper into my grief.

On January 7, 2009, the *New York Times* ran a story about a group of former sex workers breaking a decades-long silence about the South Korean government's role in setting up a sex trade for the Americans. "Our government was one big pimp for the U.S. military," one of them said.[6] The number of women speaking out would grow, and eventually 120 of them would file a lawsuit against the South Korean government for enabling systematic abuse against thousands of women and girls.

It would take eight years, but a panel of three judges would rule in favor of fifty-seven of the plaintiffs—workers who had serviced the US military in the 1960s and 1970s, the same time period in which my mother worked on the base. The court determined that the government had illegally detained the women by locking them up in rooms with barred windows and forcing them to undergo medical treatment for sexually transmitted infections, constituting what one judge described as a "serious human rights violation that should never have happened and should never be repeated."[7]

According to Park Young-ja, one of the plaintiffs mentioned in the article, "They never sent us to doctors even when we were so sick we almost died, except they treated us for venereal diseases . . . not for us, but for the American soldiers." Park also challenged the popular notion that she and her fellow sex workers at the American military bases were "willing" prostitutes. She pointed out that some women had been tricked by job-placement agencies, but even those who knew what kind of work they'd be getting into had never consented to the abusive conditions. "I was only a teenager and I had to receive five GIs a day with no day off. When I ran away, they caught and beat me, raising my debt." The plaintiffs would later file a lawsuit against the US government.

I heard my mother's voice chanting as I read the article from the *New York Times. Januaryseventhjanuaryseventhjanuaryseventh* . . . I had always thought it was in reference to my birthday, but then I wondered if the date was also her vision into the future, the voice of her solidarity with the plaintiffs.

Jenny came to visit me in February. She was my rock from the past and the only friend in my adult life that knew my mother. One night we went to a gay club called Generation X that was housed in an old industrial warehouse at the end of my street. Although it was just one block away, it was a challenge to get there without slipping on patches of compacted snow and ice as we walked downhill. We sat down at the bar, and after I warmed up with a cocktail, I told her what I'd learned about my mom.

She covered her mouth and began to cry, yet didn't break eye contact with me. She cried for a long time like that, muffling sobs and staring at me through her loose blond curls. When she was finally able to speak, she shook her head and said, "That's so unfair." It was the most satisfying response I had gotten from any of my friends, perhaps because she was the only one who knew my mother as a real person who had once loved her, not as a hypothetical mother, always hidden away behind her psychosis.

In the years to come, after my father died and I became my mother's cook, Jenny would say to me on the phone, "Oh, Gracie. When it's all over, I want you to know that you did right by her."

There were a lot of things we didn't know about schizophrenia in the 1990s, when my mother first entered the mental health care system. We didn't know that "psychoses have a briefer duration in the Third World,"[8] or that people in non-Western countries were ten times more likely to experience "nearly complete remission,"[9] or that the "normative treatment for schizophrenia in American culture may significantly make things worse . . . that it does so by repeatedly creating the conditions for demoralization and despair."[10] We didn't know that it was possible to recover from schizophrenia in some parts of the world, but that the United States wasn't one of them.

It wasn't simply the bad luck of a faulty gene or an incurably diseased brain that made my mother suffer. She also had the bad luck of having schizophrenia in the United States, the very place she dreamed would bring her good fortune.

The last big snow of the season fell in March, on the night that I began my first meaningful long-term relationship.

I had met Cesar during college and admired him from afar whenever his salsa band played near campus. He was a slender six feet with thick, wavy, chin-length hair, a few strands of white gleaming amid the black.

The summer after graduation, we started working together at

a branch of the university—a center for ESL and bilingual education—but by this time his hair was shaved to half an inch. Cesar
had graduated from Brown a year before me and already had a
year of postcollege professional experience working there, even
though it was just a day job to support his music career. Both of us
were basically doing clerical work, but we had some sort of fancy
titles so that the administration could report diversity in their
hiring practices. He was Chicano and I was Asian, and together
with the Cape Verdean secretary, we were token representations
of several racial and linguistic minorities of Rhode Island.

I had been nurturing a crush on Cesar since graduating, and
it began to blossom into something more the night of the snow-
storm, when he invited me to a party at his friend's house in Fox
Point.

A squall rattled my bedroom window as I was getting dressed
for the party—a pair of purple jeans, a black top, and a pair of
Italian leather ankle boots that were about to get ravaged. If I had
been the least bit rational, I wouldn't have even entertained the
idea of getting in my car and driving across town in five inches of
snow, let alone shoveling my driveway first.

When I arrived at the party, I barely needed to search the faces
in the crowd before Cesar spotted me from across the room and
smiled, the corners of his dark-brown eyes turning downward.
"Hey, Grace. Glad you could make it." I scanned the room to
make sure he had come alone before giving him a hug. He handed
me a cup of sweet rum punch as we sank into one of couches that
his friend had salvaged through dumpster diving. The cushions
sagged in the middle, pulling our bodies toward each other so
that our legs touched. I felt the energy between us but wondered
if I was reading too much into it.

A few rum punches later, sometime around 4:00 a.m., he
blurted out, "I think I love you, Grace." It was clear that he had
had too much to drink, and I probably had too, yet his confession

jarred me into sobriety. I led him over to one of the mattresses that the host had set up on the floor so that his guests could pass out for the night, and told him to go to sleep. I lay down next to him and dreamed of a future in which his sunny disposition would be the light to my darkness.

I woke up the next day around noon to the sound of a coffee pot hissing and party guests chatting. Cesar was still asleep, but I got up and walked out to the front porch, where two women were basking in the sudden arrival of spring. It was 60 degrees, and the sun was melting little rivers through the snow.

"*Glorious! Glorious!*" one of them sang as she tilted her head back and opened up her arms.

The forsythias lining the streets of Providence that spring burst into raucous yellow blooms, followed by the daffodils. Cesar and I kissed for the first time in April. He moved into my carriage-house apartment in May.

Our collection of food magazines steadily populated our living room shelves: *Food & Wine*, *Gourmet*, *Bon Appétit*, *Saveur*, *Cook's Illustrated*, *Chile Pepper*. We cooked decadent meals on our 1940s white porcelain stove: saucy French dishes or fiery Asian or Latin ones. Cooking became the incarnation of our desires and hopes, and trips to Stop & Shop were infused with the romance of building a life together.

I lost myself to the fever of falling in love and spent entire days not thinking about my mother.

One day in June, I picked up the phone to the sound of my sister-in-law's voice. *Grace, your mom . . .*

I didn't want wake from my reverie. I wished that I could mute her, just this once, and not hear the end of the sentence.

It was probably close to 11:00 p.m. that night when a state trooper pulled me over on I-95. I rolled down the driver's-side window as I heard his heavy boots clomping up to the car.

"Do you know how fast you were going?" he asked.

I began to tremble and could see my hands shaking against the steering wheel.

"You were doing almost ninety."

"My mom's in the hospital," I said, choking on tears. The officer's face softened.

"Where?"

"New Jersey," I said. We were somewhere in Connecticut.

"Be careful, or you'll end up in the hospital too."

I nodded and croaked out the words "thank you" as the officer walked away.

Six months after she started taking Haldol/Mellaril, my mother tried to kill herself. Suicidality was another common side effect of antipsychotic drugs, but it wasn't until the second suicide attempt in July that I would wonder if the drug treatment itself might have made her do it.

When she regained consciousness that first time, I grabbed her hand and begged her not to die, made promises I'd struggle to keep. I said I'd go to grad school. Maybe Harvard. Get a PhD. Anything to make her happy. With her hand in mine, I started down the path of finding things I didn't even know I'd been looking for.

1O. CRUST GIRL

Princeton, New Jersey, 1994

"WORTHLESS." THAT WAS THE WORD my mother used in the hospital, after she swallowed four bottles of antipsychotic drugs and was delirious from the chemical residue.

"Why, Mama? Why would you do something like this?"

She giggled and lolled her head from side to side against the pillow, reached her hand out and tweaked my nose as if I were a little girl and not a young woman starting my adult life. "Grace has a cute ko. Not big American nose like Abeoji." She then lapsed into a mixture of Korean and gibberish before answering my question in clear, sober English: "Because I feel worthless."

That word, "worthless," insinuated its way into my psyche and took up residence there like a disease. I spent the next fifteen years driven to find out where my mother's feelings of worthlessness came from, to get to know that place intimately, and to somehow rid myself of the malady.

After my mother died I spent agonizing years puzzling over the cause of death, the possibility—no matter how remote—that she might have taken her own life. Just as painful was the knowledge that I'd never find out the truth.

When my anguish finally subsided, I started baking pies—
twenty to thirty a week in a commercial kitchen. Until then I
could count on one hand the number of pie shells I had made
from scratch. The first one I made at age five, when my mother
reluctantly let me use her dough scraps to bake a baby pie. It was
the first and only time I was ever allowed to cook as a child, lest
I derail my path toward academia.

For a time, I did drift away from that path. It was when I
became "ABD" ("all but dissertation") in my doctoral program, a
time when many students stray, and sometimes never come back.
I put my studies on hold after taking the second of my three PhD
qualifying exams, also known as "the orals": two hours of speaking fluently on three different literatures.

Public speaking had always been a weakness of mine, one
of my biggest fears, and leading up to the exam I spent months
buried in jargon-filled prose and self-doubt. When I passed the
exam, Cesar, always my cheerleader in those days, gifted me with
the shiny red KitchenAid stand mixer I had been saving up to buy
with my $236 weekly income as an adjunct instructor at Brook-
lyn College. The mixer revolutionized my life. Gone were the
days of hand-mixed doughs, half-beaten meringues, and whipped
cream in a can. I started making cakes like never before, with
perfectly structured crumbs and tight fluffy icings.

The mixer was a gateway. Three months later, I enrolled in a
professional pastry program. I dreaded telling my mother, but
she was living with Cesar and me in our co-op apartment in
Queens at the time, so I couldn't exactly hide it. When I finally
worked up the courage to tell her, she crossed her arms and
turned her back to me. "I think someone is brainwashing you,"
she said. Although I assured her that I would finish my PhD, she
loathed the idea that I had temporarily exchanged a life of letters
with late nights in an industrial kitchen, up to my elbows in flour.

It was in pastry school that I baked four more pies from scratch. None of them came out perfect, but because we worked in pairs, the success or failure of the pies was not mine alone. I tried to explain this to my mother when she tasted one of them and said, "The filling is not bad, but that crust needs to be more flaky. It is not flaky." Overall I did well in culinary school, but pie was neither my strength nor my passion, and when it was over I went back to using frozen pie shells because I doubted that I could produce anything better. I just kept them on hand for whenever the occasion might arise.

Once, when I was invited to cook a three-course meal for a fundraising party, I pulled those crusts out of the freezer to fill with frangipane and fresh raspberries. I passed the crust off as my own, too embarrassed to admit I hadn't made it myself when one of the diners complimented me on it. If my mother had been there, she would have seen me as lazy, just as she had when she discovered the grease stains on the sides of my cookware.

"You need to clean your pots, Grace, or else people will think you don't have ambition."

"No, Mom. It has nothing to do with ambition," I said then, and would repeat again and again during the imagined conversations with my dead mother about my failure to execute a pie from scratch.

That's not it. I'm just a cake person.

Cake had never been a part of my mother's baking repertoire. Every cake that entered my childhood home had been from Safeway—butterless and cloying.

The world of gourmet cakes was uncharted culinary territory for me and became something I wanted to master. Cake was a delight, something whimsical, and at the same time, serious business. I continued to study cakes, like the good student my mother raised me to be. Even after culinary school ended, I took specialized workshops in icing and decoration. I practiced until I achieved the silkiest buttercream, the richest ganache, the most delicate piping around the borders. I baked until I earned a reputation for making the best cakes my friends and associates had ever tasted. *You see, Mom. I do have ambition.*

Apple Pie

MY MOTHER USED TO bake dozens of pies each month, hundreds of pies each year, her final pie count landing in the thousands. This proliferation of pie must have started with a taste somewhere of tender crust and sweet-tart filling, both completely foreign to her Korean palate. That first taste was probably on a US military base in Korea, where the foods were all-American: hamburgers, hot dogs, and apple pie.

There was a time when my mother believed that she'd be able to melt into the homogeneity of my father's hometown, and to that end, she embarked on a project of assimilation through the mastery of American cooking. Maybe she just got tired of the relentless interrogations from our neighbors. "Do they have this in your country?" "Is it true that they eat dogs in your culture?" Maybe she really believed that her role as wife and mother was to cook the things that were familiar to my father or to feed my brother and me things that would not mark us as foreigners. Whatever the reason, American cooking became something she took on with messianic zeal. Of course, she did not abandon Korean food in favor of American food but learned to eat some things in secrecy instead.

"If American people see us eating this, they will be scared," my mother said to me once as we chewed our way through a whole dried-roasted squid, clusters of tentacled legs dangling from our mouths. We laughed about it at the time, but decades later when I was on the tenure track, a student knocked on my office door and caught me eating dried squid legs. A rush of blood lit up my cheeks as I remembered her words. *If American people see us eating this . . .*

She learned to make a distinction between her private eating and her public performance as a cook and eater. The performance featured her as a slightly off American housewife who tested new recipes from ladies' magazines and found mentorship from the octogenarian spinsters who lived across the street. This was before the days of the "USO Bride School" in Korea, a training program for the Korean girlfriends and fiancées of American servicemen that taught them how to be good wives—first and foremost through lessons in American cookery. My mother's cooking training was informal, and her immersion in small-town America left little room for error.

But she did make mistakes. Ovens, for example, are not typically part of a Korean kitchen, and certainly for my mother's generation, they were completely foreign. So the first time she attempted baking, her chocolate chip cookies were burnt on the bottom and rock-hard.

"They're a little dense," my father said after gnawing on a cookie with his molars.

"What's so dense?" she replied, unfamiliar with a cookie's texture. Her answer to my father's criticism was ultimately to keep trying until she produced a proper batch. With cookies under her belt, she moved on to something more challenging, and more quintessentially American: apple pie.

Baking, for my mother, was a way to become American. Baking was a way to forget.

Blackberry Pie

THERE WERE THINGS that complicated my mother's persona as our hometown's immigrant Betty Crocker, not the least of which was the fact that she was not content with domesticity. Before she went mad, the hours she spent working outside the house in a given day exceeded the time she spent at home, and all the effort she poured into cooking and cleaning—scrubbing those grease stains off the sides of her pots—was fueled by ambition. As a woman with barely more than a middle school education, success was a tenuous thing that she could not measure by conventional means. Not by degrees completed or money earned, only by the number of superlatives her work elicited. During her years as a forager, the phenomenal quantity of wild blackberries she picked, sold, froze, jammed, and baked evoked many exclamations peppered with words like "most" and "best." "Those are the most berries I've ever seen in one place!" "You have the best prices anywhere!"

I didn't realize what a steal her blackberries were until she was living with me in Queens, and I bought her a half-pint of cultivated blackberries at the Union Square Greenmarket. They were large and plump, and a half-pint sold for four dollars. I began to calculate in my head how much more expensive these were than the wild blackberries she used to sell. Four of these in a quart, four quarts in a gallon. Sixteen times four equals sixty-four dollars a gallon. Hers were thirteen dollars a gallon fifteen years ago. I had no idea how to calculate the rate of inflation, but I knew for sure that wild blackberries were far superior to cultivated ones. There was really no comparison. I selected the juiciest-looking basket, handed four singles to the cashier, and hoped that my mother wouldn't ask me how much they cost. But when I got home and presented her with the little plastic clamshell, she just took one look at them and made the moaning sound she always made when she was disappointed. "Uuungh. The seeds are too big. Those blackberries are no good."

In the days immediately following my mother's death, I became awash in memories of her better days, long before she uttered those words, *I feel worthless*. I asked all the people who had once known her what they remembered most about her. Unequivocally, it was the blackberry pie.

It seemed as if her favorite pastime, aside from picking blackberries, was baking blackberry pies. It was, perhaps, not so much a pastime as it was a compulsion, a need to produce something with the sweat of her own labor that she could call her own, that she could choose to give away and not have taken from her. So many Sunday afternoons she spent with her sleeves rolled up and her arms immersed in giant bowls of flour and shortening, her fingers working the fat and flour together into little pearls of dough. By the end of the day, there would be a dozen hot blackberry pies cooling on the counter, waiting for someone to break open their shells.

In retrospect, I see that the blackberries were the real stars of her pies—"small wild blackberries," as my mother distinguished them from other blackberries. The ratio of crust to blackberries was always perfectly balanced, but to my immature palate, the filling was just a condiment for the crust, one that I considered optional. Sometimes I would ask if I could have just the crimped edges, and once she gave me permission to eat the entire outer crust, I took the liberty of helping myself the next time. One day, lured by the scent of caramelized blackberry juice bubbling against the flaky brown pastry, I went into the kitchen and ate the crusts of four or five fresh pies that were on the counter. My mother was somewhere else, maybe stealing a moment to nap or tending to her roses in the backyard. Later, when she discovered what I had done, she shrieked: "Graaaace! You ruined my pies! I was gonna give them away and now they're so ugly! All that work for nothing!" Despite her initial rage, she found a moment of humor in it, and dubbed me "Crust Girl."

When my brother's wife told me the big family secret, it was to explain my mother's mental illness, as if her past were an answer and not, in itself, a question.

The confluence of developments that year flipped a switch that could never be turned off. I devoured any film, novel, scholarly book, or article that engaged the theme of sex work, particularly if it was set in Asia or involved a military or an interracial romance, though much of what I consumed left me feeling queasy because of the absence of a big picture, the frame always drawing the eye toward the individual. I also became hyperattuned to the way in which people of all genders casually and frequently used the words "whore" and "slut" as pejoratives, the way in which these insults were pervasive in every aspect of popular culture. This would be the beginning of a wondering: How much had my mother's sense of worth been bound up in that stigma? The excess of shame reducing her to nothing.

I understood then why my education had been so important to her. It wasn't only so that she could live out her vicarious dream of becoming a scholar but also to make sure that I would never have to face the same choices she had. "Work with your mind, not your body!" she would urge whenever I expressed an interest in physical labor, like the first time I took a job in a restaurant kitchen. As much as I liked school, my decision to spend seven years in graduate school was largely motivated by that fleeting moment, perhaps less than two seconds, during which I heard the words *Your mother used to be a prostitute.*

By 1998 I enrolled at the CUNY Graduate Center, further committing myself to find out what could have shattered my mother's spirit to the point that she'd feel worthless. My project was to eke out every possible connection between those two sets of words: *Your mother used to be a prostitute* and *I feel worthless.*

I studied the feminist sex wars, which put commercial sex at the center of the debate. At first I was more on the side of the radical feminists, thinking that prostitution and pornography were inherently oppressive, even though I had a far more laid-back view of noncommercial sex. After a fellow student, a sex worker herself, introduced me to a group of sex worker activists, my perspective would start to inch toward that of sex radicals. Sex work was a choice, and should remain so, they said. It was an act of agency, empowering even. The things that needed to change about the sex industry were the working conditions and the lack of respect. I was sympathetic to these points of view and agreed that women could find power in their sexuality, that using it for profit or livelihood should be legitimated. But then I began to notice that the most prominent voices celebrating their choice to be sex workers belonged to white, often highly educated women. Of course the choice is less fraught if you have an advanced degree. What about the women who had been silenced because of their choices?

Again and again, I'd return to the words of Adul de Leon, a sex worker activist from the Philippines: "[American feminists] spend all their time arguing about whether or not prostitution can be a free choice. We women from Third World countries got really bored with their fighting. Our issues around prostitution are different."[1] Having the "right to choose not to be a prostitute" was more urgent.[2]

Ironically, years after publishing my first book, I'd receive an email criticizing me for portraying Korean camptown women as having been prostitutes "by choice." The person had come to this conclusion because I hadn't simply portrayed them as "forced." In my reply, I countered that I would never use that term—"by choice"—because the idea of choice was far too troubled in the context I was writing about. When sex work is sponsored by the state to service a foreign military (the most powerful military in the world), when the relationship between the two countries is profoundly unequal, then the working conditions are already rooted in a place of coercion. It was true that many of the women who were sex workers for the US military were not tricked or trafficked, but neither did they have other good options.

I had written that, despite how limited one's choices are, there is always possibility for resistance. Maybe some of the women had embraced their roles as "bad girls"—a "fuck you" to patriarchal expectations of wifedom and motherhood—or maybe some had seized an opportunity to get closer to America. Working in the camptowns was the most likely path there for young Korean women in the 1960s. Even sex work for sheer survival is a way of defying a power structure that might otherwise leave you for dead. Survival is an act of resistance, but performing an act of resistance within an imperialistic order is not the same thing as "being a prostitute by choice." *Forced or free* is a false dichotomy.

While I had already spent years thinking about my mother's situation, the work of systematically breaking it down began in my first-year sociological methods class, in which we were asked to write weekly research questions. I never explicitly mentioned her in the assignments, but she was present in the subtext of everything I wrote.

What structures and systems and geopolitical events created a social context in which she dared to transgress her societal norms to enter the sex industry? Once there, what small actions and gestures slowly eroded her self-esteem? What large-scale transactions crushed her psyche? Once out, did the same things happen all over again, just in a different time and place?

The answers to these questions were not at all obvious.

Later, after I had spent a decade on my investigation, my sister-in-law would say that she had only told me because I "ought to know." Because she was speaking "woman to woman." Somehow she expected me never to do anything with those words except to lock up the secret myself and never speak of it again. When I had made it my life's work to openly interrogate the words that had haunted me, when I had written hundreds of pages about them, my sister-in-law revised the storyline: "Your mother was a cocktail waitress. Nothing else."

But it doesn't matter. It doesn't matter whether she was a cocktail waitress or a prostitute or something in between, because those words, when they were first spoken, changed me. *Your mother used to be a prostitute.* That bit of new information was so huge that it erased my old memories. It made me forget all those years when she was my mama, the woman who called me Crust Girl and was famous for her blackberry pies.

Mincemeat Pie

AFTER MY MOTHER'S first suicide attempt, she moved back in with my father. According to my sister-in-law, it was my brother and father's idea, and my mother acquiesced. It was a disastrous plan. Neither of my parents was capable of taking care of the other, and although I knew this to be the case because I had witnessed their dysfunction together, my opinion didn't matter. Why should it have, when I was the youngest, the daughter, and in no position to provide my mother a home?

The rationale for my mother returning to my father was that he would somehow prevent her from trying to kill herself again, but she tried again just a few weeks later.

She had asked him to buy her a bottle of wine. Although he thought it a strange request because she didn't drink, he did it anyway. She then went upstairs to the attic and hid in the crawl space, in the deepest corner where she stored things she would never use again: bolts of fabric, kimchi jars, foraging gear, all the remnants of her old life. Securely hidden away where no one would even think to look, she washed her pills down with a glass of the wine and waited to die. (She later admitted that she drank the wine only because the warning label on her medication told her not to mix it with alcohol.) The police came to the house the next day to investigate my mother's disappearance, but found no trace of her, even when they checked the attic. But just as they started back down the attic stairs, my mother—unconscious and half-alive—let out a long moan. The police turned around and found her just in time.

After her failure to carry out the suicide the first two times, she swore she would "never try *that* again." There was disgust and conviction in her voice when she said it. "No, I am *never* gonna try *that* again."

It was less a promise to herself to survive than it was an attempt to avoid another failure, to shield herself from further humiliation. Regardless, it was somewhat reassuring.

Our last Christmas together as a family took place in 1997, by which time my parents were still living together but no longer speaking. We flew to my brother's house in North Carolina, me from New York and my parents from Seattle. For six hours they sat next to each other on the plane in silence. I wonder if the other passengers thought that my parents were strangers. My mother had become so good at tuning my father out, the way she tuned out other kinds of background noise so that she could listen to her voices, that she was able to sit next to him and show not even a glimmer of recognition.

When they arrived at my brother's place, my father took his things to the guest room while my mother unpacked a mincemeat pie from her bag and turned on the oven. I was happy to learn that my mother could still bake for special occasions. My brother and I sat down at the kitchen table, sinking our forks into the fragrant pie, but as soon as he took a bite, he hesitated.

"Did you put meat in this?" he asked.

"What's the matter?" my mother said, puzzled by his question. "It's good."

Apparently he hadn't taken the name of the pie literally, nor had he been aware of the culinary history of mincemeat pie, which was traditionally made with a mix of meat and fruit, before it gave way to more common fruit-only versions. It wasn't my favorite, but I ate it anyway. It didn't stand up to her blackberry pie, but it tasted of Christmas with its spices and winter fruits. The bits of meat took the edge off the sweetness of the raisins. Perhaps my father, who had always been a fan of fruit and meat together, would have enjoyed the pie, but he didn't sit at the table with us because he was avoiding my mother.

I had warned my sister-in-law that having both my parents there for the holiday was a terrible idea, but she insisted, saying that it would have been cruel to invite one parent without the other. My father slept in the guest room while my mother slept in the living room, neither of them making any effort to thaw the mountain of ice that had built up between them. The day after my parents' arrival, my father began complaining of constipation and asked me to buy him an enema at the drugstore. "Make sure it's Fleet," he said. "F-L-E-E-T." I did so dutifully, and when I handed him the enema, he took off his pants and lay down on the living room floor where my three-year-old niece was watching a *Madeline* cartoon.

"Dad? What are you doing?" I said below my breath. "Do that in the bathroom."

"There's not enough room for me to lie down in the bathroom."

"But what if you don't make it to the toilet in time?"

"Oh, balls! I'll make it. I've done this a hundred times."

This is not my responsibility, I thought as I walked away, but no sooner did I enter the next room before I heard my father shouting, "Grace! I didn't make it!" The stench of his feces, trailing behind him as he ran to the bathroom, triggered my gag reflex and I ran outside to heave over the side of the porch. My mother and brother were outside enjoying the warm southern winter when I ran out.

"What's wrong?" they asked in unison.

"Dad . . . just shit . . . all over your house," I said to my brother in between gasps of air.

My mother waved her hand in the air. "Oh, that. He's doing it all the time at home and leaving for me to clean up."

The incident sabotaged our Christmas Eve dinner preparations. My mother's mincemeat pie sat on the counter with two slices taken out of it, only one of them eaten.

That mincemeat pie was the last my mother ever baked. For the next eleven years, the remainder of her life, she never turned on the oven again. I don't know if it was the Christmas gone wrong, the lack of enthusiasm for her mincemeat, or the realization that no matter how many pies she baked, no matter how good they were, she could not resurrect the sense of accomplishment that she had once garnered from her pies. Baking had turned into a worthless pursuit.

From that point forward, I began to bake in earnest, as if to salvage my mother's crumbling legacy. Over the years, I put together little pieces that helped me come a bit closer to the things that fed her sense of worthlessness. She must have been immersed in messages of how little value her life had—when she was no longer regarded as a person, but as a thing. These messages came from the people around her, from Korean society, maybe even from her own family. She escaped Korea only to find that American society devalued her, too—*this gray country, this violent foster home . . . land where they stuff our throats with soil & accuse us of gluttony when we learn to swallow it.*[3]

PART IV

The world begins at a kitchen table. No matter what,
    we must eat to live.

The gifts of the world are brought and prepared,
    set on the table. So it has been since creation, and
    it will go on

. . . .

Our dreams drink coffee with us as they put their arms
    around our children. They laugh with us at our
    poor falling down selves as we put ourselves back
    together once again at the table.

This table has been a house in the rain, an
    umbrella in the sun.

Wars have begun and ended at this table. It is a place
    to hide in the shadow of terror. A place to celebrate
    the terrible victory.

We have given birth on this table, and have prepared
    our parents for burial here.

At this table we sing with joy, with sorrow. We pray of
    suffering and remorse. We give thanks.

Perhaps the world will end at the kitchen table,
    while we are laughing and crying, eating of the last
    sweet bite.

—JOY HARJO, "Perhaps the World Ends Here"

11. ONE TIME, NO LOVE

Chehalis, Washington, 1980

MY MOTHER PICKS UP a sizzling-hot mushroom with her fingers and pops it into her mouth. The scalding temperature never seems to dull her taste buds. She reaches toward the ledge of the stove, past my grandmother Grace's pig-shaped ceramic saltshaker, and grabs the big glass one instead. She adjusts the seasoning and tastes another mushroom before moving the pan off the glowing electric coil, pulling broiled sirloins out of the oven, and fluffing the steamed white rice with a wooden paddle. Another meal is cooked and about to be served, signaling the passage of time with surgical precision. The clock strikes six, and her voice booms through our one-story house. "Dinner ready!" She bellows it the same way she summons our cats to come home after a night of prowling through the wilderness, as if we are miles away and not in the next room.

My father, brother, and I scurry in to gather at the white rectangular table affixed to the wall in the corner of the kitchen. Only two sides of the table are open, so we are unable to sit facing each other. My seat is on the end closest to the stove; my father's is on the opposite end beneath the wall phone, which is mustard yellow to match the appliances; and my mother's is in the middle. My brother sits on the short side of the table, and together we form an L.

She stands at the stove, plating steaks onto white Corning-Ware dishes, while the rest of us sit down in squat oak chairs. "One time, no love," she says as she piles a giant mound of rice and mushrooms next to the meat. In other words: *If I only give you one serving, I am not giving you enough love.* It is her mealtime mantra, her way of foreclosing anyone's protest about the double portion. The unspoken rule is that we reciprocate by eating. I look at my plate and wonder how I can possibly eat that much, but I always manage to finish it.

There's only dinner conversation during the first few minutes, when my father asks what my brother and I did at school that day and then tells my mother that the food tastes good. Instead of saying thank you, she says, "I know." For the rest of dinner we are so busy eating that we hardly talk. Instead we eat to the sounds of forks and knives clinking and the buzzing of the long fluorescent light bulb that's mounted above the table. When we're almost done, my mother breaks the silence by getting up to serve more rice and mushrooms. "Let's eat it *all* because leftovers are no good." If anyone refuses, she smiles and gives her stock response, "One time, no love."

The scene will repeat the next night, except that she'll cook bibimbap with seasoned soybean sprouts and gosari, and the night after that, it will be spaghetti and meatballs with a salad, and the night after that, Cornish hens and roasted root vegetables. Sometimes my father's chair will be vacant, if he's out to sea, and by the time I turn eleven, my brother will be away at college. Even when it's just my mother and me having dinner at our white Formica table with its two sides attached to the wall, we'll sit side-by-side in our usual places, she'll call "Dinner ready!" when I'm standing ten feet away, and urge me to eat more and more.

When I was young and stuffing myself full of my mother's food, I never once gave a thought to the meaning of our mealtime rituals or the possibility that cooking family dinners was anything more than a maternal obligation. Maybe only my father fully appreciated what my mother did. He knew that it was a symbolic act of how far she had come—how far they both had come.

Although his life as a young man revolved around producing food, he never spoke of moments from his past when someone lovingly prepared food for him. Whenever he talked about his early memories of food, they were about hardship. "I would get a whipping if I turned my nose up at the food. We had to eat whatever was on the dinner plate!"

Once he told me a story of a destitute family whose plight captured the hardships of the Depression. "They were so desperate . . ." His voice became strained, but he forced out the rest of the sentence. "They had to eat their own dog." And with these final words came a gush of tears. After all those years, it still pained him to remember that kind of hunger, and I would always wonder if the family in the story had been his own.

When he sailed to Korea and met my mother, he found a new horizon. Her food was the link to the places my father had traveled, a magic wand that allowed him to be both here and there at the same time, savoring the exotic from the comfort of his home. She fed him the spicy, pungent flavors of Korea alongside his American favorites. When he wanted to remember his trips to Goa, he gave my mother a bag of spices and a recipe. She whipped up a fragrant chicken curry with coconut and cashews, which quickly became part of her growing repertoire. She experimented with new recipes, cooked comfort food on weekends, made sumptuous feasts on holidays. She always kept the refrigerators full. Perhaps her cooking made my father feel like a wealthy man.

For my mother, too, eating this way represented a world of possibility. Feeding others allowed her to transcend her origins. It was a testament to her survival and her hope for the future.

The moments when I most experienced my mother's food as love were during my first few visits home from college, after months of her fretting over whether I'd been nourished well enough by the "American college people." The outpouring of affection would begin the moment I spotted both of my parents waiting for me at Sea–Tac Airport. Her first greeting, before saying hello or giving me a hug, before asking me how my flight was or how I was doing in school, was to reach her hand out and present me with a peeled orange. "Ja. Eat. I made chaltteok," she said, raising the bag of sweet rice cakes in her other hand. "You can eat that in the car."

But soon—maybe after the third or fourth trip—there was no peeled fruit, no mother, to greet me at the airport.

"Where's Mom?" I asked my father the first time she was absent.

He let out a long, exasperated sigh. "Beats me! Hell if I know why your mother does anything anymore."

We arrived home, and I saw the tree stump in the front yard, the remains of the old oak my mother had somehow managed to cut down a few months earlier. I remember my father complaining to me about it on the phone: *She chopped down all the trees! What the hell was she thinking?*

Along the walkway leading up to our front door, the shrubbery was slightly overgrown and weeds were popping up in the soil. I walked into the house, through the dining room, and into the living room at the back of the house to find her on the beige sectional. She said hello but made no effort to get up, so I hugged her while she was still sitting.

I saw that the pantry had withered down to a few dusty jars of jam and the refrigerator was almost empty. There was virtually no food in the house.

My mother had been subsisting on the simplest fare of rice and kimchi and perhaps one other side dish of spinach in oyster sauce or green chili peppers stewed in doenjang. "Doenjang is made of soybeans. That's protein, you see," she said when I told her I was worried she'd become malnourished. Once in a while she went out to the Burger King and treated herself to a Double Whopper with cheese, but she had stopped cooking for my father. He got by on a combination of spaghetti, canned soup, steamed vegetables, and Meals on Wheels, where he was both a driver and a recipient of whatever meals they had left at the end of the day.

Because neither of my parents had been eating well, I went to Safeway and loaded up on groceries, including a pork roast and potatoes that I had planned to bake that night. I hadn't yet learned how to cook, but I had seen my mother do it enough times to know how to season the meat and heat the oven. And salad, I could make: chop some iceberg lettuce, tomatoes, and cucumbers, and cover with bottled salad dressing. My parents and I then sat side by side at the kitchen table, eating the meal that I made.

"Tastes good," my father said about the pork.

"Sorry I overcooked it," I said.

While my father and I exchanged only a few words during the meal, my mother was silent the whole time, her eyes vacant. My desire to hear her voice amplified the sounds of the fluorescent light buzzing and the three of us chewing and swallowing and washing down the dry meat with gulps of water. The silent meal reminded me of my childhood dinners, but this time, it wasn't bookended by my mother's joyful refrain of "One time, no love." The absence of her words made me aware of how much she had used cooking as a form of communication, and now her silence made her seem like an apparition. Although I could see that she was there, I could hear her eating, I could even smell the faded lilac scent of the White Shoulders perfume that clung to her clothes, it still felt like she was in some other world beyond my reach. It had finally registered on a visceral level that the mother I once had was gone. *One time, no love.* Part of me wanted to say it, but I hadn't earned the right to take her place as the family cook, nor did I want to. I wanted those words to be hers and only hers, and if I didn't say them, maybe she'd come back. Besides, the food hadn't turned out very well, so I just cleared the table and washed the dishes.

"Thank you, honey," my father said as my mother returned to her place on the couch. It was the first time I cooked for my parents and the first of a thousand meals I would cook for my mother.

Each time I visited them after that, I took on the responsibility of cooking while I was home, but my mother never said a word about my food. I wasn't sure if her silence was a way of discouraging my culinary interests or if her mind had become so disturbed that she was completely indifferent to food. My early attempts to cook for her were bitter reminders of her unhappiness, leaving me to wonder if things could ever change.

It was sometime after her second suicide attempt, after she had moved back to Chehalis from New Jersey, that she began seeing a therapist in Olympia, thirty miles north of Chehalis on I-5. Her therapist was Dr. Jeon, another Korean immigrant woman and the first Korean adult outside of our family that my mother had spoken to in fifteen years. "I feel I can really talk to her," my mother said with optimism in her voice. "She is not like a therapist, more like good friend to me." Her words brought tears to my eyes, and for the first time in years, I dared to imagine a radically different future.

But things changed once she started taking my father with her for couple's counseling. Being in that intimate space of the therapist's office, where he felt heard and seen again, my father began to crave the therapist's attention. He started seeing Dr. Jeon independently of my mother, and sometimes outside of the office.

My mother quit therapy, probably once she caught on to what was happening. I can't say for sure whether his relationship with Dr. Jeon was sexual, but it was personal. He saw her on a regular basis, gave her gifts of money, and made no effort to hide his attraction to her. In fact, he shamelessly bragged about their friendship and once asked me to send her my first published journal article, as if she were a stand-in for my mother, who would never be literate enough to read my writing. I recoiled at the proposition.

"No way! I don't want anything to do with her!"

"Now, now. What's all that about? She's a good person," my father said.

"Are you kidding me? She's Mom's therapist! What's the matter with you that you think this is okay? It's totally unethical of her to have a relationship with you."

More than anger or betrayal or disgust, I felt an overwhelming sense of defeat. I never brought up the affair with my mother, but I was certain that it must have destroyed her fragile trust in mental health professionals. After all those years, we would have to start over. The trajectory of her mental health once again would be always and only downward.

My sister-in-law continued to be the person in my family to take the most prominent role in my mother's situation, as the one who made things happen—the cross-country moves, the psychiatric visits—but also as the arbiter of information. It was never clear to me whether this was a self-appointed role or if my brother had asked her to be his proxy. Regardless, she was almost invariably the one who would break news to me about any new developments.

224   TASTES LIKE WAR

As I was on my way to visit my parents in late 1997, she warned me that my mother's mental health was taking another turn for the worse. This time the news was about a mouse that had been running wild around the house. "Your dad says she thinks it's a pet." I didn't know what to believe, because my father was prone to embellishment and fits of confusion, and my sister-in-law had a tendency to overemphasize some of my mother's behaviors because she thought I didn't take them seriously. The truth is that I did sometimes shrug off her alarm because I was afraid of validating the stereotype that people with schizophrenia are dangerous or erratic, afraid of my own fear.

I had forgotten about the alleged mouse until one day when I found my father trying to vacuum behind the couch.

"Dad, what are you doing?" I asked, concerned that he was overexerting himself.

"Dammit, your mother! She has a pet mouse that lives under the couch. She throws all kinds of *crap* back there for it to eat," he said, pushing the word "crap" out through clenched teeth. He half sighed, half grunted as he struggled with the furniture. I helped him move the couch and saw the droppings mixed with hollowed-out sunflower shells, breadcrumbs, and bits of dried apple peel. Oh my god, it's true, I thought. Perhaps feeding the mouse was related to a "bizarre delusion," one of the symptoms listed in the diagnostic criteria for schizophrenia, which unlike a "nonbizarre delusion," had no basis in reality. What significance did that mouse have for her? Was she like the man who believed his "kitten was retreating into an alternate universe when she went behind the refrigerator"?[1]

That night I confronted her. "So, I heard that you have a pet mouse."

"Oh yeah?" She sounded annoyed. "Did your father tell you where that mouse came from?"

"Uh, no."

"He got it for his cat to play with. It ran away and I been feeding it."

"Did you name it?" I asked, trying to discern whether she really considered it a pet.

"Well. I call it Bol-jwi. You know what that means? It means 'smart mouse.' Smart enough to get away from that cat . . . My mother used to call me Bol-jwi when I was a little girl. Aigu, dap-dap-eu-rah. I miss my mother." She smiled faintly and her gaze wandered off.

Although I had initially agreed with my sister-in-law that the mouse was a bad sign, I considered my mother's situation carefully. She was a recluse and could have used the company of a pet, so when the mouse took refuge under her couch, she chose to take care of it instead of return it to the cruel fate that my father had intended for it. Like her, this vulnerable creature was a survivor. She identified with it because my grandmother, whose death she still mourned, used to call her "mouse." It did not seem at all like a "bizarre delusion." But this was a rodent on the loose, and without a cage, it delegitimized my mother's logic and compassion in the eyes of others. A cage would have clearly drawn the line between rational and crazy, between pest and pet, but my mother hadn't been well enough for years to leave the house. Who knows if she would have caged it anyway? Maybe the presence of an uncaged animal allowed her some small measure of vicarious freedom. Perhaps more than anything, what made me see the mouse as an *improvement* in her mental health was the fact that it rekindled her desire to feed another being. If my mother still had that in her, then maybe she still had some fight left.

I thought back to our family dinners. It was a time of togetherness that both my parents enforced, yet neither of them used it as an opportunity for dialogue. The awkwardness of our seating arrangement mirrored the awkwardness of our sparse mealtime conversations. I began to see the currents running through the silence, and they were all flowing back to my mother's early life and the things she would not, could not, talk about. I wanted to assemble a coherent narrative, but how was I supposed to artic-ulate the things she couldn't say? All I had to cling to were the things she *could* say. *One time, no love.* There was something about the memory of her standing in front of our mustard-yellow stove and piling our plates with food that sparked my desire to know more. Simmering beneath the surface of my consciousness was some inchoate story about my mother that I needed to tell. Who fed her then? Who was feeding her now? If food is love, how must the experience of going hungry have deprived her heart and mind? I had seen the scarcity of her pantry, but I still didn't know enough to ask these questions. Nor did I know what it felt like to be starved of affection. How many years had it been since she had been nourished by human touch? Were the hugs from me and my brother the only times she ever got to feel the warmth of another body, a few minutes or seconds out of the year? One could ask the same questions about my father, but he remedied his need for affection by buying it from a few young women in town, sometimes bringing them into our house while my mother sat on the couch with her eyes closed, tuning out the external reality. What was it like for her to be reminded of her own past that she wanted to forget, of how she and my father had met in the same way, when he was lonely in Korea and willing to pay for a woman's touch?

My mother, too, found companionship in unorthodox places, but while my father's actions may have been distasteful by normal societal standards, they were not considered insane. My mother's companions were a feral mouse and a set of voices that only she could hear.

It went on like this—my father's company paid, my mother's hallucinated—for a year or so until he kicked her out again in August 1998.

Again, my brother would make her flight arrangements, find her another place near him in New Jersey. This time, things would be different, because there'd be no one left to want her to return to Chehalis.

I would pick up the phone on Labor Day weekend as a steel-pan band was practicing on the street below my apartment for the West Indian Day Parade in Brooklyn. On the other end, I would hear the sound of my father's labored breathing, his gruff voice. "When's your mother going out there?" he would ask, then snarl at my answer. "I hope the goddamn plane crashes."

This time, my mother would live in a three-bedroom house instead of an apartment, with a large eat-in kitchen and a sparkling new linoleum-tiled floor. The size of the house, the kitchen, were largely aspirational. I would be the only person to ever cook in it.

12. OAKIE

New York and New Jersey, 1998

MY MOTHER LANDED SAFELY in New Jersey during the second week of September and moved into her new house, a few blocks away from my brother's. It was a time of transition for me, too, as I was in the first semester of my doctoral program.

My schooling had always been something my mother thought would put distance between her past and her present, whitening the stains of her history, but the more I pursued it, the more my sense of social justice became intertwined with my family history.

In 1995 I had enrolled in a one-year master's program in education at Harvard, initially to fulfill my mother's lifelong dream to have a child at Harvard. While I found the climate there to be elitist and somewhat retrograde when it came to issues of race, I was fortunate enough to have studied with a couple of visiting professors whose radical perspectives on education pushed me further toward openly interrogating my family history. I read bell hooks's *Teaching to Transgress*, and upon graduation, moved to New York to study with her and to seek out an intellectual community. After two years of taking graduate classes at CUNY as a nonmatriculated student, I enrolled in the Graduate Center's PhD program in sociology with the explicit intent of studying my mother's past as a sex worker for the US military. I had even said so in my admissions application. It was a peculiar coincidence that she would move back to New Jersey at the same time that I was starting my program, becoming the flesh-and-blood shadow to my academic life.

At first, I didn't feel compelled to visit her more than once a month. The nearly three-hour commute took a lot out of me considering the demands of my first year in the doctoral program. I was also working full-time as a Head Start director at a community center in Cypress Hills, Brooklyn. Cesar was touring with an off-Broadway show that year, and the occasional weekend he came home I spent with him.

Door-to-door, the trip from my apartment in Brooklyn to her house in Princeton took forty minutes on the subway, one and a half hours on New Jersey Transit, and forty minutes walking from the train station—all while carrying a backpack full of schoolwork and a bag of groceries in each hand. She would always comment on how many books I brought with me, how thick they were, how small the print. "Hwaaa, that is a lot of reading. I could never in my life read that much."

It was between the first and second visit to my mother's new house that my father died.

On Friday, October 2, 1998, I went to work and had just started an in-service training for the teachers at my Head Start program. I had gotten a call earlier that morning that two sisters who were teachers in my program had just lost their father to a heart attack. "I have sad news," I told the other teachers. "Constance and Adriene won't be joining us today because their father died." I choked on the words because the voice in my head said *my* instead of *their*. I had just heard the sound of my own voice speaking two things at the same time. *Their (my) father died.*

Two nights earlier I had a dream that he was lying in a hospital bed, glowing. The body wasn't his though; it belonged to an old college girlfriend who had died of Hodgkin's that summer. I was sitting by his side in a translucent metal chair that looked like silver jelly. There were no lights in the room, but the white bedsheets and the aura around him were so brilliant that they illuminated everything, and I could see that the room had no walls or floor or ceiling. Just beyond us was pitch black. We were floating in space, holding hands. The light emanating from my ex-girlfriend's body was a radio, sending me my father's thoughts: *Forgive me for being cruel to you.* The words came to me as the sound of a meditation bell.

The feelings from the dream stayed with me that day and the next, and were still on my mind when I choked up on the words, "Their (my) father died."

About two hours into my workshop, I was interrupted by an urgent phone call. I ran downstairs to my basement office and picked up the phone to hear my sister-in-law's voice. "I'm sorry, Grace. Your dad died. He went peacefully in his sleep . . . Wednesday night—" but just then, the J train rumbled by on the elevated tracks above my office building, drowning out the rest of her words.

"Okay. Thank you for telling me," I said, and hung up the phone. I stood there, unable to cry, unable to feel much of anything, let alone grief. I just felt mildly stunned.

I returned to the room of teachers and said, "The rest of the workshop is canceled. My father died." Gasps and murmurs rippled through the room. *You too?* How uncanny that two of our fathers could die on the same day. But in fact, my father had not died that day, but on September 30, in the middle of the night when I was dreaming about him.

Outside, Fulton Street was a cacophony of merengue blaring from car stereos, Spanish chatter of passersby, and the J train rolling over the tracks above, but the sounds were muffled, as if I were hearing them from under water.

Back in my dim two-room apartment on Eastern Parkway, I sat on the futon and stared out my second-story window at the building superintendent throwing trash into the dumpster, and wondered what to do next. I had grown so accustomed to my father's absences from my life that the finality of this one wouldn't fully register for months to come. Because his death had been drawn out over decades of heart disease and hospitals and constant low-grade misery, decades of him talking about and planning for his own demise. "This is for when I expire," he used to say. Because his mortality had loomed over me my whole life. I had grown numb to the idea of him dying, and perhaps the numbness was also borne out of our years of conflict and estrangement, his neglect of my mother, and my growing consciousness about social injustice and the way he symbolized the power that my mother didn't have. With all of that, what was my grieving supposed to look like?

I think it was the following weekend that I went to visit my mother again, my first time speaking to her since my father's death. In a rare display of maternal warmth that I hadn't felt for years, she greeted me by reaching her arms out to hold me, to soothe me for having lost my father. "Sesang-eh, sesang-eh." *What in the world?* I wish I could have accepted her affection, but instead, I pushed her arms away because I still wasn't ready to mourn him.

It would be two years before I learned what horrible misunderstanding had transpired in that split second, that the voices had told my mother that I thought she was "dirty."

Although I had known about the voices since I was in high school, I first heard that my mother had named them Oakie from my sister-in-law. They were ethereal beings spawned by the trees on our property in Chehalis, whose lineage began with the ivy-covered oak in the front yard. I wondered if this was the reason my mother had cut the trees down. I don't know if she was

trying to free herself from the voices or free the voices from
the trees. Regardless, chopping them down didn't make the
voices go away. Over time, I would learn that they talked to her
during every waking minute, guiding all of her decisions. Some
of them took the form of beeping electronic sounds and others
barked like dogs. Although my sister-in-law always referred to
the voices as "the Oakies," my mother called them "Oakie" singular—preferred pronoun, "they." They were a multiplicity, the
many parts that made up a whole, the source of both torment and
comfort.

Each time I spent the weekend with her in New Jersey, I cooked
a big dinner, enough for a generous portion of leftovers, but she
began to complain bitterly about it. *Cooking is a waste of time. I get
by just fine on what I have.* But what she had was a paltry selection
of five items: a bag of rice, two cases of Top Ramen, a can of
Planters mixed nuts, a jar of kimchi, and a pitcher of apple juice
that she mixed from frozen concentrate. The more I tried to talk
her into eating other things, the more stubborn she became, and
I wondered if she sometimes threw away the food I left for her.

Toward the end of my first year of grad school at CUNY, my
sister-in-law would call to say that ramen was the only thing my
mother had eaten for weeks, and that I needed to visit more
often. I was initially frustrated. Did she understand that cooking
for my mother was already so fraught? That it was challenging for
me to travel there and shop for groceries without a car? If they
had expected me to do this regularly, why couldn't my mother
live closer to me? And yet, I relented out of guilt. I gradually
increased the frequency of my visits and quit my full-time job
at the community center, until I was going to New Jersey every
weekend.

Something must have happened behind the scenes, my brother
telling my mother that she had to accept my cooking, his voice

overpowering the others. Or maybe it was Oakie that talked some sense into her: *You can't let that food go to waste.*

It was on the night I cooked chicken paprikash that I first asked her about Oakie. I had been working my way through the recipes in a *Bon Appétit* international cookbook, each meal a new culinary experience for her, and often for me too.

"Pah-pree-kash. Pah-pree-kash. What a funny name," she said, taking delight in both the sound and the taste of it.

"It's a Hungarian dish," I said.

"What is this? You gonna open up a restaurant named after me? Koonja's Kitchen." She laughed, and the smile remained for the next few bites. It pleased me immensely that she seemed to be enjoying our culinary excursions around the globe, and that despite my being the cook, she still thought of the kitchen as hers.

After dinner, I put on an Ozomatli CD. It was a Latin band from Los Angeles that Cesar and I had just discovered and had been listening to incessantly. "Let's dance!" I said, on a whim. "I'll teach you how to salsa!" I expected her to protest, but she got up and grabbed my hands as I showed her the steps. We moved exuberantly to conga beats and brass, doing spins on the linoleum floor.

"One more time, Ma?" I asked when the song was over.

"No, I better not." Suddenly, she looked tense, and I wondered if she regretted dancing, if I had disrupted the rhythms of her "work," as she called the act of listening to her voices. She had once told me that Oakie forbade her from moving too much. *If I even lift my finger the wrong way, bad things will happen*, she once told me.

We sat back down at the kitchen table and listened to the rest of the album, a mixture of hip hop, pop, and Latin folk. There was a brief pause after the end of the last song, then a child's voice said, "Ozomatli is in the house." My mother jumped at the sound of it. "Omo! That voice scared me! I thought it was real." There was fear in her eyes, and she had a hard time shaking it. I was frightened, too, by whatever disturbance the music and dancing might have unleashed, but I was also curious. She was so clear in distinguishing the voice on the record from the ones in her head. What did it mean for her to hear a voice that was "real"? Could a voice be real without belonging to an embodied person? Was Oakie real?

"Mom, do you still hear Oakie?" I knew that she did, but it was the most innocuous question I could think to ask.

"Yeah. Sometimes."

"Are they talking to you right now?"

"Well, actually, they are always talking to me."

"I want them to go away," I said, not knowing if saying so would offend her or Oakie.

"Me too. I wish they would just leave our family alone!" Her face flushed, and her eyes welled with tears.

I wondered what exactly she meant, how the rest of the family was involved, but she was already so agitated that I didn't ask. As much as I wanted to know every detail about my mother's experience, I was always careful to tread lightly.

After I finished my doctoral coursework, I began reading books on hearing voices, sometimes as part of my dissertation research. According to Leudar and Thomas's work on the cultural meanings ascribed to verbal hallucinations, contemporary psychiatry views these voices as "errors in perception": *in some versions of this episteme, the experiences reflect no more than a confusion about what is real and what is imaginary, and therefore are a dangerous source of psychotic delusions.*[1] But in fact, *voice hearers do not mistake hallucinatory voices for other people speaking*; they use the same methods of reality-testing that nonvoice hearers do.[2] Contrary to popular belief, the voices in Leudar and Thomas's study did not typically "make" their hearers do things against their will, but rather influenced decisions in the same way that the ordinary inner dialogue of a "normal" person does.

My sister-in-law recommended that I read a memoir about a man who heard voices coming out of the objects in his day-to-day environment. The lion statues in front of the New York Public Library would hurl expletives and insults at him each time he walked by, pulling him down into his deepest traumas. What I remember most about that book was that he also talked about living with the stereotype that schizophrenics are violent, when the truth of the matter is that the vast majority of schizophrenics are not violent, that the vast majority of violent crimes are committed by people without schizophrenia. People who hear voices are far more likely to be victims of violence than perpetrators of it.

While it is a common experience of voice hearers to be harassed with violent imagery by their voices, it is not universal. Cross-cultural research on schizophrenia has shown that voices in the United States are more likely to talk about violence. *Americans spoke of "war," as in, "They want to take me to war with them," or their "suicide voice" asking, "Why don't you end your life?"* By contrast, those in India instructed their hearers to do domestic chores— *cook, clean, eat, bathe, to "go to the kitchen, prepare food."*[3]

The Hearing Voices Network, a self-advocacy group, has also shown that engaging with voices can make them more peaceful. *Voice-hearers are invited to focus on the voices, recount what they are saying, to record them, document them and integrate them into their lives. In short, the style of living changes from one of denial to acceptance, through which individuals begin to transform their relation to the experience.*[4]

The process of becoming my mother's cook allowed me to let go of my fear long enough to ask about her voices, and it was as if acknowledging Oakie's place at the table changed something between us. I was preparing one of the last recipes in the *Bon Appétit* cookbook when she said, "How 'bout next time you make me some sogogi soup?"

Sogogi is a spicy beef and radish soup in a clear, aromatic broth, which she taught me to make by barking out the directions from five feet away. "Use more sesame oil. Don't be ashamed to use it. Now put garlic in. More. More. Okay, that's enough!" Like other Korean dishes she would teach me to cook, it was simple and flavorful and tasted of my childhood. It became part of my regular rotation of dishes and was the entrée for other requests. "You make me some kong-nameul each week. I always gotta have that, you know."

It was always after she had begun to eat, as her hunger was being sated and she was swimming in nostalgia, that I would peri-odically check in about her voices.

"Mom, do you still hear Oakie?"

"Yeah, but they are not really bothering me anymore."

My mother lived by herself in that house for two years before my brother and his wife decided that it was both too isolating and too burdensome for her. So they sold the house and moved her to his Tribeca studio, where she slept on his couch for several months. It was a small, spare apartment in a luxury high-rise that served as his crash pad for the nights he worked too late to make the commute back to New Jersey.

Now that she didn't live three hours away from me, I some-times made impromptu visits during the week when my brother was there. I could just hop on the downtown R train from Thirty-Fourth Street after school and arrive at her door fifteen minutes later. She ate well during those months: takeout that my brother brought home after work and the meals I cooked for her on the weekends. It seemed as if her days of rejecting food were over.

She also developed a new interest in baseball. My brother usually had sports on in the background, and the Mets and the Yankees were facing off in a Subway Series.

"How often do two New York teams play each other in the World Series?" my mother mused. "That is really something!" I was delighted by her sudden engagement in the outside world, and it gave me hope that one day she'd be able to go out again.

There was one time when it almost happened. Upon arriving at my brother's apartment and unpacking a bag of Korean groceries from Han Ah Reum, she eyed the packages of bean sprouts and said, "Grace! I have an idea. Let's go shopping!"

"Shopping? You mean you want to go out?"

"Yeah! You take me to that Korean grocery store."

I was shocked and elated by the request. For the first time in months, she changed out of her pajamas and bathrobe, put on makeup, and curled her hair. The whole time she talked about everything she was going to buy. "Misu-garu. Oh, I can't wait to taste misu-garu," she said, practically salivating at the memory of the sweet toasted-grain drink of her childhood.

The anticipation in the room was palpable. She was one beat away from opening the front door and taking a step outside before she suddenly changed her mind.

"Oh, never mind. It's a bad idea," she said, her eyes beginning to go blank.

"C'mon, Mom. Let's go. It'll be fun."

"I'd better not."

"Please, Mom. Let me take you out. I promise everything will be all right."

"No, it's okay." Her smile evaporated and she returned to her usual place on the couch. I silently cursed Oakie. Though I was crushed by disappointment, I also recognized that something inside her was waking up. The rumblings of her desire to eat Korean food were getting louder.

It was in my brother's Tribeca apartment, over a bowl of sogogi soup, that my mother would make a confession.

I ladled the soup over bowls of rice and set them down on the coffee table in front of the couch. She moved onto the floor, and we sat across from each other eating the soup. After dinner we made small talk for a while before our conversation trailed off into a familiar silence.

"Grace?" she said, her voice higher than normal, with a kind of tenderness and vulnerability I hadn't heard since I was a young child. It was the same tone she used when she was trying to comfort me.

"What is it?" I felt nervous, like she was about to break bad news.

"I realize now that you love me."

"Why are you saying this? You thought I didn't?" I was hurt and touched at the same time.

"I used to think that you hate me."

"Why would you think that?"

"Because you put me in jail."

"Mom," I gasped. "I only did that because I thought I could help you." I started to cry. No one in my family had ever spoken about what had happened that night or my motivations for taking such drastic measures. Over time, the gravity of the police incident faded away, and it became just another segment in a string of dramatic events that made up the course of my mother's mental illness.

"And when your father died and I try to hug you, you pushed me away, like I was *dirty*." She grimaced when she spat out the word, as if it were a piece of rotten fruit.

"What? No, I . . . I . . . Did Oakie tell you that? It was because I couldn't admit that I was sad."

She grabbed my hand and looked into my eyes. "Now I realize they are wrong. You really do love me."

I didn't know of a single person outside my family that had a schizophrenic relative, not until I began writing and speaking about it publicly, and then they started coming out in droves—approaching me after talks, looking up my school email, to say "me too." Yet, despite not having had firsthand experience with schizophrenia, my friends in grad school were a huge source of support, especially Hosu. Although she had never met my mother in person, she did once speak to her on the phone. "Let me talk to Umma," she said when I was talking to her from New Jersey.

"Mom, Hosu wants to say hi." My mother began shaking her head in protest, but I held the phone up to her ear anyway. Hosu was a small person but she had a large presence, and I could hear her voice projecting into the room through my flip phone. She was speaking to my mother in Korean, in the honorific. "Eommeonim jal jinaeseyo?" *Respected mother, are you doing well?* My mother clapped her hand over her mouth, as if to keep her voice from escaping. Oakie had long forbade her from talking on the phone, or to anyone outside of our family, but she began to smile and nod her head as she listened to Hosu speak in their native tongue. Having come from the same region in Korea, Hosu could even speak my family's dialect. Despite my mother not responding, there were no awkward silences; Hosu already knew that it would be a one-way conversation. *I am thankful for Grace's friendship. Be in good health, respected mother.* And with that, my mother lifted her hand from her mouth and gestured for me to take the phone back.

I could tell Hosu anything about my family without feeling the least bit of stigma. Her research on Korean birthmothers often intersected with mine on sex work in US camptowns, so she was highly attuned to the social forces that shaped my mother's life. "That is so interesting," she said when I told her about Oakie. "It sounds just like Ok hee, you know? Popular girl's name of our parents' generation."

I wondered if Oakie was a double entendre, a manifestation of another lost sister, or maybe a lost child, someone my mother once loved but couldn't bear to talk about. I kept thinking of Maxine Hong Kingston's aunt that drowned herself in the village well, the woman whom the family was sworn to never speak of after her shameful death.

Though I could never be sure of what they meant in her mind, in mine, Oakie/Ok-hee was a ghost from my family's past, and I would soon begin to feel their presence in my everyday life when my mother moved in with me.

13. QUEENS

Jackson Heights, New York, 2001

THE BEGINNING OF CESAR'S TOUR coincided with my mother moving to New Jersey, my father's death, and the start of my doctoral program. Although I wished for Cesar to be with me then, during some of my life's biggest transitions, he always reminded me that his absence was for the benefit of our relationship. "Keep your eyes on the prize, Gracie. We can buy a place when I get back."

On tour he was frugal in a way that both of my parents would have admired. For lunch he would buy a foot-long Subway sandwich, eat half of it, and save the other half for dinner. That way, he could put most of his per diem toward our nest egg, along with his regular salary. While the other performers on his tour drank all their money away at hotel bars, Cesar continued to pay half our $700 rent during the three years that he was away and still returned home with $40,000.

In January of 2001, a couple of weeks after my thirtieth birthday, we closed on a spacious three-bed, two-bath apartment (with a patio!) in Queens and said goodbye to our shabby little Brooklyn rental. Having the luxury of space was going to be a game changer. I could host parties, big dinners, out-of-town guests. I could even host my mother.

My first overnight guests were Jenny and her husband, who had flown in from Seattle for a babymoon when she was six months pregnant. One day I brought her with me to see my mother in Tribeca. My mother was startled when we first walked in and appeared to have been taking a nap. She smoothed down her bedhead for a minute before easing into her old familiarity with Jenny.

"Oh, Jenny. You are having a baby. Let me see," she said in a sleepy voice. Jenny approached the couch, and my mother placed a hand on her belly. "It's a boy."

"You think?" Jenny said.

"Oh yeah. I can tell by the shape."

They talked about the pregnancy and Jenny's imminent motherhood for a few minutes and then she asked about my apartment. "Is Grace's place all right?

"Yeah, it's really nice! It's a lot bigger than her last place."

Although I had already told my mother that it was huge by New York standards, hearing it from Jenny must have reassured her.

"Come see it for yourself, Mom," I said. "Maybe you can stay with me for a while."

And then a month later, she did. When my brother called to let me know that his finances had become tight and he'd have to give up his Tribeca apartment, I was excited about the prospect of having my mother come live with me.

"Yes. Yes!" I said.

"It's only going to be a few weeks until the renovations on her new place are done," he said, referencing the work they were doing to convert the space above their garage into an apartment.

"Yeah, no problem. I'm happy to do it. It'll actually be easier for me if she's here."

The advent of my homeownership, along with turning thirty, made me feel adult enough to accept the challenge of caring for my mother full-time. I hadn't anticipated that the renovations would keep getting delayed, turning the six-week estimate into seven months, or that a few weeks into her stay, she would begin refusing food again.

The day before my mother's arrival, Cesar and I rearranged our apartment to make room for her, and he didn't show the least bit of worry or resentment that she was moving in with us or that he'd be losing his music studio.

"She's probably just going to stay in here the whole time, so you should take out anything you need," I said, reminding him that interacting with new people made her extremely uncomfortable.

"No problem, Gracie," he said as he smiled and picked up a conga and moved it into our bedroom. I exhaled a sigh of relief, grateful for his laid-back Southern California attitude, and started rolling our old cotton futon out on the gray-carpeted floor. Even though Cesar and I had been living together for years, he had only seen my mother once in 1999, and only after he had gently prodded me to introduce them.

"Will I ever get to meet your mom?" he had asked during one of his tour breaks. "We've been together five years." His question made me wistful, thinking about how quickly the days had turned into years. Two of those five years we had been together, my mother had been living in New Jersey, and I had never taken him with me to visit her. I didn't know what to say, but Cesar, ever patient with my silence, waited a moment before adding, "I wish I could have met your father before he died."

"Really?" I asked, wondering why this was the first time he expressed an interest in meeting my family. I had always thought that he understood that I was trying to hide my parents' dysfunction, shield him from the tension between my father and me, or protect my mother from her phobia of strangers. Yet his question made me insist to her that it was time for them to meet. She argued for a while but ultimately accepted my final word, and I felt guilty for the stress I knew it was causing her.

Just a few weeks before their first meeting, I went to her house in New Jersey to supervise a plumbing job. The doorbell rang, and she frantically looked for a hiding spot while murmuring, "Oh no, oh no." The plumber walked in and saw my mother crouching behind the couch, one hand clutching the white damask slipcover and the other covering her head. Like a young child playing hide-and-seek, she seemed to think that because she couldn't see him, he wouldn't be able to see her either. But she soon figured out that he was standing right next to her, so she said, "Oh! Hello!" but without once moving or looking up.

When the moment arrived for her to meet Cesar, she showed none of her typically phobic behaviors, and even greeted him with a handshake and said, "Welcome." He stood ten inches taller than her, but she didn't look up. At no point did she look him in the eye, but she did look in his direction several times, her line of sight just skimming the side of his face, perhaps getting a good glimpse of his mahogany skin, his shorn black hair and goatee. By taking out the photo album and showing him old family pictures, she managed to carry on a conversation with him for thirty minutes without ever having to look at him. Although Cesar and I had just traveled three hours to see her, I knew that staying longer than that might have pushed her beyond her limit, and I didn't want her performance to end in failure. It was time to save face and go. As I hugged her goodbye, I whispered in her ear, "You did a really good job, Mom. Good job."

I looked around the room that Cesar and I were setting up for her and knew that none of it matched her taste. But at least I could give her a private room and her own bathroom. There was even a door that closed off the back of the apartment from the rest, so she could move freely between her bedroom and bathroom without anyone seeing her.

The next morning, I borrowed Cesar's car to pick her up from my brother's place. It was a twenty-year-old Chevy Citation II that smelled of must, the powder-blue exterior lightly chipping away.

She walked outside into the warm breezy air of late June, and it was one of those rare occasions when she saw direct sunlight. She didn't pause to feel the warmth of it on her skin, but there was a brightness in her eyes that I perceived as a look of defiance. I tried to imagine the conversation she was having with Oakie during that fleeting moment of freedom, whether they cheered her on for stepping outside or warned her that she was putting others in grave danger by breaking the rules. A wrong move could set off a chain reaction of catastrophic events, and therefore, she needed to be extremely careful. She got into the passenger seat of the Chevy, and I drove off toward Queens with the windows rolled down. Suddenly, she looked behind her, and I worried that something had frightened her, but then she cracked a smile and the twinkle in her eye returned.

"Boy, this is a nice car," she said.

"Really?" If I had ever known her to use sarcasm, I would have thought it was a joke, but instead I was mystified. "I'm surprised you think so."

"Well, no. It is not really. But it's nicer than I thought it was going to be. Not bad for an old car," she said as she ran her hand along the vinyl upholstery of the bench seat.

We exited the BQE onto the bustling streets of Jackson Heights with its twenty-four-hour ethnic food shops, representing dozens of countries in Asia and Latin America. I turned into the parking lot of a large Korean grocery store to stock up on some staples.

"Do you want to come inside with me?" I asked as I turned off the engine.

"No, I'll wait here."

There was a slight gap between my question and her answer, and in those seconds of silence I heard an opportunity to persuade her. It had only been a few months since our near outing, and I felt certain that a part of her still longed to shop for Korean food.

"Come inside with me. You'll love it."

"No, I better stay here."

"What difference does it make if you're in the car or in the store? You're still outside."

"No, no."

"But people can see you either way," I pleaded, frustration now spilling through the cracks in my optimism.

"I am staying right here." Her fists were balled up and pushing down against the seat cushion, as if to root herself into the blue vinyl.

"Okay, fine," I sighed. "What do you want me to get you besides rice and kimchi?"

"Kong. Pa. Gochu-garu. Soy beans, misu-garu . . . Maybe some mackerel . . . No, maybe not. It'll stink up your kitchen."

"It's okay, Ma. I don't mind."

"No, no. You don't have to get it," she insisted.

Inside the store, a blast of cold air circulating the scent of dried red peppers and garlic woke up my senses. This market was at least three times the size of its Manhattan counterpart, with aisles as wide as city sidewalks, giving it the feel of a suburban supermarket. I put the hot pepper powder and toasted grain into my basket, and moved back toward the produce for the scallions and bean sprouts. Then something caught my eye. I saw a sign in Korean that said "suk."

I looked at the bundles of greens and remembered how she had salivated over the wild suk that was growing along the Northeast Corridor line of the New Jersey transit. I thought that this could be my chance to offer a temporary antidote to her psychic pain of living a life of confinement, to satisfy some small desire of hers to taste the wilderness again. I grabbed a couple bunches and put them in my basket, yet doubted that this was the same plant that she had been dreaming of. It didn't exactly look like what she had described, but I figured there was no harm in getting it.

I then walked up to the fish counter, pleased that I would surprise my mother with mackerel after she had told me not to get it. I worked up the courage to speak in my most confident-sounding Korean and said, "Go-deong-uh seh-geh juseyo."

The middle-aged man at the fish counter let out a throaty laugh. "Seh-geh?" he huffed, shaking his head and picking up the fish. I had used the wrong counting word at the end of "seh," *three*. "Geh" is the counter for most inanimate objects, while "mari" is the counter for animals.

"Seh-*ma-ri*," he said in the kind of loud, slow voice that one uses with the native speaker of a foreign language.

"Mi-an hamnida. Hanguk-mal jal mot-hcyo. Go-dcong-uh seh-mari juseyo." I apologized to the man. *I'm sorry. I can't speak Korean well. Please give me three mackerel.*

"Seh-geh," he repeated under his breath, looking slightly disgusted as he gutted the fish.

Then I interjected before he could chop off the heads, "Meu-ri do juscyo." *Give me the heads, too, please.*

He looked up, studying my face. I wondered if he was perplexed that a fish-head-eating Korean American could have butchered the language so badly, or if he saw my freckled skin and the whiteness of my features and recognized me as a "Western princess's bastard." That was the name that Koreans of his age, of my mother's generation, called the biracial children of Korean women and American men. We had no legitimacy either in law or in public opinion to call ourselves Korean, so I wondered why this Korean man who was serving me expected my speech to be flawless. Or maybe upon realizing that I was not "pure Korean," his perception of my Korean improved. Could he have thought that it was not so bad for a non-Korean? But everything I knew about how Koreans regarded those among us who were mixed race—the systematic societal exclusion of children and their mothers that I had read about in my research, coupled with my vague early childhood memories of being in Korea— whirled in my head.

An image surfaced: the little girl in my nursery school in Busan who stared me down, alternating her glare between my face and my yellow patent-leather Mary Janes before she grabbed one of the butterfly bows and tried to rip it off. Suddenly, I realized why she did it. I was the only child not wearing traditional shoes. I was brazenly Western, just like my mother, and even a four-year-old knew that she was authorized to keep me in line, to contain the foreignness that my being represented. My attention returned to the fish counter, and I saw the little girl's hateful stare on the man's face. I grabbed the bag of fish and rushed to check out.

I tried to shake off the shame that the fishmonger had projected onto me as I got back into the car. My mother relaxed into her seat when she saw the paper bags packed with her familiar foods. I forced a smile and said, "Mackerel for dinner!"

We arrived at my apartment and Cesar greeted us at the front door. My mother bowed her head almost imperceptibly as she said hello and avoided making eye contact. He knew enough to give her space, so he kept his distance as I gave her the grand tour of our new apartment: a long, rectangular living room with ample space for our oversize eggplant-colored couch on one wall and a wide L-shaped storage bench topped with twin futon mattresses built into the opposite wall. The living room opened up to a dining room, which now housed the six-seat country-style dining table that she had had to get rid of nine months earlier when my brother sold her house. She had put the dining set and my childhood piano in storage until I could get a place that was big enough for them, and now they were here in the open living space of my Queens co-op apartment.

"Look up, Mom," I said, pointing to the clouds painted on the dining room ceiling. "The previous owners were interior decorators." I then walked us into the adjacent galley kitchen and set down the groceries. "The kitchen looks a little dated. We might renovate it," I said.

"What's so dated?" she asked, genuinely perplexed. "There's nothing wrong with it." Though I sensed her disapproval at my desire to spend money on the kitchen, I also felt relieved that it was up to her standards. Of course. The eighties style fit her aesthetic because that's where she was frozen in time. The 1980s was the last decade in which she spent any significant amount of time in a kitchen.

"It doesn't look very modern, but you're right. There's nothing wrong with it," I said, unpacking the groceries. Then I pulled out the greens. "Look, Ma. Is this suk?"

She shook her head. "*Sukat*. Sukat. Not suk."

I felt myself deflate. I wasn't literate enough in Korean to know the difference between suk and sukat. This was yet another instance of my language skills betraying me. Twice in one shopping trip.

"Sukat is good too," she said, sounding upbeat. "We make salad out of that for dinner." If she had been disappointed, then she recovered quickly, perhaps because sukat was another thing she hadn't tasted for ages. I put the fish and vegetables in the fridge. "Help yourself to anything in the kitchen. I'll be around to make breakfast and dinner, but you'll have to help yourself to lunch when I'm out. Don't be shy, okay?" She nodded and followed me down the hall to the back of the apartment. Cesar popped his head out of our bedroom as my mother and I passed by, and for a brief instant she looked straight at him and said, "Thank you for letting me stay here." I would later look back at that moment and be struck by how she thanked him and not me. I would wonder if it was because I didn't need to be thanked, because I was performing a filial duty, while he was a virtual stranger.

We passed through my office to the room in the back that was now her sparsely furnished bedroom. I looked at the cotton futon on the floor and remembered our trips to Korea, when we would sleep on thin pads on the floor of Halmeoni's house. "Let me know if there's anything I can do to make your room more comfortable," I said as she sat down on the futon. She didn't say anything but gestured with her hand that I could go.

That night, as per my mother's instructions, I rinsed the mackerel in cold water, then braised it in a broth of soy sauce, dashi, garlic, and a splash of water; tossed the sukat with vinegar, sesame oil, red pepper powder, and salt. I also made some kong-nameul, heavy on the scallion, and set it out in a bowl along with kimchi to accompany the greens. For a Korean table, it was a meager selection of banchan, but compared to how my mother had grown accustomed to eating, it was a feast. I piled steaming white rice onto her plate, placed the mackerel next to it, and spooned the spicy braising liquid over the rice, just as she liked it.

"Hwaa, that's too much!" she said, feigning protest as I set the plate in front of her. She smiled and lifted a forkful of fish to her mouth, then nodded her approval.

Cesar joined us for dinner. It was one of only two times she came out of her room and ate dinner with us at the dining table, the second being for her sixtieth birthday. It was one of only three times in the seven months that she lived with us that she would interact face-to-face with him.

It took only two days before it became clear that my mother was not going to come out of her room, though she still had an unusual interest in food, and that made me happy. The previous night's mackerel dinner must have sparked her desire to taste her old favorites, because she asked for yet another dish I had neither cooked nor tasted before.

"Graaace!" she called from her room. "Let's make some kong-guksu!" Soybean soup with noodles. I could feel her anticipation as I walked into the room.

"Sure," I said. "How do you make it?"

"First you make soymilk. Boil the soybeans in a pot—just for a few minutes. Then you put 'em in the blender and strain it. Put salt in it. Plenty of salt. Sometimes you don't put enough salt in."

"Okay."

"You have to put salt, because otherwise it don't taste good."

"Yes. I'll be sure to add enough salt. What else?"

"Then you just put the kong-guk in a bowl and add some cooked noodles and shredded cucumber and sesame seeds. So easy. Oh, and ice cubes. It's summertime dish, you see."

"Why don't you come to the kitchen so you can show me how to make it?"

"Oh, it is so easy to make. You do it. I'll stay in here."

I went to the kitchen, took out a pot for the beans and a blender, and put water on to boil. A few minutes after I poured the beans into the pot of bubbling water, my mother yelled from the back of the apartment, "Make sure you don't cook the beans too long! Only a few minutes!" I wondered if she had timed it, visualizing each move I made in the kitchen, so that she could instruct me from a distance.

"Okay!" I shouted back, cutting off the flame. I poured the hot beans and liquid into the blender and gave it a long whirr. I strained and salted the bean mixture, tasting it after each pinch. The richness and the depth of flavor was astounding. I had always used soymilk on my cereal and in my smoothies. How could I not have known earlier how far superior fresh soymilk was and how easy it was to make?

I assembled the dish in two wide pasta bowls and set them on a large tray along with spoons and forks. The customary Korean table setting uses spoons and chopsticks, but in our adaptation to American life, my family always used spoons and forks for noodle soups. I carried the tray into my mother's room and set it down on the floor next to the futon. She leaned over and inhaled the nutty fragrance rising from the bowls, then picked up a spoon and pushed one of the glistening ice cubes around in the bowl before tasting a spoonful of soymilk. We both became completely focused on slurping up the cold soup until there was nothing left but half-melted ice cubes and a few sesame seeds stuck to the sides of the bowls.

"Wow, that was good," I said, astonished by how so few ingredients, seasoned only with salt and sesame seeds, could produce something so flavorful. It didn't even have any garlic or scallions, which I used liberally in nearly every Korean dish my mother had taught me to make. This was the soybean truly exalted. "How come you never made that when I was growing up?" I asked.

"Huh? I don't know. I guess I just never craved for it until now."

I made another batch of kong-guk, this time adding several pinches of sugar and a capful of vanilla extract, to use for breakfast on the next few busy weekday mornings. The richness of the soymilk on my cereal reminded me of how Halmeoni used to eat her cornflakes with half-and-half, dairy being a luxury and novelty for most older Koreans.

A couple of days later, I hurriedly served my mother a bowl of cereal with the sweetened soymilk as I was getting ready to leave for the Graduate Center. I was teaching a seminar on social theory and incarceration for a group of women who had recently been released from prison, and that day was our first meeting. I was preoccupied with making sure I had everything I needed: the syllabus and copies of the excerpt from Michel Foucault's *Discipline and Punish*, which would be the first reading assignment.

Although it wasn't my first time teaching a college-level class, it was my first time teaching theory, and I doubted whether I knew it well enough to teach it, whether I could make it relevant to women who had spent half their lives locked up for nonviolent offenses. What did *I* have to teach them? I had enjoyed every freedom in the world, but I reminded myself that my interest in incarceration was rooted in the experience of caring for my mother, who, under slightly different circumstances, could also have been institutionalized in a "correctional facility."

She had two children who housed and fed her, and she would never live behind bars, but then again, not all bars are physical. When she moved in with me, she was in the eighth year of her psychic prison sentence. The walls and prison guards were invisible, but the rules were very real. Oakie gave her clear boundaries about where she was allowed to go, how she could spend her time, who she could talk to, and what she could eat. Sometimes, instead of being granted permission to eat good food, she was mandated to eat things that were awful, given "disgusting commands."[1] That's what I think happened the morning of my first seminar meeting.

Everything was packed in my book bag, and I was as ready as I'd ever be, so I poured myself a bowl of mango passion Yogi Peace cereal with some of the soymilk. I shoved a spoonful in my mouth and instantly gagged. The soymilk had turned sour and fizzy. I dropped the bowl into the sink and spit out the cereal, then ran into my mother's room. The TV was on in the background, a New York 1 recap of the day's local news followed by the weather forecast. She sat in the middle of the futon with her knees bent and head down, not looking at the TV.

"Mom, the soymilk went bad!" My heart was racing as I looked down at the tray and saw the empty bowl by the door. "No, please don't tell me you ate it."

She didn't answer, and kept her eyes focused on a spot on the floor.

"I can't believe you ate it!" I began to shout. "Why didn't you tell me it was bad? Now you're going to get sick!"

She still didn't acknowledge me. I felt flames of panic begin to consume me, and I was on the verge of crying. I had just served my mother rotten food and she ate it. Maybe I hadn't stored the kong-guk properly. Maybe this dish was never meant to be stored, but simply eaten. Since it was my first experience with fresh soymilk, I had no idea it could spoil so quickly. She waved her hand for me to go away, without once lifting her head or speaking. I took her dirty dishes to the kitchen and started to clean up the mess in the sink. As I lifted the strainer full of soggy cereal, the smell of rotting fish rose up from inside the pipes and hit me square in the face, making me retch. It had been lingering ever since I cooked the mackerel a few nights earlier, the oil from the fish having coated the inside of the drain. Now I knew what she meant when she said it would stink up the kitchen. Maybe the distress of having just fed her spoiled food had heightened my senses, or maybe it even triggered an olfactory hallucination, but the fish smell was overwhelming. I grabbed a sponge and some Comet and scrubbed furiously until the scent faded, but I still couldn't get it to dissipate completely.

That night I dreamed of mackerel. A pile of blue-and-silver fish in the sink, their dead eyes glistening in the moonlight, shining through the dining room window and into the kitchen. How many did the fishmonger give me? Seumul-mari? Seoreun-mari? There were at least twenty or thirty. Many more than the three I asked for. Did I try to say "seht" and instead said "seoreun"? Did my Korean fail so egregiously that I ended up with ten times the amount of fish I wanted? Why didn't the fishmonger correct me this time? In my dream, I can think of only one way to deal with this: I take out all my pots and pans and begin cooking, call up everyone I know, and beg them to come over and help me eat the mackerel. Soon, my apartment is flooded with fish and people. The mackerel are multiplying in the sink faster than I can cook and serve them, and I've run out of people to invite, so I urge my guests to eat seconds and thirds. I refill their plates again and again. *Eat, eat, or it'll go to waste. Mackerel is good for you. Please, I can't let this fish go to waste.*

Over the next few days, the smell of rotten fish and the taste of spoiled soymilk followed me everywhere and tainted everything I ate. Although my mother didn't appear to get physically ill after the cereal incident, things were taking a downward turn, and I feared I wouldn't be able to get them back on track. I suspected that Oakie had told her to eat the bowl of cereal, or maybe this was some residue of the Korean War, when hunger overpowered the risk of getting sick. I also discovered that she had been eating the leftover mackerel straight from the fridge, not bothering to warm it despite the layer of solidified oil that had formed on top of the container. My stomach churned at the thought.

There were other signs that she had regressed to the scavenging mentality of her days as a war survivor. One day, I came home from school and heard her footsteps scurrying down the hall from the kitchen.

"It's just me, Mom!" I called out.

I walked into the dark kitchen and found a bottle of Log Cabin syrup on the counter and the garbage can out from its usual place under the sink. "What's going on in here?" I asked.

She slowly crept back toward the kitchen and stopped in the entryway. "I was eating a piece of bread. The end piece with some syrup on it. You know, the end piece is still good. You don't have to throw away."

"Did I throw it away? You didn't pull it from the garbage, did you?"

"No, I was just eating over the garbage so the crumbs don't fall all over the place."

"Mom, you can use a plate, you know. And there are other things to put on the bread. Syrup doesn't sound very good."

"It's okay. I like it."

I let it go at that because I didn't want to argue, but I wondered if she had lied about not recovering the bread from the garbage or if she had anticipated that I was going to throw it out. Either way, it was stale, and my mother was eating like someone who was starving. I became meticulous about making sure every bit of food was consumed before it had a chance to spoil, and I took out the garbage immediately after putting any food scraps in it. These tricks worked to keep her from eating stale or rancid foods, but she was still eating cold leftovers, congealed fat and all.

After 9/11, she started a new hunger strike. On some nights, I would get so frustrated by her refusal to eat that my temper would explode and I'd yell at her. On others I'd collapse on the floor crying, begging her to eat until she finally took a few bites.

Cesar observed all this from a distance. After one of my screaming fits I apologized to him. "I'm sorry. This must be really stressful for you."

"It's stressful for *you*," he said. "You're the only one who ever sees her."

14. COUNTING GHOSTS

Princeton, New Jersey, 2002

TWO MONTHS AFTER SHE MOVED OUT of my Queens apartment into the granny flat above my brother's garage, my mother was admitted to Princeton House, an upscale private psychiatric facility, because she had stopped eating. I felt both grateful that she was going to get treatment and slightly jealous that I wasn't the one to help her get it.

We were by her side when the ambulance arrived. It was a frigid February night, and she plodded outside in her slippers, a thin coat over her robe, keeping her head down, eyes on the ground. Then she said something in a low, muffled voice.

"What was that?" asked one of the paramedics.

"I want to go with my children," she repeated. Her voice was audible this time, but it was still so small, like that of a little girl using all her strength to not cry. It was one of very few occasions that she was able to express that she needed someone.

"I'm sorry. We can't take them," he said.

She looked petrified and stood frozen for a minute or two as my brother and I tried to reassure her, then climbed into the back of the ambulance. It pained me to see her so scared and vulnerable, being handled by strangers.

During her weeklong stay at the hospital, I borrowed Cesar's car to visit her every night or two. It was only a couple of days in when I noticed a marked contrast in her mood and demeanor.

I arrived at the visitor's desk, and the receptionist greeted me with a big smile. "You're Koonja's daughter?" he asked. "She talks about you all the time."

"She does?"

"Oh, yeah. She's really proud of you."

She is? In thirty-one years, I had never heard her say this explicitly.

He escorted me into the rec room, where she was sitting at a table, beading necklaces with a group of other residents around her, abuzz with excitement. They seemed to be hanging on her every word.

"Mom?" I approached tentatively, not wanting to disrupt what appeared to be her most triumphant moment in decades.

"You're Koonja's daughter!" one of the residents shouted. "Oh, we *love* your mom."

There was a devilish grin on her face. All these years she's been terrified of people, and now she's the belle of the ball? Have they been giving her new meds? The only thing the nurse had mentioned the last time was the laxative. Whatever it was, the charismatic mother of my childhood had momentarily returned, and I was thrilled to see her.

She led me to her room so that we could talk privately as we drank apple juice in plastic cups with tinfoil lids. When I asked how it was going, she immediately told me about her roommate, a sixtysomething woman whose son and husband died in a car crash. "She's here because she's very sad," my mother said, her voice soft with compassion. I was moved by her empathy and felt grateful that she had had the chance to hear other people's stories of loss and hardship.

The doctors had in fact started her on a new drug regimen. This time she was taking one of the "new generation" of antipsychotic drugs that had fewer side effects, along with an antidepressant, but I knew it wasn't just the drugs; it was too soon for them to have made much of an impact. She was benefiting from being around other people, from being reminded that she was lovable. And surely, group therapy at a nice facility like this one must have given my mother's experiences a kind of validity that they had never had before. I tried to imagine how she presented herself, what she had told the others about why she was there. *I'm here because Oakie gave me too much work to do, and I got kinda burnt out. I made mistakes and people died.* I imagined that whatever she had to say was treated with respect and not dismissed as psychotic nonsense.

We dined on tuna sandwiches from the vending machine and talked for a while, and then I apologized that I needed to go back to New York. "Tomorrow is my proposal defense," I said, wondering if she would ask me what my dissertation was about, but she didn't. As usual, it was enough for her to know that I was getting a doctorate, and too much for her to know the details of it.

"But I'll come back the day after tomorrow."

"Oh, don't worry about me."

"No, Mom. I'm coming back."

"No, no. It's okay."

"Mom—"

"Oh, all right."

My defense was scheduled for 10:00 a.m., and although I was on time, I felt harried and disorganized after having gotten home late the night before. I walked into the small, windowless seminar room at the CUNY Graduate Center to defend myself before the sociology faculty. Patricia, my adviser, was already there, and I beelined it for the seat next to her.

"Hello, my sweet. How are you?" she said, in her soothing, sultry voice.

"Well, I've been in the psychiatric hospital all week if that gives you any indication," I said, trying to make light of the situation but also acknowledge that my mind had not been focused on the proposal and I was feeling pretty vulnerable. My palms were sweating, and I kept wiping them on my pants under the table. I had never had the easiest time in this sociology department—my interests were more on the side of cultural studies, while many of the professors were wedded to mainstream notions of sociological empiricism. Patricia, however, was a champion of students who were drawn toward creative sociology and the unorthodox research methods that seemingly unanswerable questions demanded. Because of that, the defense turned out to be at least as much about her as it was about my proposal.

"My dissertation will analyze the figure of the yanggongju, literally 'Western princess' but more commonly translated as 'Yankee whore,' as a ghost that haunts the Korean diaspora," read the first sentence. Some of my proposed methods were dream work, experimental writing, and performance—methods of the unconscious—to make unspeakable traumas audible and hauntings visible.

There was a taut silence as the faculty reviewed my proposal, which was broken by the department chair, a middle-aged white man and one of the "quantoids," as the qualitative sociology students called them. "Somehow I don't think you're using this word 'ghost' just to be cute. I think you really mean it."

Then another white professor burst out, "You're not doing any interviews! It's incumbent upon you as a researcher to interview your subjects!" She then turned to Patricia and shouted, "How could you let her do this?"

"Wait, wait, wait," interjected a third professor, the only Black faculty member and the one who had supervised my oral exam on the literature of sex work. He turned to the professor who had just spoken. "Let me explain something to you. If I'm writing about the figure of Aunt Jemima, I'm not going to interview Aunt Jemima."

I exhaled a long breath knowing that there was at least one person in the room that got what I was trying to do, but his comment did nothing to change the tone of the conversation. Faculty continued yelling at one another about my proposal, often talking about me in the third person as if I wasn't even there. Each time someone took a jab at my proposal, or warned Patricia of my impending "career suicide," I shrunk a bit more in my seat and heard my voice fading, until I felt myself disappear completely.

Later, I would be able to see that much of the aggression had been directed toward Patricia for having encouraged me to experiment with what "counts" as sociology. Another professor would explain the politics of the department to me by picking up a plate and balancing a pencil on the edge. "If this is the discipline of sociology," he would say about the plate, "then the pencil is Patricia. They don't want her students to push the boundaries any further."

After the meeting was adjourned, the chair emailed Patricia: "I don't think your student is mentally stable enough to get a PhD." While Patricia and I laughed about how absurd it was that the word "ghost"—a word that was utterly commonplace and taken for granted in Asian American studies—had set off the alarm bells of an old-school sociologist, I also felt shamed and brutalized. I had already spent so much of my life thinking about misconceptions of madness and the silencing of women, and here was a white male professor suggesting that my place was not in academia but in the loony bin alongside my mother.

As Patricia and I sat in her office continuing to process the defense, she scoffed at the other sociologists. "They think you should be counting ghosts," she said, as if transgenerational haunting were quantifiable in such a way. And in the next breath, she expressed regret. "I know I encouraged you to do all this, but somehow I didn't think you were going to listen to me," she said as she put her head in her hands, messing up her wiry black hair.

"I'm glad I listened to you!" I said defiantly, as a reminder to us both that she had made the margins the most livable place for me. "I don't want to be a straight sociologist. I don't even want to be an academic."

My professional desires had long gravitated toward becoming a pastry chef, and Patricia would sometimes fret, "Oh, Grace. Are we going to lose you to cakes?" She knew that what drove me in graduate school was not a love of sociology but a traumatic legacy so deep that I would never be able to find the bottom. She had been my adviser through my struggles to feed my mother, to confront the past—all of it tied up with my doctoral work.

I had lamented profusely to Patricia about my mother's agoraphobia, all those days she spent in my apartment wrapped up in a little ball, rocking herself on the futon. She had been doing that in one form or another for years, but to see her illness on a daily basis devastated me all over again, almost to the point of dysfunction. There had been instances at school when I felt like I was on the verge of a nervous breakdown, unable to think about anything but my mother stuck in that little room. Then one day Patricia delivered a bit of psychoanalytic tough love.

"Grace. Maybe *you're* keeping her in the room."

"What did you say?" I thought she was accusing me of hyperbolizing my mother's condition as a shut-in. Or maybe she was suggesting something even worse.

"*You're* keeping her in the room."

I heard these words not in Patricia's voice but in the piercing sound of my own self-doubt and criticism, the one that for years had been reminding me of the debacle I had made out of trying to get help for my mother when I was fifteen.

And now, she was stuck in the room because I had failed.

The day after my defense, I fired up the Chevy and drove to the psychiatric hospital for my mother's discharge. There was a crowd gathered around her waiting to say goodbye. One man reached out to hug her and she pulled away. "Oh, no, no, no," she said while backing up, but with each step back, he stepped forward and almost put his hands on her shoulders. They danced across the floor like this, but she reached the front desk without ever letting him touch her. Then she whispered something in the receptionist's ear that made him blush. "We're gonna miss you, Koonja," he said as we walked out the door.

Back in her apartment, she sat down on her cream-colored couch and stared off into space. I marveled that just a few minutes earlier she had been working the crowd down at Princeton House, and now she was back to her lonely days of doing nothing.

"Mom, you know, I could see that socializing was really good for you. What do you think of finding a day program?"

"Hah! No," she snorted, and waved her hand at me.

"Well . . . do you want me to get you some beading supplies so you can keep making jewelry?"

"No, no. That's okay."

I began to feel frustrated by her stubborn refusal to do anything but sit on the couch, as if all the progress I'd just witnessed had never really happened. Again I had gotten my hopes up, only to have things return to the way they had always been. Yet something was different. She was in a better mood and more talkative. It could have been the new meds or the impact of the positive social contact. Or maybe it was me who had changed. Maybe I would finally be able to let her out of the room.

"Do you understand that you have a mental illness, Mom? That you're schizophrenic?"

"Yes. However"—she raised her index finger in the air with an imperious gesture—"*I* am no *ordinary* mentally ill person."

A psychiatrist probably would have said that her declaration was further evidence of her delusional thinking, but I chose to believe that it was a sign that her self-esteem was on the rise. Everyone at Princeton House could see what I had seen as a child—that she was extraordinary, the most charming and charismatic of the bunch.

Despite the few members of the sociology faculty who continued to see my work as having "absolutely no empirical basis in reality"—much in the same way that psychiatrists spoke about hallucinations—I started writing my dissertation in 2003, by which time my mother had taught me to cook about fifteen Korean dishes. Each time I visited, the pungent smells of garlic and fermentation would fill the air, bringing Korea into the room. The tastes and smells sometimes prompted her to tell me some tidbit about her youth that I hadn't heard before. "You know, my father used to make the best bulgogi of anyone I know," she once confided. "He used to feed me with his chopsticks straight from the fire. I was his favorite because I was the youngest, you see."

These meals with my mother and her minor revelations about the past punctuated my research and writing, but the boundaries between these two aspects of my life often blurred.

When I was four or five, a ghost-child would sometimes visit me in Chehalis. On clear moonlit nights, it would appear by the camellia bush in the backyard and summon my body to float out my bedroom window. I knew it wasn't going to hurt me, but its appearance frightened me. Downy white fur covered its skin, and there was a small hole in the middle of its forehead. As I got a little older I began to wonder if the ghost-child was perhaps a spirit in the guise of a living human or just a trick that my mind had been playing on me. Over time, it receded into the depths of my unconscious until I began researching civilian experiences of the Korean War. Amid reading survivors' aggrieved tales of massacre—of witnessing their loved ones murdered and then later having to recover the rotting remains for burial—alongside the cold rationality of US military memos—"Policy on Strafing Civilian Refugees" as "an excellent method of clearing road-ways"[1]—the vision of the child flashed back with a vengeance. I wondered if it was an apparition that had crossed the Pacific with us, one of my mother's relatives perhaps, or someone she had seen dead or dying on the side of the road. At that moment, its unusual physical appearance ceased to be a mystery. Suddenly, I saw it as a child that had been shot in the head and had begun growing mold on the surface of its decomposing flesh, an image that could have been taken straight from the pages of my research.

As I was reenvisioning the ghost-child, I then contemplated how popular culture depicted children who could see and hear things that others couldn't as highly perceptive, gifted with a sixth sense, yet adults that had the same experiences were simply crazy.

Once, as we were eating dinner, I asked my mother directly what she remembered about the war. She answered, but her eyes went vacant as she spoke. "I remember traveling through the mountains and seeing North Korean soldiers. Girls. Girl soldiers. It was scary to me. I never imagined girls with guns." She seemed so troubled by it, but it couldn't have been the most horrific thing she had ever seen. Maybe it stood out in her mind precisely because the other things were *too* traumatic to remember.

For a chapter I wrote on the ways the figure of the camptown sex worker haunted the cultural productions of diasporic Koreans, I read Nora Okja Keller's novel *Fox Girl*. The story is set in 1960s South Korea and revolves around Hyun Jin and Sookie, two teenage girls whose lives bear the consequences of US imperial war. Sookie is the older one who introduces Hyun Jin to prostitution for American troops and teaches her to dissociate. *You can do*

anything if you have to . . . it's easy. It's easy because the more you do it,
the more you know it's not the real you. The real you flies away.[2] She is
the ghost that haunts Hyun Jin's dreams, the voice in her head,
the imprint of her trauma. Did my mother have a Sookie? Was
her name Ok-hee?

There's one scene in *Fox Girl* that I've never been able to forget, in which three mixed race children are singing a song that
they had heard from American GIs. One of the few words the
kids understand is "whore," because they *knew whose mothers they*
were.[3]

> *I saw a whore by the side of the road.*
> *Knew right away she was dead as a toad.*
> *Her skin was all gone from her tummy to her head.*
> *But I fucked her, I fucked her even though she was dead.*[4]

Although Keller's book is fictional, it is not unlike things I had
found in my scholarly research, which made the song all the
more horrifying. As much as I tried, I could not unhear the voices
of these children blithely singing about the murder and rape of a
woman who could have been their mother.

I also read similarly disturbing accounts of former wianbu,
the "comfort women" who were conscripted for the Japanese
military, to look at the continuity between the two systems of
militarized sexual labor. In one testimony, a woman named
Okpun told of being abducted at the Korean age of twelve
(American age eleven) and sent to a "comfort station" in Taiwan.

> *On weekday evenings we were made to sing, dance and play the vio-*
> *lin. . . . If we couldn't play well, we were beaten. . . . The song dedicated to*
> *life in the comfort station went something like "my body is like a rotting*
> *pumpkin left out in summer."*[5]

I was struck that I had found a recurring theme of the army
song that depicted the woman's rotting body, the woman whose
purpose was to provide entertainment to imperial soldiers.

One night, when I was in the middle of writing a chapter on the violence of the camptown, I lay on my mother's couch trying to sleep, but the harrowing images from my research kept me awake. Yun Kumi splayed out on the floor of her ramshackle apartment, her body desecrated after having been murdered by one of her clients. The camptown worker who said she had witnessed an American GI throwing a woman's body into the dumpster, then lighting it on fire. The smell of singed hair and smoldering flesh.

It was pitch black except for the little red light of the smoke detector on my mother's ceiling. The light seemed to grow brighter and brighter, burning my eyes with red.

When I finally fell asleep, I dreamed that I was trapped in a dark room, searching for a door. I could see my face, distressed and crying out, "Please! Somebody get me out of here!" I didn't know where I was at first, then realized that it was a brothel, and I knew that my body would stay there until long after my mind had fled, until no one on the outside remembered me.

Her skin was all gone. . .

Voices had gotten into my head too.

You can do anything if you have to. . .

They gave me instructions: Put the flesh back on the body.

The body that had decomposed beyond recognition.

15. CHEESEBURGER SEASON

Princeton, New Jersey, 2002–2008

AS IF SANCTIONS HAD BEEN LIFTED, my mother's appetite completely returned. No longer skin and bones, her body looked healthy again, her eyes bright.

Her discharge from Princeton House marked the beginning of the best years of her late life. It was during this period, while I was working on my dissertation, that she resembled the mother of my childhood, eating so intently that beads of sweat would form on her nose.

I had seen glimpses of the first mother before, and perhaps my most concrete understanding that she was still there, ready to be resurrected by the right meal, had been on her sixtieth birthday when she was living with me in Queens.

It was only a week or so after she moved in, but she had already established a pattern of staying in her room, curled up in her little ball. The day before her birthday, I approached her as she rocked herself.

"Mom?"

"Hm?" she said without looking up.

"I'm going to make galbi for your birthday," I said.

The little ball began to unfurl as she lifted her head. "Be sure to put plenty of garlic in it."

"I'm also going to barbecue some chicken."

"I haven't had that for years . . . Why you go to so much trouble? Don't cook all that."

"Mom, it's your birthday."

"Big deal."

"It's your sixtieth birthday." Among Koreans, sixty is the age that deserves the most fanfare, as a person has achieved a milestone measured by the completion of the entire lunar zodiac. "There'll be cheeseburgers too."

She had avoided smiling since her front tooth had fallen out a couple of years earlier, but this time she couldn't help herself. She sat straight up and covered her mouth to hide the missing tooth. "Cheeseburgers, huh? That sounds good!"

When the moment arrived, I set the big dining table for three and filled it with plates of galbi, grilled chicken, potato salad, kimchi, kong-nameul, spinach nameul, cheeseburgers, sliced tomatoes and onions, baby lettuce, grilled corn on the cob, seedless watermelon, and a four-layer lemon cake.

"It's time for your birthday party!" I said from the doorway of her room.

"I'll just eat in here."

"No. I already set the table. Come out."

I was anticipating a struggle, but instead, she stood up and shuffled down the hall toward the dining room. When she came face-to-face with Cesar, she stopped and said to him, "It is my birthday, after all." Then she walked up to the edge of the table, sized up the spread, clapped her hands, and shouted, "Manta! Lots of goodies!" The three of us feasted together and she relished everything.

It comforted me to see the look on her face at the end of the meal, as she milked the corncobs with her teeth and sucked the last shreds of meat off the galbi bones.

"Did you enjoy the food?" I asked.

"Yeah. I been wondering if I was gonna get a birthday party

this year." Her big smile returned and she said, "Oh boy! That cheeseburger is good!"

The mother who had raised me was still alive.

By the time I finally learned to listen to my mother's cravings, she stopped making me guess what she wanted. She made regular requests for Korean dishes she hadn't eaten for ages, like jangjorim (beef and spicy green peppers stewed in soy sauce) or chapssal tteok (a sweet red-bean rice cake). The flavors transported me back to my childhood, to my first mother's embrace.

Though it took years for me to fully absorb the significance of these meals, it was saengtae jjigae that would make me understand that feeding her had the effect of gently releasing the past.

It was a dish that I had never tasted or heard of before, but I cooked it as per my mother's instructions. Sautée radishes in sesame oil until they begin to soften. *Don't be ashamed to use sesame oil. Put in garlic, plenty of garlic. Now don't be ashamed to use that either.* Her recipes were like incantations against a history of being rendered inferior. Add fish, dashi broth, scallions, gukganjang, and gochu-garu. Bring to a low boil and serve with rice.

We sat down on the floor around the glass-top coffee table to eat the fragrant fish stew, and I contemplated the balance of flavors—spicy, smoky, pungent, and sweet.

"I haven't tasted this in forty years," she said. Her voice was soft, dreamy.

"Wow! It's so good! How come you never made this when I was little?"

"I guess I just never craved for it until now." That was always her answer when I asked why we were eating something now but not then. What was it about the now that stirred up her cravings?

"Does it taste the same as when you used to cook it?"

"I never cooked it," she said between slurps of garlicky broth.

"Really? How did you know how to make it?"

"It's how I remember my mother making."

I couldn't believe that she had successfully taught me how to make such a delicious dish based on a forty-year-old recollection of watching someone else cook it. Throughout her life, saengtae jjigae was something that others cooked for her, the most comforting of comfort foods. The recipe—the memory of her mother's hands—had been lying dormant on her tongue for all those years. Tasting it must have been a kind of homecoming.

The experience of awakening her memories moved me so much that saengtae jjigae became a family treasure, something that I didn't want to cook too often so as to not diminish its importance. I made it only when she specifically asked for it. After one such request, I heard from my sister-in-law that she had been thinking about it all week long. "Are you making your mom that fish stew?" she said to me. "She keeps talking about it, how she's really looking forward to it."

Our Korean dinners became beacons around which her uneventful life was structured. From the moment I walked out the door, the countdown to the next meal would begin.

That Monday, when I returned to the Graduate Center, Hosu and her girlfriend asked me what I had cooked for my mother over the weekend. They would always take delight in hearing about our dinners, but this time, as soon as I told them it was saengtae jjigae, they screeched, laughing so hard they doubled over.

"What's so funny?" I asked.

"Nobody from our generation makes that!" Hosu said, breathless from laughing.

Visits with my mother were like culinary history lessons, encounters with Korea of the 1950s and 1960s. Everything we ate together during those last years of her life must have reminded her of her youth, but the cheeseburger stood out as the lone American dish in my old-school Korean repertoire.

During my childhood, despite all the experience she had acquired with different kinds of food, her favorite meal was always a cheeseburger: medium rare with tomato and cheddar. Every year, when the Washington rains gave way to drier days, she would fire up the charcoal grill, throw some patties on it, and declare the commencement of "Cheeseburger Season."

The timing of Cheeseburger Season was different in the Northeast. We would kick it off sometime in April, as soon as it was warm enough for me to cook on the fourteen-inch Weber charcoal grill that we kept on her balcony. Though I could never get her to come outside with me, at least she'd let me keep the curtains open so she could supervise from the couch. Sometimes she'd get impatient waiting for spring to come and ask me to jumpstart the season: "You can cook 'em in a pan, you know. Not as good as barbecue, but they are still good."

At first I thought that the cheeseburgers were some throwback to my childhood, some residual fondness for her life in America, but then I remembered that this dish, too, she had first eaten in Korea.

Her love of cheeseburgers went way back to the US military occupation of Korea. As a bargirl at a US naval base, she had access to luxurious American foods that most Koreans could only dream of; it was sort of a fringe benefit of serving American soldiers.

My father used to tell this one story about how he fell in love with my mother because of her passion for cheeseburgers. He took her out on a date (the only one I had ever heard him talk about) to an American restaurant at the base.

She had long been out of school and had never formally studied English, but she was a woman driven to learn. She compared her speech to that of other English-speaking Koreans and felt certain that she did not have an accent. Indeed, she pronounced many English sounds correctly. The Zs that most Koreans pronounced as Js did not intimidate her. She had little trouble with long As or words ending in consonants, except for words ending in both R and L, which were especially difficult if they were followed by another consonant. Nonetheless, the fact that she believed she spoke English without an accent illuminated her voice with the unmistakable sound of confidence.

My father looked across the table at this young beauty, and wondered if she could possibly love an aging man like him. "Order anything on the menu," he said. "Anything at all." My father was frugal, but he believed that some things were worth the money. It was a much fancier restaurant than the other ones my mother had been to before. An irrepressible smile spread across her face, revealing her huge dimples. She was rapturous. The waiter arrived to take their order. My mother swung her feet back and forth and wiggled slightly in her seat. Her smile grew larger as she enunciated each word clearly, "I'll have a cheeseburg, please." She clasped her hands together and said to my father, "Oh boy! Cheeseburg is my favorite food in the whole worl!"

At this point in the story, my father would always get dewy-eyed and often his telling would end there. But if he still had a handle on his emotions, he would conclude with the words "Your mother was the cutest thing I ever did see."

Before that, she was like any other Korean, whose first taste of American food probably came from scavenging in the dumpsters outside US Army mess halls. Right after the war, the American bases became a destination for hungry Koreans looking to buy bags of leftover food scraps, which were often mixed up with all kinds of inedible trash. I would learn about this when I was working on Still Present Pasts, an oral history project with Korean War survivors, many of whom talked about how common it was for people to get meals out of the Americans' garbage. Their stories

illuminated the dark side of my mother's desire for cheeseburgers. I tried to picture the moment she first found a half-eaten
cheeseburger beneath a layer of crumpled napkins and cigarette
butts, and in her malnourished state of mind, thought it was the
most transcendent thing she had ever tasted.

The cheeseburger was a complex symbol of survival and
subordination, a luxury item that the Americans could afford to
throw away while Koreans starved. For my mother, it also symbolized all the hope and possibility that America had to offer.
US imperialism seemed to be writ large on her unconscious,
expressing itself through her alimentary longings. At the same
time, taking pleasure in food offered her some relief from the
stress of her militarized psychic space. The cheeseburger just
happened to represent both symptom and remedy.

I went through my own process of psychic decolonization
during those years of cooking for her. The meals we shared nurtured me through the emotionally taxing work that I was doing
in graduate school. *She* nurtured me. After dinner, she would
massage my feet and calves as I stretched out on the couch. "Your
legs must be tired," she'd say about my long walk from the train
station. Before heading back the next day, she would always
encourage me to take a ten-minute nap. "It's okay. Go to sleep. I
watch the time for you."

It wasn't until after I had defended my dissertation and was
revising it into a book manuscript that we ever had a conversation about my research, though it didn't happen the way I had
intended. My sister-in-law spilled the beans, which I was ultimately thankful for. I just couldn't bring myself to do it on my
own.

When I walked upstairs to find my mother in her usual place
on the couch, there was a tense look on her face.

"Is everything okay?" I asked.

"Are you writing a book?" Now that she knew, there was nothing left for me to do but tell her as much as she could bear to hear.

"Yes . . . I've been wanting to talk to you about it for a long time . . . It's sort of inspired by you, your life." I went on to try to explain the thesis as concisely as I could, but when I got to the word "yanggongju," she interjected.

"Oh, that is a bad word," she said, turning her eyes away.

"I know it was used that way," I said, "but I'm trying to change the meaning of it by writing about it. I don't want it to be a shameful word anymore. That woman, to me, she's a hero." My voice began to falter. "Mama . . . I don't want you to feel ashamed of anything you've ever done. There's nothing about you that I'm ashamed of."

She didn't look at me, but I thought I saw a faint smile appear on her lips.

"I won't publish it if you don't want me to," I added. She paused for a few seconds, and in that silence I surrendered to the possibility that my writing might never see the light of day.

"I want you to," she said.

Nearly every time I saw her after that, she would ask about the progress of my book, sometimes reiterating her wish for it to be published.

It was that same year that she surprised me with a Christmas present, the only gift besides money she had given me during her fourteen years as a shut-in. After opening her gifts from me—a knife sharpener and a pair of tongs, both of which she had asked for, and some moisturizer—her face lit up. "I got present for you too!"

"What? How?"

She scurried over to the closet, pulled out a red metallic gift bag, and handed it to me with a huge smile on her face. Inside was a liter of olive oil, several different types of candies and cookies, and two pairs of multicolored fuzzy socks—a gift that I would have appreciated from anyone, but receiving it from my mother made me ecstatic.

"Oh my god! Where did you get all this stuff?"

"I been saving up for you!"

She'd spent months squirrelling away things that my brother and his wife had been bringing to her so that she could give me something more personal than a check. As always, she was ingenious in her resourcefulness.

She had transformed into a new mother—present once more, and at the same time open to the past, able for the first time to talk to me about Korea.

For six good years she consistently enjoyed the dinners we shared, the food she taught me how to cook. Little by little, meal by meal, she traced her legacy. It was the most magnificent gift.

After my mother's death, I replayed our final moments together on loop. I obsessed over the exact sequence of events, minor details of the weather, the sound of her voice.

"Surprise me," she had said when we were planning that night's menu, as if the suspense would add some excitement to her week, and maybe it was precisely her wish for excitement that told me she needed a meal that could lift her spirits.

The air was cold but smelled vaguely of budding flowers. With the change of seasons on the horizon, I had the thought that it might be the last time we'd eat saengtae jjigae for months.

As soon as I walked in through the ground-level entrance, I heard her call down the stairs as she always did. "Professor is here?"

"Hi, Professor's mom!" I called back.

"What are we eating tonight?" she asked as I approached her studio at the top of the stairs.

"Saengtae jjigae."

"Sounds good."

At dinner she nodded her approval of the stew, but something about her seemed a little off. Her short hair was greasy and flattened on one side, as if she hadn't gotten out of bed for days, and her energy seemed low.

"Are you sick, Ma?" I asked.

"I had some diarrhea the other day. My stomach been bothering me a little. It's no big deal." It didn't worry me, as gastrointestinal distress wasn't unusual, and certainly nothing that registered as life-threatening. Plus, she was eating the spicy stew without any apparent discomfort.

After dinner we talked about how the demands of the tenure track were eating up all my free time. "I have to work the next two weekends, Ma. I'm really sorry. I won't be able to come back until March 22. Will you be okay until then?"

She pursed her lips together and nodded. "It's okay. You do what you have to do."

We covered all our usual topics of conversation—teaching, the status of my dating life now that I was single again, her visits with my brother and his family, the menu for next time—and then she asked about daylight savings.

"When does the time change this year?"

"Next weekend."

"Oh! Why so early?" She seemed troubled and furrowed her brow.

"They're doing it in March now, but I can't remember why."

"Why does it have to be so soon? Why does it have to be so soon?" The way she said it under her breath made me think that she was talking to Oakie, but I didn't think much of it at first. Her preoccupation with the time had been a constant through all her years with schizophrenia.

The visit was shorter than usual because I wasn't spending

the night, and the few hours we had together had already slipped away. My commute to campus in Staten Island took almost as long as the two-hour-and-forty-minute trip to her house in New Jersey, and I needed that Sunday to rest and prep my classes.

As I began packing to go back to New York, she stopped me. "You don't have to leave right now, do you?" I had never known her to be clingy with me, so the very fact that she had asked me to stay made me want to do it.

"I can take the next train," I said as I pulled the schedule out of my bag and studied it. "Yeah, I'll take the 7:54."

Later that night, as I was walking toward the train station, I would call my best friend to tell him the foreboding in my gut.

"I just have this feeling that she's not going to be around much longer, and I wish I could spend more time with her," I would say with a tremor in my voice.

"I know you're super busy, but you can go see her more once the semester is over."

"Yeah . . . yeah, but I want to be able to spend more time with her *now*."

All we could really count on was *now*, and if I knew that, why didn't I turn around and stay the night? In the coming weeks, I would torture myself with this question, then try to extinguish it by telling myself that it wouldn't have made a difference. What's another night compared to forever?

As it was, we had another sixty-seven minutes.

"Get comfortable. Put your legs out," she said once I sat back down.

Both of us stretched out on the couch, facing each other from opposite ends. She spread her orange floral blanket over our legs, the one she had brought back from Korea in the 1970s. Beneath the blanket she held my right foot in her hand, gently rubbing it with her thumb. The blanket, the sensation of her touch, reminded me of being a young child strapped to her back, my cheek resting between her shoulder blades. It reminded me of all the occasions when we slept together on heated floor mats while visiting my grandmother and cousins in Oregon. An intense, almost unbearable longing to lie next to her again washed over me, and then I realized that the very thing I wished to happen was already happening.

Except for a few words here and there, we spent most of our sixty-seven minutes quietly lying on the couch. Relaxing into the warmth of each other's bodies under the fuzzy Korean blanket. Listening to the ticking of the grandfather clock, the rise and fall of our breath. Being together in the now. We continued like that until the clock struck seven, announcing that our time was up.

"I guess I should go now," I said as I leaned forward and wrapped my arms around her. "I'll see you in three weeks." She nodded and gestured with her hand that it was okay to go.

As I started to leave, I felt a sharp pang of remorse. I had already said goodbye and had taken two steps down the stairs when something compelled me to turn around.

"Mom, just think that the next time I see you, it'll be spring," I said. "And then it will be Cheeseburger Season."

NOTES

PROLOGUE

1. Throughout this text, I use the terms "mad" and "madness" to reference the work of people who have challenged the psychiatric dogma that hearing voices is always and only an "illness," "disorder," or "dysfunction," but I also use the terms "schizophrenic" and "schizophrenia."
2. Esme Weijun Wang, *The Collected Schizophrenias* (Minneapolis, MN: Graywolf Press, 2019), 50.
3. Maggie Nelson, *The Argonauts* (Minneapolis, MN: Graywolf Press, 2015), 114.

1. TASTES LIKE WAR

1. Charles J. Hanley, Choe Sang-Hun, and Martha Mendoza, *The Bridge at No Gun Ri: A Hidden Nightmare from the Korean War* (New York: Henry Holt and Company, 2001), 127.
2. Chong Suk Dickman, "Thank You," in *I Remember Korea: Veterans Tell Their Stories of the Korean War, 1950–53*, ed. Linda Granfield (New York: Clarion Books, 2003), 75–76.
3. Kyla Wazana Tompkins, *Racial Indigestion: Eating Bodies in the 19th Century* (New York: NYU Press, 2012), 4.

2. AMERICAN DREAMS

1. BBC News, "Korea Reunion: Mother and Son Reunite after 67 Years" (video), August 20, 2018, https://www.bbc.com/news/av/world-asia-45249821/korea-reunion-mother-and-son-reunite-after-67-years.
2. Arissa H. Oh, *To Save the Children of Korea: The Cold War Origins of*

International Adoption (Stanford, CA: University of Stanford Press, 2015), 27.

3. Oh, *To Save the Children*, 121.

4. This quote derives from an oral history with a birth mother who had been a camptown sex worker in the 1960s, conducted by the Sunlit Sisters Center in Seoul, translated by Hosu Kim.

3. THE FRIENDLY CITY

1. These are the two postings I remember most from my adolescence in the 1980s.

2. Sarah Kershaw, "Highway's Message Board Now without a Messenger," *New York Times*, November 28, 2004, http://www.nytimes.com/2004/11/28/us/highways-message-board-now-without-a-messenger.html?_r=0.

3. *Senate Judiciary Committee Hearing on the Nomination of Brett M. Kavanaugh to Be an Associate Justice of the Supreme Court, Day 5, Focusing on the Allegations of Sexual Assault*, September 27, 2018 (statement of Christine Blasey Ford).

4. T. M. Luhrmann and Jocelyn Morrow, eds., *Our Most Troubling Madness: Case Studies in Schizophrenia across Cultures* (Oakland: University of California Press, 2016), 21.

5. Adam Pearson, "Forget Friendly—Chehalis Happy Being the Rose City," *Daily Chronicle*, May 11, 2010, http://www.chronline.com/news/forget-friendly-chehalis-happy-being-the-rose-city/article_9874fcc4-5d20-11df-a354-001cc4c03286.html.

6. "The Ku Klux Klan Was Strong in Lewis County," *Daily Chronicle*, August 13, 2008, http://www.chronline.com/editorial/the-ku-klux-klan-was-strong-in-lewis-county/article_9a3f2a84-a35a-557e-b23f-6e3641e2e722.html; Brittany Voie, "Voice of Voie: Lewis County No Stranger to Far Right, Supremacist Groups," *Daily Chronicle*, August 18, 2017, https://www.chronline.com/opinion/voice-of-voie-lewis-county-no-stranger-to-extreme-right/article_5bda9aa4-8490-11e7-81da-97c03aeb6b52.html.

4. UMMA

1. In the words of a former prostitute, "The more I think about my life, the more I think women like me were the biggest sacrifice for my country's alliance with the Americans." Choe Sang-Hun, "Ex-Prostitutes Say South Korea and U.S. Enabled Sex Trade Near Bases," *New York Times*, January 7,

2009, https://www.nytimes.com/2009/01/08/world/asia/08korea.html.

2. James L. Watson and Melissa L. Caldwell, eds., *The Cultural Politics of Food and Eating: A Reader* (Malden, MA: Blackwell Publishing, 2005), 1.

3. Anne Allison, *Permitted and Prohibited Desires: Mothers, Comics, and Censorship in Japan* (Boulder, CO: Westview Press, 1996).

5. KIMCHI BLUES

1. Ji-Yeon Yuh, *Beyond the Shadow of Camptown: Korean Military Brides in America* (New York: NYU Press, 2004), 127.

2. Yuh, *Beyond the Shadow*, 128.

3. Yuh, *Beyond the Shadow*, 130.

4. Yuh, *Beyond the Shadow*, 127.

5. Yuh, *Beyond the Shadow*, 128–29.

6. Yuh, *Beyond the Shadow*, 129.

7. This quote derives from archival film footage of Korean War orphans eating American treats such as chocolate and chewing gum with the text from an International Social Services pamphlet that was provided to American adoptive parents in the 1960s. Deann Borshay Liem, "Practical Hints about Your Foreign Child" (video), 2005, http://www.stillpresentpasts.org/practical-hints-about-your-foreign-child.html.

7. SCHIZOPHRENOGENESIS

1. T. M. Luhrmann and Jocelyn Morrow, eds., *Our Most Troubling Madness: Case Studies in Schizophrenia across Cultures* (Oakland: University of California Press, 2016), 197.

2. "Talkin' John Birch Paranoid Blues," Bob Dylan, recorded October 26, 1963.

3. "Talkin' John Birch Paranoid Blues," Bob Dylan, recorded October 26, 1963.

4. Lisa Miller, "Listening to Estrogen," *The Cut*, December 21, 2018. https://www.thecut.com/2018/12/is-estrogen-the-key-to-understanding-womens-mental-health.html.

5. A study in Ghana found that one-third of women with schizophrenia first developed it after menopause, while others seem to have been triggered by the stress of marriage. Luhrmann and Morrow, *Our Most Troubling Madness*, 8.

6. Ann Olson, *Illuminating Schizophrenia: Insights into the Uncommon Mind* (Newark, NJ: Newark Educational & Psychological Publications, 2013), 15.

7. *Diagnostic and Statistical Manual of Mental Disorders: DSM-III* (Washington, DC: American Psychiatric Association, 1980), 188–89.

8. Luhrmann and Morrow, *Our Most Troubling Madness*, 2.

9. Luhrmann and Morrow, *Our Most Troubling Madness*, 3.

10. Olson, *Illuminating Schizophrenia*, 20.

11. Miller, "Listening to Estrogen."

12. Miller, "Listening to Estrogen."

13. "Schizophrenia Onset: When Do Symptoms Usually Start?" WebMD, accessed January 22, 2020, https://www.webmd.com/schizophrenia/schizophrenia-onset-symptoms#1. The National Alliance on Mental Illness website also states that it is "uncommon for schizophrenia to be diagnosed in a person . . . older than forty." The data shows, however, that almost 20 percent of first-time diagnoses are among people over forty. "Schizophrenia," National Alliance on Mental Illness, accessed August 31, 2019, https://www.nami.org/learn-more/mental-health-conditions/schizophrenia.

14. John M. Glionna, "A Complex Feeling Tugs at Koreans," *Los Angeles Times*, January 5, 2011, http://articles.latimes.com/2011/jan/05/world/la-fg-south-korea-han-20110105.

15. Sandra So Hee Chi Kim, "Korean *Han* and the Postcolonial Afterlives of 'The Beauty of Sorrow,'" *Korean Studies*, 41 (2017): 256.

16. Deanna Pan, "Timeline: Deinstitutionalization and Its Consequences," *Mother Jones*, April 29, 2013, https://www.motherjones.com/politics/2013/04/timeline-mental-health-america/.

17. Allen Frances, "World's Best—and Worst—Places to Be Mentally Ill," *Psychiatric Times*, December 29, 2015, https://www.psychiatrictimes.com/worlds-best-and-worst-places-be-mentally-ill.

18. Benjamin Weiser, "A 'Bright Light,' Dimmed in the Shadow of Homelessness," *New York Times*, March 3, 2018, https://www.nytimes.com/2018/03/03/nyregion/nyc-homeless-nakesha-mental-illness.html.

19. "Rampant Sexual Abuse at the Green Hill School in Chehalis," Pfau Cochran Vertetis Amala Attorneys at Law (website), accessed September 6, 2018, https://pcva.law/case_investigation/rampant-sexual-abuse-at-the-green-hill-school-in-chehalis/.

20. Natalie Johnson, "Lawsuit Alleges 'Culture' of Sexual Abuse by Female Staff at Green Hill School," *Daily Chronicle*, March 8, 2018, http://www.

chronline.com/crime/lawsuit-alleges-culture-of-sexual-abuse-by-female-staff-at/article_f56fe2d4-226d-11e8-9157-3f71631484e5.html.

21. Olivia Messer, "Staffers Raped Teen Boys at Juvenile Detention Center, Lawsuit Claims," *Daily Beast*, March 8, 2018, https://www.thedailybeast.com/staffers-raped-teens-at-juvenile-detention-center-lawsuit-claims.

22. "Rampant Sexual Abuse," Pfau Cochran Vertetis Amala Attorneys at Law.

23. Johnson, "Lawsuit Alleges 'Culture' of Sexual Abuse."

24. Rebecca Pilar Buckwalter-Poza, "Teen Who Says He Was Raped by Juvenile Detention Center Staff Fights Back through the Civil System," *Daily Kos*, March 12, 2018, https://www.dailykos.com/stories/2018/3/12/1748449/-Teen-who-says-he-was-raped-by-juvenile-detention-center-staff-fights-back-through-the-civil-system.

25. Andy Campbell, "Culture of Sexual Misconduct Alleged at Green Hill School," *Daily Chronicle*, July 16, 2009, http://www.chronline.com/news/culture-of-sexual-misconduct-alleged-at-green-hill-school/article_42b8b61d-1acc-5e6d-b369-c15a7f40a03c.html.

26. Campbell, "Culture of Sexual Misconduct."

8. BROWN

1. Peter Applebome, "Duke's Followers Lean to Buchanan," *New York Times*, March 8, 1992, https://www.nytimes.com/1992/03/08/us/the-1992-campaign-far-right-duke-s-followers-lean-to-buchanan.html

2. Michael Ross, "Duke Ends Presidential Bid, Blames Hostile GOP," *Los Angeles Times*, April 23, 1992, http://articles.latimes.com/1992-04-23/news/mn-1312_1_duke-s-campaign.

3. Trevor Griffey, "KKK Super Rallies in Washington State: 1923–24," Seattle Civil Rights & Labor History Project (website), http://depts.washington.edu/civilr/kkk_rallies.htm.

9. JANUARYSEVENTH

1. Ralph Ellison, *The Collected Essays of Ralph Ellison*, ed. John F. Callahan (New York: Modern Library, 2003), 148.

2. Michael Rembis, "The New Asylums: Madness and Mass Incarceration in the Neoliberal Era," *Disability Incarcerated: Imprisonment and Disability in the United States and Canada*, eds. Liat Ben-Moshe, Chris Chapman, and Allison C. Carey (New York: Palgrave-Macmillan, 2014), 139.

3. Jonathan M. Metzl, *The Protest Psychosis: How Schizophrenia Became a Black Disease* (Boston: Beacon Press, 2010), xiv.

4. Metzl, *Protest Psychosis*, xiv.

5. David A. Karp and Lara B. Birk, "Listening to Voices: Patient Experience and the Meanings of Mental Illness," *Handbook of the Sociology of Mental Health*, eds. Carol Aneshensel and Jo Phelan (New York: Springer), 28.

6. Choe Sang-Hun, "Ex-Prostitutes Say South Korea and U.S. Enabled Sex Trade Near Bases," *New York Times*, January 7, 2009, https://www.nytimes.com/2009/01/08/world/asia/08korea.html.

7. Choe Sang-Hun, "South Korea Illegally Held Prostitutes Who Catered to GIs, Court Says," *New York Times*, January 20, 2017, https://www.nytimes.com/2017/01/20/world/asia/south-korea-court-comfort-women.html.

8. Richard Warner, *Recovery from Schizophrenia: Psychiatry and Political Economy*, third edition (New York: Brunner-Routledge, 1997), 148.

9. Warner, *Recovery from Schizophrenia*, 169.

10. T. M. Luhrmann and Jocelyn Morrow, eds., *Our Most Troubling Madness: Case Studies in Schizophrenia across Cultures* (Oakland: University of California Press, 2016), 25.

10. CRUST GIRL

1. Saundra Pollock Sturdevant and Brenda Stoltzfus, *Let the Good Times Roll: Prostitution and the U.S. Military in Asia* (New York: The New Press, 1992), 300.

2. Sturdevant and Stoltzfus, *Let the Good Times Roll*, 302.

3. Franny Choi, "Choi Jeong Min," Poetry Foundation (website), accessed December 17, 2018, https://www.poetryfoundation.org/poetrymagazine/poems/58784/choi-jeong-min.

11. ONE TIME, NO LOVE

1. Ann Olson, *Illuminating Schizophrenia: Insights into the Uncommon Mind* (Newark, NJ: Newark Educational & Psychological Publications, 2013), 27.

12. OAKIE

1. Ivan Leudar and Philip Thomas, *Voices of Reason, Voices of Insanity: Studies of Verbal Hallucations* (London: Routledge, 2000), 3.

2. Leudar and Thomas, *Voices of Reason*, 3.

3. T. M. Luhrmann, "The Violence in Our Heads," *New York Times*, September

19, 2013, https://www.nytimes.com/2013/09/20/opinion/luhrmann-the-violence-in-our-heads.html.

4. Lisa Blackman, *Hearing Voices: Embodiment and Experience* (London: Free Association Books, 2001), 189.

13. QUEENS

1. T. M. Luhrmann, "The Violence in Our Heads," *New York Times*, September 19, 2013, https://www.nytimes.com/2013/09/20/opinion/luhrmann-the-violence-in-our-heads.html.

14. COUNTING GHOSTS

1. Colonel Turner C. Rogers, "Memo: Policy on Strafing Civilian Refugees," July 25, 1950, declassified June 6, 2000, US National Archives, College Park, MD.

2. Nora Okja Keller, *Fox Girl* (New York: Penguin, 2002), 131.

3. Keller, *Fox Girl*, 81.

4. Keller, *Fox Girl*, 81.

5. Yi Okpun, "Taken at Twelve," *True Stories of the Korean Comfort Women*, ed. Keith Howard (London: Cassell, 1996), 100–101.

CREDITS

American Dreams (p. 23) and **The Friendly City** (p. 42). Portions of these chapters originally appeared as "Disappearing Acts: An Immigrant History" in *Cultural Studies Critical Methodologies* 18, no. 5 (2018): 307–13.

Kimchi Blues (p. 88). A version of this chapter originally appeared in *Gastronomica: The Journal of Food and Culture* 12, no. 2 (2012): 53–58.

Madame Mushroom (p. 105). A version of this chapter originally appeared in *Gastronomica: The Journal of Critical Food Studies* 15, no. 1 (2015): 77–84.

Crust Girl (p. 197). A version of this chapter originally appeared in *PMS poemmemoirstory*, no. 15 (2016): 87–96.

Oakie (p. 228). A portion of this chapter was originally published as "American Movies" in *WSQ* 47, nos. 1–2 (2019): 83–88.

Cheeseburger Season (p. 268). A portion of this chapter was originally published in *East Asian Mothering: Politics and Practices*, eds. Patti Duncan and Gina Wong (Bradford, Ontario: Demeter Press, 2014), 53–58.

ACKNOWLEDGMENTS

I began writing this book in fits and starts back in 2008, as I was mourning my mother's sudden and untimely death. Writing was equal parts therapy and eulogy, and at some point, it started to take the shape of a book. The transformation from grief-driven unconscious thought to memoir was possible only because of the many people and institutions that supported me along the way.

I am grateful to the teachers and writers at Gotham Writers' Workshop, Sackett Street Writers' Workshop, and Asian American Writers' Workshop, especially Marie Carter, Starina Catchatoorian, Bill Cheng, Courtney Mace, Luke Malone, Bushra Rehman, Cullen Thomas, Michael Tirrell, and Alisson Wood. My friends and colleagues Jean Halley, Rose Kim, Jessie Kindig, and Christine Rague were exceptionally generous with their time and care in giving feedback on multiple chapters. Thank you all for reading my words and helping me to craft them into a bigger story.

To the people who have been by my side through the journey documented in these pages—Sandra Baptista, April Burns, Jaquetta Bustion, Patricia Clough, Rafael de la Dehesa, Jenny Hammer, and Hosu Kim—thank you for being my family. To my partner, Patrick Bower, who has been by my side through the twelve-year-long journey of writing this book, thank you for reading every word and for believing in me. You have made me a better writer and a stronger person. To my children, Felix and Isabella, thank you for your love and patience.

I am indebted to the Feminist Press for making a space for marginalized voices and publishing the multiplicity of viewpoints that is feminism. It is an honor to be in such good company. A special thanks goes to my editor, Lauren Rosemary Hook, whose thoughtful work on my manuscript infused it with energy, clarity, and compassion. Jisu Kim, Nick Whitney, and the rest of the team at FP have shown unqualified enthusiasm about my work, banishing every doubt I ever had about telling this story.

My gratitude also goes to the College of Staten Island, CUNY, and the Professional Staff Congress of CUNY for providing me with the most precious resource of time.

Above all, I am thankful to my mother for teaching me the value of an unconventional mind.